CONJURE IN AFRICAN AMERICAN SOCIETY

Conjure in African American Society

Jeffrey E. Anderson

LOUISIANA STATE UNIVERSITY PRESS

BATON ROUGE

Published by Louisiana State University Press
Copyright © 2005 by Louisiana State University Press
All rights reserved
Manufactured in the United States of America
Louisiana Paperback Edition, 2007

DESIGNER: Andrew Shurtz
TYPEFACE: Adobe Caslon Pro

LIBRARY OF CONGRESS CATALOGING-IN-PUBLICATION DATA
Anderson, Jeffrey E., 1974–
    Conjure in African American society / Jeffrey E. Anderson.
    p. cm.
    Includes bibliographical references and index.
    ISBN 0-8071-3092-3 (alk. paper)
    1. Hoodoo (Cult) 2. Magic. 3. Voodooism—United States. I. Title.
BL2490.A64 2005
133.4'3'08996073—dc22

2005004333

ISBN 978-0-8071-3348-4 (paper : alk. paper)

The paper in this book meets the guidelines for permanence and durability of the Committee on Production Guidelines for Book Longevity of the Council on Library Resources. ∞

To my wife, Lynn, and my son, Michael

Contents

Preface: Defining the Realm of Investigation   ix

Acknowledgments   xiii

Introduction: The Invisible Conjurer:
The Disappearance of Hoodoo from Conceptions of Black Society   1

1. *Vodu* and *Minkisi:*
   The African Foundation of Black American Magic   25

2. Witches and Medicine Men:
   European and Native American Building Blocks of Hoodoo   50

3. The Conjurers' World:
   The Social Context of Hoodoo in Nineteenth-Century Black Life   75

4. The Conjurers Themselves:
   Performing and Marketing Hoodoo   90

5. Conjure Shops and Manufacturing:
   Changes in Hoodoo into the Twentieth Century   112

6. The Magic Continues:
   Hoodoo at the Turn of the Twenty-first Century   134

   Conclusion:
   The Importance of Conjure in African American Society   150

   Notes   161

   Note on Sources   189

   Bibliography   199

   Index   221

   Illustrations follow page   74

Preface
Defining the Realm of Investigation

All of the hoodoo doctors have non-conjure cases. They prescribe folk medicine, "roots," and are for this reason called "two headed doctors." ... Often they are not hoodoo doctors, but all hoodoo doctors also practice medicine.
ZORA NEALE HURSTON, "Hoodoo in America"

Other names for hoodoo include "conjuration," "conjure," "witchcraft," and "rootwork." ... As you may guess by now, it is not at all correct to refer to African-American hoodoo as "Voodoo."
CATHERINE YRONWODE, "Hoodoo"

Prominent among Gullah culture was the belief in herbalism, spiritualism, and black magic. While in other places it was called "ubia," "voodoo," or "santeria," the Gullah called it "the root."
ROGER PINCKNEY, *Blue Roots*

TODAY, WHITE READERS listening to blues music or reading a book by, say, Pulitzer Prize–winning author Julia Peterkin are apt to be puzzled by some of the references they find. Peterkin's novels often refer to an African American practice known as *conjure*. Blues lyrics frequently include the words *hoodoo, goopher, mojo,* and the like. Such terms refer to a specifically African American form of magic that has been practiced by blacks since colonial times and survives today.[1] While they might be unfamiliar to modern whites, most African Americans would have little trouble comprehending them.

"Witches," "two-heads," "goopher doctors," "Voodoo priests," "root doctors," "hoodooists," and other masters of the occult have long peopled African Americans' supernatural world. As the epigraphs above suggest, however, no two authors agree on what the different names denote. Some draw sharp lines between root doctors, goopher doctors, Voodoo priests, and other classes of magic workers. Others simply condense all of these magic workers into a single group, usually known as "hoodoo doctors" or "conjurers." It is best to define a conjurer as a professional magic practitioner who typically receives payment in return for his or her goods and services. Still, three vital questions remain unanswered. First, what separates conjure from syncretic religions like Voodoo? Second, what sets conjure apart from lower-level supernaturalism, commonly called "superstition"? Finally, how are witches, two-heads, goopher doctors, rootworkers, and the like related to conjurers?

Conjure, properly defined, falls between the two extremes of religion proper and low-level supernaturalism. At one end of the spectrum of African American beliefs lie such syncretic religions as nineteenth-century Louisianian Voodoo and modern Cuban Santería.[2] Conjure is broader than such faiths. Functionally, syncretic religions seek to honor the gods and spirits who people the believers' world. For example, both Voodoo and Santería have historically included sacrifice to please such deities as Papa Lébat and Ogun. Conjure, however, pursues no such lofty aims; instead it seeks to accomplish practical objectives through appeals to the spirit world.[3] While conjurers may consider their religion to be Christian, this has not prevented some of them from calling on Papa Lébat to perform specific deeds. Likewise, Christian conjurers might try to compel God to bend to their will through selective Bible reading. For example, in a spell recorded by Zora Neale Hurston conjure clients recited Psalm 120 during "court scrapes" in order to guarantee success.[4]

In addition to conjure's functional distinctiveness, it also lacks the developed theology of syncretic religions. Though neither Santería nor Voodoo has held to rigid dogmas, their basic tenets remain much the same for all practitioners. For instance, Voodooists recognized the existence of the supreme creator god, who takes little part in human affairs. Likewise, believers in Santería, whether they live in Cuba, Miami, or New York City, place great emphasis on the powers of the dead. In contrast, while the majority of conjurers engage in many of the same practices and use similar materials, such as graveyard dirt, bones, and plant materials, their uses differ widely from practitioner to practitioner. Furthermore, some conjurers claim to receive their power from God, while others credit familiars or animistic spirits. Conjure is far less systematic than even undogmatic syncretic religions.[5]

If religion delineates the upper boundary of conjure, supernaturalism marks the lower. Conjure and supernaturalism differ in terms of the specialized knowledge or abilities required for their practice. For example, nineteenth-century Georgia blacks believed that lending salt or red pepper was bad luck. Such folk beliefs required no particular occult aptitude. On the other hand, few African Americans possessed the supernatural skills to make one of the complex "luck balls" that nineteenth-century Missouri blacks fashioned from a combination of human hair, ashes, graveyard dust, pig blood, and tail feathers from a crowing hen. Such complex and allegedly more potent spells have traditionally been left up to hoodooists.[6]

Two major exceptions to the general reliance on local conjurers for full-blown magic exist. One is the mail-order conjure companies that arose during the twentieth century. Such businesses often sell do-it-yourself kits that promise to provide users with magical powers. The second is the many traditional practices designed to remedy and prevent conjure, such as sweeping and scouring recently occupied homes to cleanse them from evil forces. These modes of supposed protection rarely reach the level of complexity commonly attached to the conjurer's art. Nevertheless, as foils of evil magic they must be classed as a form of counterconjure.[7]

Having set the boundaries to what properly constitutes conjure, what are we to make of the plethora of words indiscriminately used as synonyms? This question must be answered in three parts. First, *hoodoo* and the less well known *mojo*, *tricking*, and *fixing* are readily interchangeable with *conjure*, differing from one another only with respect to regional and personal preferences.[8]

Second, some authors treat *witch* as a synonym for *conjurer* even though African Americans sometimes distinguish between the two terms. While conjurers are human, witches are sometimes described as nonhuman beings who ride lightning and give birth to vampires. In some accounts, witches also engage in practices below the dignity of most conjurers, such as riding sleepers and stealing milk from cows. At the same time, witches can usually transform themselves into a variety of animals, an ability possessed by few conjurers.[9]

Finally, a variety of other terms refer to specific aspects of African American magic. The most common of such semi-synonyms for *conjurer* is *rootworker*. Some scholars have argued that rootworkers are a distinct class, differentiated from conjurers by their use of herbal remedies to cure medical problems. Hoodoo, they maintain, seeks to improve spiritual conditions.[10] As Zora Neale Hurston has pointed out, however, "Nearly all of the conjure doctors practice 'roots,' but some of the root doctors are not hoodoo doctors."[11] Thus, rootwork is an aspect of the repertoire of virtually all conjurers. While some root doctors understand their profession in light of modern science, many hoodooists simply attribute herbal remedies' efficacy to magic.

Some authors distinguish specialists within the broader field of conjure. For instance, Catherine Yronwode, owner of the Lucky Mojo Curio Company, argues that conjurers can be divided into three categories: hoodooists, healers, and readers. According to this categorization, readers only tell clients' futures; healers use herbal medicine to cure illnesses; and hoodooists specialize in evil and its cure. Many conjurers, however, practice all three professions, rendering any distinctions vague at best.[12] Similarly, some conjurers use epithets like *doctor* to imply that they perform only good magic or heal those harmed by malevolent sorcery. Historically, this distinction has been largely fictitious, a way for conjurers to make themselves more acceptable to clients while demonizing their rivals as workers of evil. Of course, some conjurers do specialize, especially readers, who often predict the future without offering the possibility of changing it. Such individuals, however, are the exception rather than the rule.[13]

Other terms commonly used to designate conjurers are less problematic. For instance, *goopher doctor* refers to the strong connection between hoodoo and the dead. *Goopher* is a synonym for *grave,* most commonly used in reference to *goopher dust,* which is dirt taken from a cemetery. Another equivalent of *conjure doctor* is *two-head,* which according to Hurston refers to hoodooists' ability to deal in both magic and herbal medicine. Another explanation is that it reflects a belief that conjurers possess two souls. These are but a few of the most common appellations applied to conjurers. Although many others exist, they appear only rarely and are usually confined to specific localities.[14]

The distinctions outlined above are somewhat arbitrary. The borders between religion, magic, and lower forms of supernaturalism are porous and blurred. While one person may differentiate between healers and conjurers, another may not. Still, an understanding of the terms is necessary for their study. Moreover, these distinctions reflect genuine differences that must be appreciated in order to effectively examine the practice of conjure, its origins, regional distinctions, and evolution.

Acknowledgments

I WOULD LIKE to thank the members of my doctoral committee at the University of Florida: Bertram Wyatt-Brown, William F. Brundage, Jon Sensbach, David Hackett, and Alice Freifeld. Without their encouragement and suggestions I would not have been able to complete this book.

My family deserves my thanks as well. As important as any of my committee members was my wife, Lynn, who patiently read through each and every page of my work, looking for errors in grammar and style. I thank her for putting up with my lectures on conjure and the difficulties of writing. I also thank my mother and father, Reba and William Anderson, for their suggestions.

Several people aided my research by providing information and professional know-how. Carolyn Morrow Long, who was working on a similar project, graciously gave me advice. The interlibrary loan staffs of the University of Florida and Samford University supplied me with hard-to-obtain books and articles, as did Samford's special-collections department. In addition, the hoodooists, healers, spiritual advisers, and others knowledgeable about the subject who were willing to speak with me allowed me to glimpse African American magic at work. In particular, I would like to recognize the contributions of Catherine Yronwode, Deborah, Sallie Ann Glassman, Phoenix Savage, Barbara Gore, Miriam Chamani, Felix Figueroa, F. L. Robinson, Claudia Williams,

Richard Miller, "Pop" Williams, Nancy Rhett, Eugenia Brown, "Tater Red" Allred, Elliot Schwab, Deborah Halstead, Dr. Charles Champion, and Jonell and Jazell Smith.

Finally, my faith in God encouraged me to persevere and gave me insight into the workings of the supernatural.

CONJURE IN AFRICAN AMERICAN SOCIETY

Introduction
The Invisible Conjurer: The Disappearance of Hoodoo from Conceptions of Black Society

THOMAS NELSON PAGE, one of the major architects of the "moonlight and magnolias" myth of the Old South, published his most famous novel, *Red Rock,* in 1899. Set during Reconstruction, its pages are filled with the standard characters of Page's genre: heroic southern planters, dutiful Union soldiers, and depraved carpetbaggers. One villain, Dr. Moses, is particularly overdrawn in the depiction of his physical as well as moral perversity. Rachel Welch, the novel's heroine, observes, "His chin stuck so far forward that the lower teeth were much outside of the upper, or, at least, the lower jaw was; for the teeth looked as though they had been ground down, and his gums, as he grinned, showed as blue on the edges as if he had painted them."[1]

Moses is a *trick doctor,* a term Page felt no need to define. Modern readers are left to question why the bizarrely misshapen Moses should be such a threat to the white population. Other contemporary works provide answers. For instance, Philip A. Bruce, author of *The Plantation Negro as a Freedman* (1899), described the trick doctor as "a man whose only employment . . . lies in the practice of the art of witchcraft," who "is invested with even more importance than a preacher, since he is regarded with the respect that fear excites."[2] Moreover, Moses's physical appearance is typical of the numerous descriptions of trick doctors that appeared during the late nineteenth and early twentieth centuries. For instance, in the early-twentieth-century article "Observations on the

Practice of Conjuring in Georgia" Roland Steiner recorded the African American folk belief that the spells of blue-gummed blacks invariably caused death. Likewise, folklorist Mary Alicia Owen, using the language of her informant, in 1893, described a legendary "witcheh-man" as "de mos' uglies' man in de worl', wid er whopple-jaw an' er har'-lip, sidesen er lop side an' er crookid laig an' one eye dat wuz des lak fiah an' one dat was daid."[3] In short, published accounts of African American magic were so common during the era that Page had no need to explain what he meant by *trick doctor*. After Page's time, however, literary and academic interest in black sorcery declined. The net result has been that the trick doctor, also known as the "hoodoo doctor" or "conjurer," has become virtually invisible in most Americans' conceptions of black society, even while the vocation of conjuring lives on in many African American communities.[4]

How can one explain such a drastic shift in attention to conjure? The answer lies in intellectual and cultural shifts over the course of the late nineteenth and twentieth centuries that have changed the ways both blacks and whites have constructed identity. Between the Civil War and World War II, Americans in general and southern whites in particular feared losing their cultural identity to the homogenizing effects of industrial capitalism, and conjure was one expression of peculiarity that they used to resist the threatened loss of national and regional distinctiveness. Once war catapulted America to the forefront of world politics and economics, regional distinctions became less important than national pride and a united front against Communism. For blacks, attention to hoodoo was likewise a question of identity. Unlike whites, however, they tended to view hoodoo as a negative feature of their society. Its practice, they thought, would have to be stamped out before they could hope to achieve equality. Recently, the influence of the closely linked forces of cultural pluralism, postmodernism, and the New Age movement and rising black assertiveness have made magic an acceptable expression of spirituality for many. Nevertheless, conjure remains an understudied facet of black society.[5]

Before the Civil War, southerners, white and black, were well aware of the existence of conjure. For instance, in a diary entry for 3 March 1816 the South Carolinian George Izard recorded an encounter with a sickly Mr. Perkins, who explained his illness as a result of a spell cast by a spurned admirer. After physicians' remedies failed him, Perkins turned to conjure. Izard's experience was far from unique. Many whites learned of conjure from their slaves. Such was the case with Thaddeus Norris, author of "Negro Superstitions." Writing five years after the Civil War, he admitted that he had "firmly believed in witches" as a child, a conviction he had acquired through his close relationship with an elderly "house servant."[6] Frederick Douglass, the most prominent of black abolitionists, included an account of hoodoo in his antebellum *Narrative*, spreading knowledge of the practice to northern readers. Nevertheless, few observers commented on the practice beyond pointing it out as a sign of slaves' intellectual backwardness. Slaves were to be either worked or freed, not studied for their culture.[7]

Immediately following the war southern whites were too busy restoring Democratic control of their states to devote increased attention to sectional identity and certainly to black folk religion. After all, their recent experience of military defeat and occupation had left no room to doubt their distinctiveness. One of the few whites to address black folk religions was Thaddeus Norris, who bluntly wrote that "the more refined a people, the more interesting its mythical legends. Those of the Caucasian race are attractive; while those of the negroes are repulsive, especially when connected with their heathenish religions."[8] Literate blacks generally felt the same way. A selection of letters on conjure published in the *Southern Workman* provides evidence. This newspaper was associated with Virginia's Hampton Institute, one of the nation's oldest black schools. In 1878 the school solicited reports from its students and graduates on the level of superstition among the freedmen. The response was more than one hundred letters, only six of which saw print. Most of the responders frankly stated that conjure was a negative but common feature of black society. One author, referred to as "L." in the printed version of his letter, was particularly harsh in his denunciation of hoodoo, asserting, "Conjure doctors are not so numerous now as they were before our race became so enlightened, but still they are too numerous. They are a curse to their race."[9] Overcoming racist oppression and abject poverty through education was much more important to blacks than questions of culture. With both whites and blacks disgusted by Negro ignorance, few were interested in doing more than denouncing conjure.

Since Reconstruction, interest in conjure has generally followed a wavelike pattern of increasing and decreasing interest. Since the end of Republican rule in the South, interest in conjure has crested three times. The first of these upturns began in the mid-1880s and persisted until shortly after 1900. Following the turn of the century, writings on conjure appeared less and less frequently until the 1920s, when a new wave of interest began. It had passed by the early 1940s, when conjure once again faded from public view. The second trough was much deeper than the first. With occasional exceptions, few works on hoodoo appeared until the 1970s. At that point, a new respect for black folk beliefs, including conjure, arose.

As local distinctions seemed threatened by industrial homogenization following the Civil War, whites searched for regional peculiarities in order to construct a distinct identity. Corporatism, national advertising, and consumerism threatened to transform the South into a carbon copy of the North. It is no coincidence that articles on conjure peaked in the 1890s, when a generation that had never owned slaves or fought in the Civil War came to prominence.

In addition to ending the most important distinction between the North and the South, emancipation had begun a process that would cause blacks and whites to grow more and more foreign to each other. Under the peculiar institution, members of both races had lived and sometimes worked side by side, occupying the same geographic space. Whites inevitably learned much about blacks' culture, including their supernatural beliefs, from simple observation and conversation, and the same was true for blacks. Though convict leasing, sharecropping, and other forms of "free" labor that replaced slavery resembled it in many ways, they were a first step in a growing physical separation between the races. When the temporary political entitlement and citizenship rights that blacks had gained during Reconstruction faded during the last two decades of the nineteenth century, African Americans became increasingly vulnerable to racism. By the turn of the twentieth century a rigid system of economic and social segregation had developed throughout the states of the former Confederacy. During the first half of the 1890s the white Democrats' "Solid South" had begun to crack in the face of the Populists' agrarian radicalism. In part, the implementation of Jim Crow was the work of white politicians seeking to reunite their race under the banner of white supremacy. Whatever the cause, blacks and whites lived their lives ever more separately, and each culture became less familiar to the other.[10]

Whites had long considered blacks a primitive and superstitious people. With African Americans safely cut off from political and economic power, their folk beliefs could now be used to bolster white superiority and regional distinctiveness. To white authors, the hoodoo doctor became a powerful image of the southern past, conjuring up images of aristocratic planters and their happy but dependent "servants." Moreover, by describing blacks as a backward people, whites defined what their race was not. At the same time, African Americans began to develop a class system. As members of the small but growing middle class became educated and quickly adopted the scientific outlook and social Darwinism of the larger American society, they confidently expected conjure to disappear.[11] In fact, according to many blacks' ideology of racial uplift, such backward features of black society would have to give way before the race could hope to advance. Thus, while whites used black folk beliefs as a point of contrast to display their own glories, African Americans rejected whites' self-serving characterization of blacks as superstitious.[12]

The local color literary movement typified whites' construction of identity. In the South, this impulse often found expression in collections of black folklore, relayed in the dialect of the plantation "darkie." Most prominent among these works was Joel Chandler Harris's 1880 book *Uncle Remus: His Songs and His Sayings*, a collection of African American animal stories ostensibly related by an elderly former slave to a child whom he had befriended. Over the next twenty-five years numerous authors sought to duplicate Harris's success, with the result that black folklore became staple reading for white American youths until well into the twentieth century.[13] In practice, local color works provided a bridge between the romanticism of the early nineteenth century and the realism that came to characterize the twentieth. As such, it was the perfect vehicle for whites to record the exoticism of the plantation past, dovetailing nicely with the chivalric tales of Thomas Nelson Page. At the same time, it allowed authors to glorify the region's race relations by providing "records" of friendly interaction between superior whites and dependent blacks through the medium of African American stories told in dialect. In an age when white southerners sought sectional reconciliation while maintaining their distinctiveness, local colorism helped them write their past and present racial systems in a way that made their acceptance by the rest of the nation more palatable.[14]

The growth of the social sciences, especially professionalized folklore, provided another vehicle for white southerners' search for identity. Brought to prominence in Europe by Jacob and Wilhelm Grimm during the early and middle nineteenth century, folklore quickly became a popular pursuit.[15] By the late 1870s, folklorists had begun to professionalize their field. One of the earliest signs of this development was the founding of the English Folklore Society in 1878. Ten years later, American folklorists created their own national organization, the American Folklore Society. The international expositions of 1889, 1891, and 1893, which stressed the importance of progress, hosted folklore congresses in order to emphasize the backwardness of primitive societies, while preserving their beliefs for future generations. During the 1891 exposition, Mary Alicia Owen helped bring conjure to scholarly attention by presenting a paper entitled "Among the Voodoos," which described the magical practices of Missouri's blacks.[16] The newly founded *Journal of American Folk-Lore* (later the *Journal of American Folklore*), an organ of the American Folklore Society, published numerous articles on conjure and related practices throughout its early volumes. Following an article on Haitian Vodou in its 1888 inaugural issue, the journal published W. W. Newell's "Reports of Voodoo Worship in Hayti and Louisiana" in its second volume.[17] The journal did not confine itself to Voodoo proper, however, and over the next decade and a half numerous brief notes and full-length articles appeared. Typically they resemble Roland Steiner's "Observations on the Practice of Conjuring in Georgia," an essay that combines conjure stories with instructions for using particular magical materials.[18]

After 1893 southern African Americans had their own folklore society, based at Virginia's Hampton Normal School, later to be known as the Hampton Institute. In a notice to students announcing the founding of the Hampton Folk-Lore Society, an anonymous author stated, "The American Negroes are rising so rapidly from the condition of ignorance and poverty . . . that the time seems not far distant when they shall have cast off their past entirely."[19] If a record of conjure was not preserved, blacks would become a people without a history beyond what whites chose to give them. Progress, destined to wipe out folk beliefs like conjure, would nevertheless preserve knowledge of such "savagery" for future generations through the work of professional folklorists. To this end the *Southern Workman*, the school newspaper, published numerous articles on black folklore during the late nineteenth century.[20]

Throughout the 1890s and the early years of the twentieth century the *Southern Workman* frequently included a column entitled "Folk-Lore and Ethnology," which regularly addressed conjure. Like the articles appearing in the *Journal of American Folklore*, these accounts tended to be simple descriptions of hoodoo beliefs. Nevertheless, a few accounts display a high degree of analytical sophistication. The most important example is A. M. Bacon's "Conjuring and Conjure-Doctors," published in 1895. Bacon divided conjuration into two types, those involving charms and those involving poisons, and argued that conjurers provided five primary services to their clients, roughly summarized as follows: diagnosis of afflictions caused by magic, discovery of those who had cast spells, searching out and destroying tricks, curing those who had been conjured, and turning spells back on those who had cast them.[21]

Meanwhile, other authors began to tentatively introduce new interpretations. For instance, Leonora Herron, in her essay "Conjuring and Conjure-

Doctors" (not to be confused with Bacon's article of the same title), argued that conjure functioned as a means of redressing wrongs, for which slavery had provided no other mechanism. In addition, Herron proposed that conjure was not solely of African origin but had also been influenced by "association with the white race ... till it became a curious conglomerate of fetishism, divination, quackery, incantation and demonology."[22] Despite the growing volume and analytical rigor of such articles, few authors saw conjure as a positive aspect of the black past. Instead, African Americans followed the lead of whites, condemning hoodoo as a sign of backwardness. While whites used conjure to bolster their supremacist assumptions, however, blacks saw its supposed decline as a symbol of advancement.[23]

Southerners' attempts to build a new identity brought hoodoo to national attention. Knowledge of conjure ceased to be the purview of southerners who had experienced it firsthand. Instead, a growing number of books intended for popular consumption began to treat hoodoo as an important part of black culture. Publications reporting on the progress of the black race, such as Bruce's *Plantation Negro as a Freedman*, increasingly came to address the backwardness of conjure. Likewise, autobiographies of ex-slaves often pointed to antebellum conjure to demonstrate how far blacks had risen from bondage. Such was the case with Jacob Stoyer, a former South Carolina slave, who made much of slaves' belief in magic, recording their use of red pepper and salt to repel witches. Another former slave, William Wells Brown, author of *My Southern Home*, used the semihumorous character Uncle Dinkie, a conjurer, to demonstrate the "ignorant days of slavery." In addition to being a fraud who earned his reputation by fortunetelling, love potions, and "medicine," Uncle Dinkie had learned to serve the devil instead of God "kase de white folks don't fear de Lord."[24]

Another class of publication that usually addressed conjure comprised the collections of black folklore that appeared during the years around 1900. Harris's *Uncle Remus* refers to conjure only briefly, but some of his imitators dealt with it in greater depth. For instance, in Charles Colcock Jones Jr.'s *Gullah Folktales from the Georgia Coast*, "Buh Rabbit" must contend with conjure doctors as well as wolves and tar babies. Two works appeared that were entirely devoted to stories of hoodoo. The earliest of these was Mary Alicia Owen's *Voodoo Tales as Told among the Negroes of the Southwest*, first published in 1893. As its alternate title, *Old Rabbit, the Voodoo, and Other Sorcerers*, suggests, Owen's work was a collection of animal stories in which magic was the driving force. Rabbit, Woodpecker, and the Bee-King appear as the animal kingdom's principal conjurers. Another work from the period that centers on hoodoo was Virginia Frazer Boyle's *Devil Tales*. Unlike Harris, Colcock, and Owen, Boyle recorded stories of human hoodooists, usually locked in combat with the devil. Nevertheless, her underlying aim was the same: glorification of the southern past. Describing her sense of loss at the death of her storytelling black "Mammy," she wrote, "The swaying form, crooning in low rich voice, like some bronze Homer blind to letters, a weird primeval lore into the ears of future orators, is shut within the feudal past of the old plantation days."[25]

A final group of books that began to appear during this era were fictional works built around the workings of African American magic. The most remarkable of these was black author Charles W. Chesnutt's *Conjure Woman*, which recounts a series of tales told by Uncle Julius, an ex-slave, to white Ohioan immigrants to North Carolina. Though the tales are ostensibly a collection of conjure stories from plantation days, Chesnutt's Julius uses them to persuade his white acquaintances to favor him with gifts and other considerations. For example, in the story "Po' Sandy" he persuades the Ohioan narrator and his wife not to tear down an old building because it had been built from a person whom a conjure woman had changed into a tree. Shortly after, Julius himself asks for the building, which he uses for a church. Chesnutt, who was only marginally interested in the practice of conjure, used stories of the occult to demonstrate the overriding power of whites. Only by preying on whites' sense of sentiment did Julius succeed in achieving his goals. Nevertheless, white readers used *The Conjure Woman* to bolster their own version of the pre–Civil War South, including the primitive superstitiousness of blacks.

In keeping with their interpretation of *The Conjure Woman*, white authors painted an even more negative picture of blacks' supernaturalism. Thomas Nelson Page's Dr. Moses preyed upon noble whites, especially women, and led blacks in attempts to overthrow the ruling class. As such, Moses and his kind were the opposite of white southerners. Helen Pitkin's 1904 book *An Angel by Brevet* tells the story of a white New Orleans girl who dabbles in hoodoo and of the near-tragic results. Despite its threatening nature, the presence of conjure was part of what it meant to be southern. Pitkin put it best: "New Orleans is yearning upward through Northern lights and is losing by degrees the peculiarities that have given her 'color' in high relief against even Southern cities. But for many years to come the traditions of the Congo precincts of demonry will cling to her."[26] Whites dominated the late-nineteenth-century

South. For Chesnutt conjure was one means by which blacks could deal with the injustices of the ruling class. For white authors hoodoo symbolized black barbarism, a necessary counterpart to their conception of white civilization. For both races it was part of what it meant to be southern.

Even those who had no particular interest in slave life would encounter stories of conjure in their newspapers and popular magazines. For instance, on 10 July 1889 the *Daily Equator-Democrat,* of Key West, Florida, recorded that blacks of the Carolinas believed that castor oil was made by a conjurer from human blood. The popularity of stories of hoodoo was so widespread that even national magazines carried accounts of it. Not surprisingly, New Orleans, home of Voodoo, received the most attention. In 1885 the respected *Harper's Weekly* published an obituary of Jean Montanet, a well-known Voodoo conjurer who was also known by the names Dr. John and Jean Bayou. The author of the obituary, Lafcadio Hearn, celebrated the deceased as "the most extraordinary African character that ever obtained celebrity within [New Orleans]," giving him the title "Last of the Voudoos."[27] The following year, *Century Magazine* published two articles by George Washington Cable that included much information on the music and dance of Voodoo.[28]

Though journalists gave New Orleans more than its share of attention, they were not remiss in addressing conjure in other locales. For example, in 1889 the *Atlantic Monthly* carried the article "Voodooism in Tennessee," which described the author's experience with a tricked black servant. A year earlier, Eli Shepard published a summary of conjure beliefs as "Superstitions of the Negro," which appeared in *Cosmopolitan.* In the 1890s *Lippincott's Monthly Magazine* also printed two accounts of hoodoo. In short, knowledge of conjure was difficult to escape during the late nineteenth and early twentieth centuries. Such familiarity made it acceptable for popular authors, such as Thomas Nelson Page, to use conjurers as characters in their works with little or no explanation of their persons or powers.[29]

As late as 1908 the editor of *Metropolitan Magazine* was able to state confidently, "We all know to a slight extent that the uneducated negro is a victim of superstition, believes in spells and portents, and observes certain rites to ward off evil."[30] Interest in hoodoo was, however, already on the wane. By the second decade of the twentieth century, what had once been a flood of popular articles slowed to a trickle. Scholarly interest fared somewhat better, though. While the *Southern Workman* had dropped its Folklore and Ethnology column by 1910, the *Journal of American Folklore* maintained an interest in hoodoo, but even this journal published fewer articles than in previous years. The reason for this change was that the nation at large had come to accept the South and its distinctiveness as American. Scholarly histories, following the lead of such authors as William A. Dunning, validated southerners' version of their past. The Civil War became little more than an inevitable conflict between northern industry and southern agriculture. Slaves had lived happy, carefree lives under the watchful eyes of paternalistic masters. Reconstruction was seen as a tragic era during which vengeful Republicans had forced their will upon a wronged South. At the same time, Supreme Court cases, such as *Plessy v. Ferguson,* and Jim Crow laws had legalized blacks' status as second-class citizens. African Americans' ideology of racial uplift no longer seemed so promising. As a result, using the disappearance of superstition as a benchmark of progress became less important. Alongside the plethora of articles already available, these shifts in black and white outlooks inevitably caused a decline in publications addressing conjure.[31]

While works on conjure declined from shortly after 1900 to the mid-1920s, they did not disappear. Surviving folkloric interest in hoodoo helped revive popular attention from the late 1920s through the first half of the 1940s. For instance, the single most influential work to address conjure yet produced has been Newbell Niles Puckett's 1926 book, *Folk Beliefs of the Southern Negro.* Like that of his predecessors, Puckett's primary concern was the assertion of white cultural supremacy. Indeed, his avowed purpose in writing *Folk Beliefs* was to preserve the "mental heirlooms of the Old South."[32] Though he generally agreed with A. M. Bacon's conclusion that conjure had evolved from the religions of Africa, Puckett scrutinized individual beliefs and materials involved in conjure, determining that much of African American hoodoo was of European origin and that as such, it preserved the white past by keeping alive practices that had long been absent among European Americans.[33]

Though he covered topics ranging from burial customs to prophecy, Puckett devoted almost a quarter of his text to conjure and Voodoo, making *Folk Beliefs* the longest general treatment of the subject in existence until the twenty-first century. Investigating hoodoo throughout the South, Puckett examined the initiation of conjurers into their art, dozens of individual spells, and the influence and function of hoodoo doctors in the black community. Like Leonora Herron, he determined that conjure survived as a means of obtaining justice under the system of slavery. Although Puckett's work resembled the local color books of the previous century in its aim to build a white identity around the folk beliefs of former slaves, it was well received by both blacks and whites, influencing, directly or indirectly, all those who followed.[34]

More typical of whites' identity building during the period were the works produced by the Federal Writers' Project (FWP) of 1935–39. By the mid-1920s most had accepted southerners as part of the national consensus, but the very nature of the American system seemed threatened. During the 1920s, intellectuals began to doubt the validity of American capitalism, and many turned to leftist ideologies, particularly Communism. As capitalism appeared to collapse with the coming of the Great Depression, their doubts seemed validated. Massive unemployment, resulting from the economic downturn, likewise undermined middle- and working-class Americans' faith in the American Dream. Among President Franklin Roosevelt's programs for economic assistance were several "alphabet agencies," such as the Works Progress Administration (WPA), which coordinated the FWP. The FWP's chief aim was to alleviate the economic distress of white-collar workers and literary artists by providing work. Just as important, however, its administrators used it as a means of building a "literature of nationhood," which sought to restore worth to the American democratic/capitalist system. The FWP's chief task was the publication of city and state guidebooks emphasizing America's rich heritage of diverse regional and ethnic cultures, melded together through the action of democracy and capitalism. Other minor projects, such as the collection and publication of volumes on local folklore and black life, served a similar purpose.[35]

While most of the folkloric material collected by interviewers has never seen publication, several books did result. In the study of conjure, the most important of these publications are Stetson Kennedy's *Palmetto Country* and *Gumbo Ya-Ya*, by Lyle Saxon, Robert Tallant, and Edward Dreyer, both compiled from material collected by the FWP. These works include considerable hoodoo material from Florida and Louisiana, respectively. *Palmetto Country* and *Gumbo Ya-Ya* were intended for popular audiences. To this end, they retell stories of conjure in an entertaining style, reaching broader audiences than those works aimed at scholars and helping to once more bring conjure into the public eye.[36]

With dreams of racial uplift damaged, if not destroyed, by the deepening of segregation, black Americans turned from white models for their construction of African American identity. The Great Migration of southern blacks to northern cities helped bring about this change. During World War I a dearth of white laborers impaired the productivity and profitability of northern factories, particularly in major manufacturing centers like Chicago, Detroit, and New York. To overcome the shortage of manpower, factory owners turned to black southerners. Advertisements in major black newspapers, company agents, and other forms of recruitment persuaded hundreds of thousands of blacks to flee rural poverty in the South in the hope of finding the American Dream. This folk movement to the urban North continued throughout the 1920s.[37]

The new concentrations of blacks in urban communities and the return of African American veterans from World War I led to rising black assertiveness. One consequence was the growth of largely middle-class civil-rights organizations, such as the National Association for the Advancement of Colored People (NAACP), that sought racial equality through legal maneuvering. Working-class blacks, who composed the great masses of urban African Americans, were more radical. Indeed, the 1920s was a time of widespread political ferment among laborers of both races. Industrial unions were actively recruiting new members. In 1920 the Socialist Party had an impressive showing at the polls, and by 1923 Communist organizations had become a part of the nation's political landscape. Many African Americans turned to these labor movements as a means of achieving political and economic equality as members of a unified, class-conscious proletariat. For other African Americans, being part of a white-led working-class movement was not enough. There were other options. Some chose the path of nationalism, joining such groups as Marcus Garvey's Universal Negro Improvement Association. In contrast to the labor movement, Garvey urged blacks to separate themselves from whites and work toward the unity of all dark-skinned peoples of African descent.[38]

While many African Americans of both the working and middle classes took direct action in their drive for economic improvement and political advancement, some turned to literature and the arts as a means of challenging the white-dominated system that continued to keep blacks second-class citizens. In the years following World War I a black intelligentsia gathered in Harlem. It was determined to overturn the white-defined mores of race by creating a new African American high culture. The resulting artistic flowering, which would come to be known as the Harlem Renaissance, was at heart an effort to create a new "black aesthetic" that rejected whites' denigration of the African American way of life. Participants hoped that by fashioning a black high culture they could prove their race's equality to whites, who doubted African Americans' capacity for intellectual achievement.[39] At the same time, they designed their literary and artistic productions to imbue African Americans with a sense of their own worth; a few went so far as to champion the cause of cultural nationalism.[40]

To further the cause of nationalism, many authors employed black folklore, a move partly inspired by events associated with the American intervention in Haiti. In July 1915 the United States had landed Marines in the island republic, ostensibly to help Haitians build a more stable government. During the nineteen years of occupation that followed, sensationalist books and articles on Haitian Vodou frequently appeared. By portraying the Haitian people as exotically superstitious, white authors attempted to justify American imperialism to a skeptical citizenry by demonstrating the need for a paternalistic "big brother" to protect the interests of the benighted Haitians. Many African Americans, however, opposed the occupation. Rather than perceiving a need for occupation, they saw white American racism extending its grasp beyond the borders of the United States. Many blacks, whether they supported the intervention or not, found value in the history and folklore of the only nation in the Western Hemisphere founded by a slave-led revolution.[41]

The well-known author Zora Neale Hurston was one of the most prominent African Americans to be inspired by the American occupation of Haiti. She expounded her version of black cultural nationalism in her 1931 book-length essay "Hoodoo in America." It was a typical folklore study of the time, consisting primarily of a series of anecdotes and notes on specific conjure materials. Four years later Hurston published *Mules and Men,* the last one hundred pages of which were a heavily revised version of her earlier article, now aimed at popular consumption. Three years after *Mules and Men* appeared, she directly addressed Haitian Vodou in *Tell My Horse: Voodoo and Life in Haiti and Jamaica.*[42]

Hurston's contributions to the scholarship of conjure include a comparison of hoodoo with Bahamian Obeah and her conclusion that hoodoo was primarily African in origin. Nevertheless, her most important innovation was to argue that hoodoo was a vital element of blacks' racial identity, stating, "Hoodoo, or Voodoo, as pronounced by whites, is burning with a flame in America, with all the intensity of a suppressed religion."[43] Unfortunately for the history of conjure, her contemporaries largely ignored her. Middle-class black Americans, who made up the majority of her reading public, were not yet willing to abandon the scientific outlook that drove them to seek "progress" over an identity influenced by "superstition." The working class, which continued to participate in conjure, generally gravitated to labor-based reform instead of to a less tangible cultural nationalism.[44]

Nevertheless, the movement of blacks from the rural South to the urban North did help to bring conjure to the attention of both working- and middle-class African Americans throughout the nation. For example, advertisements for conjuring materials and hoodoo practitioners aimed at the newly arrived laborers boomed in black-oriented periodicals. In the *Chicago Defender*, America's most popular African American newspaper, only one page carried advertisements for conjure goods and services on 1 March 1919. By 7 July 1928, however, twelve pages had such advertisements.

Many blues songs from the early twentieth century employed hoodoo motifs in their lyrics. References to hoodoo, conjure, mojo, charms, tricks, goopher dust, magical roots, and the like were common in the songs of the period. One example was Bessie Brown's "Hoodoo Blues." Referring to a romantic rival, she sang:

> Goin' 'neath her window, gonna lay a black cat bone
> Goin' 'neath her window, gonna lay a black cat bone
> Burn a candle on her picture, she won't let my good man alone.[45]

The other verses make similar references to hoodoo practices. Brown's song was only one of more than a hundred blues songs addressing conjure. Among the well-known artists who referred to conjure were Cripple Clarence Lofton, Champion Jack Dupree, Muddy Waters, Blind Lemon Jefferson, Louis Jordan, and W. C. Handy.[46]

At the same time that hoodoo was appearing in newsprint and music, some conjurers became nationally known figures. Chief among them were James Jordan, of Como, North Carolina, and "Doctor Buzzard," of Beaufort, South Carolina, who drew their clientele from across the eastern United States. Both men became wealthy through their work, sometimes charging hundreds, even thousands, of dollars for a single spell. In the case of Dr. Buzzard, whose legal name was Stephaney Robinson, the success was all the more notable because he relied upon name recognition to help build his reputation. Robinson was the second Dr. Buzzard. The first of that name was a white conjurer who had died in the late nineteenth century, at approximately the same time that Robinson, an African American, took up the practice.[47] While Hurston unsuccessfully sought to make hoodoo a foundation for a black identity encompassing all classes, the masses of African American laborers had never forgotten its importance.[48]

As the impact of Puckett's *Folk Beliefs of the Southern Negro* and the publications of the FWP collided with rising black assertiveness, scholars gave ever more attention to conjure. Of particular interest to historians and anthropologists of the time was the question of African survivals, the examination of which became much easier because of the oral histories collected by the WPA. Melville J. Herskovits, author of *The Myth of the Negro Past*, emerged as the most influential scholar to address this issue. Relying heavily on information from Puckett's earlier study, he argued that conjure was a relic of African religion, proving that blacks, like Europeans, were "a people with a past."[49]

As usual, however, scholarly works were not the most important influence on the wider public. Far more visible were the popular articles that once again began to appear in national periodicals. For instance, in 1927 M. S. Lea's "Two-head Doctors" appeared in the *American Mercury*. In this brief article Lea tells a series of hoodoo stories she learned from her African American maid and a black night watchman during her residence in Washington, DC. Three years later, *Scribner's Magazine* published Ruth Bass's "Mojo: The Strange Magic That Works in the South Today," an account of conjure in Mississippi and Louisiana.[50]

Despite the increasing attention to conjure in popular and scholarly publications, works addressing hoodoo were less common than in the late nineteenth and early twentieth centuries. The result was that fewer readers came into contact with them. Conjure had already begun to fade from popular conceptions of black society. Likewise, most fictional accounts of the Old South gave trick doctors little attention during the period. The two most popular books of the era, Margaret Mitchell's *Gone with the Wind* and Stark Young's *So Red the Rose*, make no mention of hoodoo doctors, who had once been common fixtures in tales of the plantation South. As a result of fading white understandings of conjure, writers from the 1920s through the 1940s treated hoodoo as a hidden part of black society. Hurston was able to refer to hoodoo as a "suppressed religion" with some justification. For instance, in "Two-head Doctors" Lea announces that before a conversation with her maid introduced her to hoodoo, she had "never supposed that its practices existed save among a handful of the swamp and plantation Negroes of the Gulf States."[51]

Popular articles increasingly carried titles intended to shock readers with their announcements of the "discovery" of conjure. Essays from the late nineteenth century were apt to have titles akin to Sheperd's "Superstitions of the Negro" or Bacon's "Conjuring and Conjure-Doctors." Works from the 1920s to 1940s were more likely to carry appellations resembling that of Bass's "Mojo: The Strange Magic That Works in the South Today" or the even more sensationalist "Black Jupiter: A Voodoo King in Florida's Jungle—Black Magic in the Turpentine Forests," by Edwin Granberry. No longer simply a peculiarity of everyday southern life, hoodoo had become a sensational mystery that needed to be revealed to a wondering public.

After the mid-1940s, conjure, already an obscure topic, disappeared from most Americans' conception of black society as it became less important as a means of identity construction.[52] For whites, World War II and the coming of the cold war played important roles. On a basic level, World War II lessened the need for such federal relief programs as the FWP. More important, however, the war revived capitalism, rendering the "literature of nationhood" less vital for the construction of American identity. Later, the Red Scare reoriented whites' search for identity away from FWP-style "unity in diversity" in favor of simple unity. As early as 1939 the fear of Communist infiltration of America's intellectuals combined with economic recovery to doom the FWP. For both northerners and southerners, Communism had become "the other" against whom they defined their revitalized system of capitalism and democracy. In such a world, blacks were simply less important to whites' identity construction than they had once been.[53]

As in the white community, the cold war limited the future visibility of conjure in black life by limiting hoodoo's importance to African American identity. During World War II the labor-led civil rights movement made substantial gains, achieving the establishment of the Fair Employment Practices Commission and the desegregation of the armed forces. Though working-class blacks never seized upon conjure as an ideological expression of blackness, they had always been more familiar with hoodoo than had middle-class blacks. A successful labor-led civil rights movement might have provided a vehicle for hoodoo to reenter American consciousness. Soon after the end of the war, however, the cold war brought the movement's promise to an end. As fear of Communism gripped America, government suppression of leftists and militant labor undermined the foundation of black efforts. While the early civil rights movement had never made folk beliefs an important part of its identity, its collapse limited the power of working-class blacks to be heard by both whites and middle-class members of their own race. Without any significant focus of resistance, Jim Crow persisted largely undisturbed until the mid-1950s.[54]

After the Supreme Court's move against segregation in the 1954 *Brown v. Board of Education of Topeka, Kansas* and a succession of nonviolent boycotts, sit-ins, marches, and other forms of protest, the civil rights movement reemerged as a more powerful force than it had been since Reconstruction.

This time, however, it was ill-suited to promote conjure as a positive element of black culture. The movement's leaders, drawn primarily from the black middle class, held to their long-term belief that hoodoo was a negative feature of their society. More important, during this phase of the civil rights movement no major effort was made to incorporate any part of black culture into its goals. On the contrary, the likes of Martin Luther King Jr. advocated a color-blind society of full social, economic, and political equality with whites obtained through Christian brotherhood. One unintentional side effect of this approach was the temporary muting of black cultural nationalism, a potential route to the rediscovery of conjure. Moreover, in its early years the movement did little more than further divide the races culturally. While only a minority of whites actively fought the movement, even fewer joined it. Though it eventually achieved its goals of ending legal segregation and halting official discrimination in the workplace and at the polls after years of struggle, it failed to erase the racism that compelled whites to reject social contact with African Americans and prevented them from appreciating the black folk culture that had once been such an important part of white identity.[55]

Professional folklorists, who had continued to study conjure on a small scale, likewise lost interest as they adopted problem solving as the focus of their work. In 1958 Vladimir Propp's *Morphology of the Folktale* was printed in English. Published in Russian thirty years earlier, the already-influential book helped reshape the field through its assertion that folktales throughout the world share common structures and underlying meanings. One result was that folklore lost much of its effectiveness as a means of asserting regional or national identities, divorcing it from popular audiences. Nevertheless, some books addressing conjure continued to see print, but these were increasingly studies of specifically black folklore, such as Langston Hughes and Arna Bontemps's *Book of Negro Folklore.* Thus, they failed to appeal to a broad audience in an era of racial turmoil. More important, articles addressing conjure became less common in such scholarly publications as the *Journal of American Folklore* and virtually disappeared from popular magazines.[56] On the rare occasion when a journalist saw fit to print such articles, they usually echoed the words of the journalist Edward D. Clayton, who referred to New Orleans Voodoo and hoodoo as "a lucrative racket ... practiced surreptitiously with weird mumbo-jumbo in flats around the city by a handful of self-styled 'doctors' and 'reverends' who prey on naive innocents."[57] Abandoned by even its most steadfast friend, hoodoo faded into invisibility.

Today, interest in conjure is again reviving. By the 1970s, black magical beliefs were becoming more apparent, largely owing to an influx of Latin Americans of African descent, who brought such syncretic religions as Santería into the United States. Whether driven from their homes by political oppression or economic distress, these new arrivals brought elements of their distinct cultures with them, including their religions. While most Latin American immigrants professed Catholicism, many also practiced some form of Afro-European syncretic religion, the most important of which has been Cuban Santería. As Santería spread throughout both northern and southern cities, most noticeably New York and Miami, it became increasingly visible in the press. Though it differs from African American hoodoo and Voodoo in its gods and central tenets, native-born white Americans have often failed to distinguish between it and indigenous American folk religions, as was clear in such works as E. Tivnan's 1979 article "The Voodoo That New Yorkers Do," which lumps Santería and other syncretic faiths under the misleading rubric "Voodoo." Other important syncretic religions that have recently appeared in the United States are Bahamian Obeah, Mexican Espiritismo, Trinidadian Shango, and Brazilian Candomble. During the 1990s Haitian Vodou also increased as a result of the flight of many Haitians from political turmoil.[58]

Despite the growing visibility of magic, most authors continued to view African American magic as a sign of backwardness. For example, in July 1976 Hamilton Bims published "Would You *Believe* It . . . Superstition Lives!" in *Ebony*, giving hoodoo a prominent place in a gallery of disreputable beliefs and practices. This dismissive approach began to decline as the ideas of cultural pluralism, postmodernism, and the New Age movement increasingly caught hold throughout the 1970s, 1980s, and 1990s, allowing Americans to construct individual and group identities free from an overarching national culture. First propounded by the philosopher Horace Kallen and adopted by the anthropologists Franz Boas and Margaret Mead, the idea of cultural pluralism proclaimed equality among the world's diverse cultures. Following the success of the civil rights movement and the arrival of the new Latin American immigrants, it had gained widespread popular support by the 1980s, opening a path to the acceptance of conjure as a valid expression of black identity.[59]

As cultural pluralism gained strength, so did the intellectual trend known as postmodernism. While scholars have yet to offer a definitive account of the meaning, influence, and worth of postmodern ideas, they tend to agree on many of its distinctive characteristics. The most important of these to the study of conjure has been the denial of any moral authority outside of the individual. In practice, this has led to an ideology that touts fragmentation, plurality, and indeterminacy as positive values. In such a world-view hoodoo is the equal of Christianity and other world religions.[60]

Together, cultural pluralism and postmodernism prepared Americans for the reappearance of hoodoo in print, but it was the revival of mysticism and magical practices during the 1970s that ultimately pushed conjure into the public eye. Known as the New Age movement, this countercultural collection of religions mirrors the secular forces of cultural pluralism and postmodernism, and like them, it rejects centralization and ultimate authority. According to author Melody Baker, New Age belief is characterized by "a commitment to spiritual growth which people pursue in different manners, many considered nontraditional in Western culture," in which "dogma and the absence of questioning are seen as obstacles to growth."[61] Beginning with imported Eastern mysticism during the late 1960s, the New Age movement quickly drew other occult practices under its wings, including forms of herbal medicine, extraterrestrial worship, and various forms of witchcraft, the most prominent of which has been Wicca, a pseudohistorical mixture of magic and goddess worship.[62]

Initially, conjure failed to attract much attention from New Agers. It was too strongly linked to American culture to be sufficiently iconoclastic. Nevertheless, a few authors have sought to merge hoodoo into the larger New Age world-view. One of the earliest of these was the South Carolinian James Edwin McTeer, author of *Fifty Years as a Low Country Witch Doctor*. McTeer, a white of European descent, also practiced African American hoodoo, working alongside the famed Doctor Buzzard. Though he claimed to be "the last remaining tie with the true African witch doctors," McTeer explained his powers in the typical New Age jargon of astral planes, extrasensory perception, and mediumship.[63] Several recent works on hoodoo also follow the same course. For instance, in *Company of Prophets: African American Psychics, Healers, and Visionaries*, Joyce Elaine Noll refers to mediums, astral projection, and reincarnation alongside traditional hoodoo beliefs. In short, by building on the foundation of cultural pluralism and postmodernism, the New Age movement has both lessened the stigma attached to blacks' magical practices and brought positive views of conjure to public awareness.

Though New Age ideology has been primarily the province of white society, it has also opened a way for African Americans to seize upon conjure as a symbol of their identity. Black cultural nationalism provided the medium through which hoodoo has regained a prominent role in African American literature. As the equality-based civil rights movement declined following its string of legal and political victories during the early 1960s, the Black Power movement took its place. Inspired largely by the writings of Malcolm X and Stokely Carmichael, its militant adherents sought African American autonomy and self-reliance. Some joined militant organizations like the Black Panther Party, which was prepared to use force to advance its aims, which included equal political and social rights, exemption from military service, and full employment for blacks. More important to the study of conjure, however, many proponents of Black Power worked to construct a version of African American history and culture that placed blacks' achievements on par with those of whites. By doing so, members of the Black Power movement engaged in a form of identity politics that offered an alternative to Eurocentric ideas of civilization and progress.[64]

In an environment of New Age ideology and black cultural nationalism, hoodoo became a symbol of African American resistance to white culture. The works of the poet Ishmael Reed exemplify this trend. To Reed, the hoodoo doctor is a trickster who subverts white dominance through apparent acceptance of his or her assigned role, while "driven by a mocking wit that subverts white authority and destroys white illusions of superiority."[65]

The influence of Reed's highly intellectual writings pales in comparison with that of works aimed at black popular audiences. The most important of these has been James Haskins's *Voodoo and Hoodoo*, which offers a brief history of conjure—a summary of works by Puckett and other earlier authors—followed by a lengthy collection of spells. Later writers have followed Haskins's example, providing both general information on the history and practice of conjure and "practical" knowledge of herbal remedies, spells, and divination. In such works conjure is an integral part of blacks' African heritage, to be celebrated, not condemned.[66]

While Haskins and his imitators have helped to make hoodoo an acceptable part of blackness, a few have followed the example of Ishmael Reed, making individual conjurers symbols of African American strength. Marie Laveau, the famed nineteenth-century "Voodoo Queen" of New Orleans, has been most commonly cast in this role, becoming a personification of black feminine strength. For example, for a 1983 issue of *Ms.* Jewell Parker Rhodes wrote that it is Laveau's "spirit that, generation after generation, enters a woman's body whenever a woman assumes power."[67] Khephra Burns followed a similar course in her 1992 article "The Queen of Voodoo," stating that "no woman was ever more feared and revered than Marie Laveau, the Voodoo Queen of New Orleans." Recently, Martha Ward has enshrined a similar viewpoint in *Voodoo Queen*, a scholarly biography of Laveau. Hoodoo has come a long way from the late nineteenth century, when it was but a survival of Negro primitiveness.

How does this third wave of interest compare with those that came before? Its growing importance to blacks can be seen by comparing two dictionaries of African American colloquialisms compiled by Clarence Major. In 1970 Major published his *Dictionary of Afro-American Slang*. It has only a few entries that describe conjuring practices, most notably "conjuring lodge," which the author defines as "a place where mediumistic practices could openly take place." Entries for such terms as *hoodoo, mojo, tricking,* and even *Voodoo* are absent. Twenty-four years later Major produced a revised version of his dictionary, renamed *Juba to Jive: A Dictionary of African-American Slang*. Not only does the new version include the missing terms but it expounds upon them in ways that emphasize the importance of conjure to black history and culture. For instance, *Juba to Jive* defines a conjuring lodge as follows: "sacred house; church; stemming from their belief in the power of the conjurer, black Americans during slavery held this as a place in which mediumistic rites and principles could be respected and practiced. It is not unlike the Zuni and Hopi kiva."

Although books on conjure, ranging from Haskins's *Voodoo and Hoodoo* to *Doktor Snake's Voodoo Spell Book: Spells, Curses and Folk Magic for All Your Needs* (with a free "Lucky Mojo Doll"), are readily available in bookstores and on the Internet, hoodoo is beyond the sphere of most Americans' conception of black society.[68] Gone are the days when major news magazines carried tales of conjure as common fare. Moreover, those works that do appear aim at African American and New Age audiences, excluding most white general readers. Nevertheless, hoodooists have begun to make occasional appearances in bestselling works, most notably John Berendt's *Midnight in the Garden of Good and Evil*, a fictionalized history of a Savannah, Georgia, murder in which a conjure woman is an important character. Such works are the exception, however. Conjure has not become the important factor of regional and racial identity that it was during the late nineteenth and early twentieth centuries. Its study has likewise failed to become an important part of public works projects, as it was during the days of the FWP. The hoodoo doctor, though perhaps not fully invisible, remains at best translucent in popular conceptions of black culture.

Scholarly interest in conjure has fared even worse. For instance, hoodoo receives minimal attention in the standard works on slave culture, most of which appeared during the 1970s and 1980s. Conjure commands only brief mentions in such works as John W. Blassingame's *Slave Community*, George P. Rawick's *From Sunup to Sundown*, and Charles Joyner's *Down by the Riverside*. Other books, such as Eugene Genovese's *Roll, Jordan, Roll*, Lawrence Levine's *Black Culture and Black Consciousness*, and Albert J. Raboteau's *Slave Religion*, devote more space to conjuring. Nevertheless, these accounts are largely descriptive, and their analyses generally summarize the conclusions set forth in *Folk Beliefs of the Southern Negro* and other early works.[69]

Scholars in general and historians in particular are reluctant to delve more deeply in their studies of hoodoo for a variety of reasons. First, relatively few primary documents address conjure; in contrast, sources on topics such as slave society, black culture, and even African American Christianity are plentiful, making their study much simpler. Far more important than the lack of primary materials, however, is religious prejudice. Scholars tend to shy away from supernatural topics because of their own secular world-views. They prefer to rely on race, class, gender, and the like to explain historical development. The result is that they often minimize the role of religious beliefs in history, particularly in their treatments of the modern world. While intellectuals tend to be irreligious, they respect magic even less. After all, virtually no one, scholar or layperson, would admit to believing in sorcery as an effective practice. A paucity of historical scholarship has been the consequence.

Racial issues have also kept hoodoo outside of mainstream scholarship. For some African American scholars conjure retains its negative image from years past. They are unwilling to tout "superstition" as a major force in black history. On the other hand, those who have accepted conjure as part of their African American identity frequently oppose any attempt by white authors to address the topic.[70]

Four notable exceptions to the scholarly trend have appeared.[71] The first of these to appear was Harry Middleton Hyatt's *Hoodoo—Conjuration—Witchcraft—Rootwork*, published in five volumes from 1970 to 1978. This massive work is a collection of transcripts of interviews addressing hoodoo, mostly undertaken during the 1930s and 1940s.[72] Though it contains a wealth of primary material, its chaotic organization and brief printing run of only six hundred copies for the first two volumes have minimized its influence.[73]

Theophus Smith's investigation of African American theology, *Conjuring Culture: Biblical Formations of Black America*, has likewise had little impact on studies of conjure. Smith argued that West African religions mingled with

European Christianity to produce a "conjuring culture," still evident in modern black society. Conjurers, he maintained, must be recognized as more than sorcerers; their magic offers a means to magically heal, or transform, society. Within this world-view the Bible has become the chief conjure tool. Like the work of A. M. Bacon, almost one hundred years earlier, *Conjuring Culture* outlined an underlying logic to black folk beliefs through its classification of the books of the Bible by their specific magical function.[74] Smith's book has largely failed to influence historians owing to its highly specialized approach. In addition to its narrow focus, its prose is difficult for those who do not have a specialized knowledge of theology.

At the same time that Theophus Smith was studying the relics of conjure in African American theology, archaeologists were recovering the physical artifacts of hoodoo. One prominent scholar who took an early interest in conjure was Eric Klingelhofer, who identified conjuring paraphernalia among the items excavated from the slave quarters of a Maryland plantation. Another archaeologist who found evidence of hoodoo in excavated items was Leland G. Ferguson, best known for his discovery of African American conjuring symbols on colonial pottery. By the mid-1990s brief archaeological studies of eighteenth- and nineteenth-century hoodoo had become plentiful, and the trend continues today. Unfortunately, historians are more comfortable with written documents than with physical artifacts. Few of them have incorporated the recent discoveries into their understanding of African American society.[75]

By far the most readable and innovative work to appear in recent years has been Carolyn Morrow Long's 2001 book *Spiritual Merchants: Religion, Magic, and Commerce*. Following brief summaries of antebellum and early-twentieth-century hoodoo, Long examines the development of conjure as a commodity, manufactured and distributed to "spiritual supply stores" for the use of do-it-yourself conjurers. Long's work has been one of the most important works on hoodoo yet produced, but its author is not a professional historian, which will hamper its acceptance by the academic community. Only time will reveal the extent of its influence. Despite the efforts of Hyatt, Smith, and Long, conjure remains unfamiliar territory to most students of black culture.

Though studies of conjure have grown more numerous over the past three decades, they have failed to return hoodoo to most Americans' conception of black society. Moreover, the third wave of interest in conjure does not yet compare to the two that erupted during the late nineteenth and early twentieth centuries and during the years between the world wars. Hoodoo's continued obscurity leaves a fertile field for historians, who have yet to answer several important questions. For example, the old problem of whether conjure is primarily an African or European legacy has yet to be satisfactorily resolved. Recent authors addressing hoodoo have tended to uncritically assume that it is of primarily African origin, giving little attention to other influences. In addition, so far, only Carolyn Morrow Long has examined hoodoo's regional variations in any detail. Most important, almost all authors, scholarly or popular, have treated conjure as a timeless phenomenon. On the contrary, it has adapted to changing circumstances, remaining an important part of African American society from antebellum times to the present.[76]

1
Vodu and *Minkisi:*
The African Foundation of Black American Magic

DURING THE FIRST half of the twentieth century scholars debated the degree to which African beliefs and practices survived in the New World. Over time those arguing in favor of substantial African survivals prevailed.[1] In light of this current scholarly consensus, it is surprising that historians have done little to systematically trace conjure's multiple African roots.[2] Nevertheless, its transformation from African religion to American magic made it into a microcosm of the African American experience that combined elements of loss with a persistent drive to survive in the face of persecution. Nineteenth-century hoodoo was a result of creolization and syncretism, the mixing of multiple African, European, and Native American cultures, which together resulted in a form of magic unique to the American South. Ultimately, however, the origins of hoodoo lie in the traditional religious beliefs of the land from which the slaves' ancestors hailed.

The roots of conjure extend deep into sub-Saharan Africa, where magic has long been a feature of everyday life throughout most of the region. Moreover, no one tribe or people group can claim to be *the* origin of hoodoo.[3] Instead, certain groups played greater or lesser roles, depending heavily on the demographics of slave importation into particular areas. African influences on hoodoo fell into two primary cultural zones corresponding roughly to the distinct areas settled by Latin and English colonists.

Modern American conjure is a mixture of magical beliefs originating in the two zones of European settlement, which remained quite distinct during the seventeenth, eighteenth, and nineteenth centuries. The first of the areas to be settled by substantial numbers of European colonists was the Atlantic Coast, encompassing Maryland, Virginia, North Carolina, South Carolina, and Georgia. These British colonies received shipments of slaves beginning in 1619, and the trade accelerated in the late seventeenth and eighteenth centuries. The primary element that set this area apart from the rest of the South was the strong English influence that shaped it from the early seventeenth century onward. Within the English-settled region, the Sea Islands of South Carolina and Georgia proved the most important. High black-to-white ratios and relative isolation from the rest of the South set these locations apart. From their initial settlements along the Atlantic coast, Anglo-American settlers moved west to occupy the lands of the central South and the trans-Mississippi region, as far as Texas.

The second area included French and Spanish settlements, chiefly on the Gulf of Mexico and the lower Mississippi River. A handful of Spanish troops and settlers arrived in 1565, founding St. Augustine, Florida. Shortly thereafter small numbers of Spanish settlers moved into what is now Texas. The French did not reach the American South in significant numbers until the early eighteenth century. Their largest settlement was New Orleans, but smaller ones also occupied the Gulf Coast as far east as Florida. During the late eighteenth and early nineteenth centuries the Latin cultural area grew far more slowly than the English domain. The chief area of expansion was the Mississippi River. Along its banks, French settlers gradually advanced northward. In other regions, Latin influence declined as the Protestant English moved westward. Louisiana, which fell under American control in 1803, retained much of its Latin culture because of its large French population. South Florida, which had a very small colonial population, likewise escaped rapid assimilation to the American culture, primarily because few American settlers wanted to move into an area with such a climate and terrain.

In the lands settled by the French and Spanish, the Fon, Yoruba, Ewe, and Mande speakers of northern West Africa laid the groundwork for an African American culture, partially through their heavy importation during the colonial period. In Louisiana, in particular, these and closely related peoples made up more than half of all Africans brought into the area. During the early republican and antebellum periods the number of slaves from northern West Africa declined drastically. West-central Africans replaced them, the largest number of whom hailed from the Kongo kingdom. Despite the shift in importation patterns, the early presence of slaves from the closely related cultures of the Fon, Ewe, and Yoruba and the more distinct Mande defined the area's magical practices. Later arrivals modified but could not replace them. Moreover, in both French Louisiana and Spanish Florida brief spurts of immigration from the Caribbean bolstered the influence of the earlier groups. In Louisiana these were Haitian refugees fleeing revolution. In Florida the late-nineteenth-century arrival of Afro-Cubans seeking economic opportunity not only bolstered existing beliefs but also created large black communities in areas where none had existed.[4]

While west-central Africans proved only a secondary influence in the Latin area, they were the primary influence on the magic of the region settled by the English. Their numbers were particularly pronounced in coastal South Carolina and Georgia, where they made up more than half of all imports throughout the period when slavery was legal. Once again, the Kongo people were the largest contingent among the unwilling arrivals from west-central Africa. Also, as in Louisiana, the Mande were a significant, though minority, presence. Although the chief features of conjure derived from the Fon, the Ewe, and the Yoruba in the Latin area, the Kongo in the lands settled by the English, and the Mande in both, other groups, including the Igbo, the Akan, and the Ga-Dangme, played important roles in the creation of African American conjure, especially in particular aspects of hoodoo.[5]

The ethnic differences between the settlers of the Latin and English cultural zones led to persistent differences between the areas. One of the most obvious of these distinctions was the difference in words used to refer to conjure. In New Orleans, where French influence dominated, whites knew African Americans' syncretic religion and its associated magic as *Voodoo*, while blacks called it *hoodoo*.[6] Male practitioners were typically known as *wangateurs*, and female practitioners as *wangateuses*. *Gris-gris* and *zinzin* denoted charms and spells, while *tobies* and *wangas* were more specific words for good and evil charms, respectively. In Missouri *noodoo*, a variant of *Voodoo*, was the favored term for the practice of African American magic. In southern Florida, an area long ruled by Spain, a Voodoo-like religion and magical system developed from the Santería and Palo Mayombe faiths practiced by Cuban immigrants to area. It was known as *Nañigo*, and its priests and priestesses were known as *papa-lois* and *mama-lois*, respectively. Conjurers were termed *brujas*. Along the English-settled Atlantic seaboard, black sorcerers called themselves *conjurers*, *rootworkers,* and *double-heads.* The performance of their art was known by such words as *conjure, rooting, tricking, fixing,* and *goophering.* In some cases terms were localized. For instance, Maryland blacks knew conjurers as *high* men or women. Likewise, *rootworkers* was a designation particularly popular along the Georgia and South Carolina coasts, as was *goopher,* a term almost unknown outside of the English cultural area. In Mississippi, African Americans used *mojo* to refer to benevolent magic. Virginian blacks sometimes called conjuring *Gombre-work.* Though the words used for conjure varied widely throughout the South, terms deriving from European languages were more common in the area settled by Anglos.[7]

The influence of specific African cultures is readily apparent in some of the unique terms applied to conjure, particularly those of the Latin zone. *Voodoo* derived from the Fon and Ewe term *vodu,* meaning "god" or "worship or fear of the gods." *Hoodoo,* originally used in the Latin area to identify conjure, is most likely a variation of *Voodoo.* However, Zora Neale Hurston claimed that it was a corruption of *juju,* another West African term, meaning "magic" or "charm."[8] The Louisianian terms *gris-gris, zinzin,* and *wanga,* denoting various types of spells and charms, likewise derive from West African terms. *Gris-gris,* a general term for magic, came from the Mandingo tribe, a subgroup of Mande speakers, who used magical items know as *gerregerys* or *gregory bags,* to harm others. Mande-speaking members of the Bambara tribe introduced the term *zinzin,* which referred to positive charms designed to confer strength or power on their possessors.[9] *Wanga,* denoting malevolent magic and charms, and the derived terms *wangateur* and *wangateuse* were probably also of Mande origin. *Toby* reflected the early republican and antebellum influx of west-central African Kongos, whose *tobe* charms brought good luck to their owners. In Florida the titles *papa-loi* and *mama-loi* were the African American creolizations of the Yoruba word for a diviner-herbalist, *babalawo.*[10]

Conjure terminology with African origins was rare outside of the Latin cultural area. *Goopher,* used in such combinations as *goopher doctor* or *goopher dust,* was an exception to the rule. Employed in coastal Georgia and the Carolinas to designate items derived from the dead or persons dealing with them, it most likely developed from the Kongo word *kufwa,* meaning "to die." *Mojo* and its variant *Joe Moe* were Kongo-derived terms found in both cultural zones that described magic and charms usually designed for positive ends. In the Kongo kingdom *mooyo* referred to spirits that dwelt within magical charms and was easily transferred to the spirits' dwelling place.[11]

More than simply words survived the Middle Passage, however. In the Latin area, African deities continued to play a role in the lives of blacks. According to Kofi Asare Opoku, author of *West African Traditional Religions*, traditional northern West African gods and spirits were of six sorts. First, there was a unique being, often far separated from humanity, who gave life and power to all other beings, including lesser gods and spirits. Among Fon speakers this being was known as Mawu-Lisa, an androgynous god/goddess incarnate in the moon and sun. Among Yoruba speakers Olorun filled the role of supreme being. Virtually every other West African people had such a god. While Africans prayed to these supreme beings, they rarely offered sacrifices or otherwise sought to win their favor; beings so perfect had no need of such mundane acts of service. The next tier in the spiritual hierarchy was filled with ancestral spirits, whom West Africans believed existed alongside their living descendants. The living honored the dead with offerings of food, celebrations, and sometimes deification. Next followed a variety of lesser deities, who, unlike the supreme being, could be relied upon to take direct action in the lives of their followers, for good or ill. Each god and goddess played a particular role. Among the Fon speakers of Dahomey, Da, chief of the earth deities, was a snake god, worshiped in the form of sacred pythons. Da was also recognized as an early ancestor of the Dahomey kings. An important god of the Fon and Ewe, Legba, served as a divine linguist, interpreting the decrees of the gods to mortals, and trickster. Da was primarily confined to Fon speakers, but Legba-like gods appeared in most West African pantheons. For instance, among the Yoruba, Elegba or Eshu fulfilled the same role.[12]

Below the ancestral spirits and deities were a variety of lesser beings. The most important were totemic animals and plants that were important to particular individuals, families, and tribes. Usually these were reputed to have had a prominent place in the lives of their forebears. Two final types of spiritual beings were closely associated with magic. Occupying the fifth level of the spiritual hierarchy were beings who assisted sorcerers in the performance of both good and evil spells. One of the more well known of these was Sasabonsum, a cannibalistic spirit who aided Tshi-speaking witches in working evil. The sixth tier was filled by the indwelling spirits of the charms made by workers of magic.[13]

Kongolese traditional religion had a similar hierarchy. At the top was Nzambi, the supreme being. Below Nzambi were four types of spirits, all of which had once been living humans. Together these roughly corresponded to the second tier of northern West African belief. *Bakulu*, or "ancestors," were the most important type of spirit and were honored in various ceremonies and sacrifices performed by the heads of clans, chiefs, and smiths. Next in the ranking were a variety of gods or spirits called *basimbi*, who occupied specific territories, localities, villages, and even physical objects such as bridges, bends in roads, and rivers. Another type of beings, *minkisi* (singular *nkisi*), occupied charms made by priests and magicians. While all types of the foregoing beings were generally benevolent, a final group of spirits, the *min'kuyu*, were malevolent ghosts. In life *min'kuyu* had been witches, and after death they had been refused entrance to the dwelling place of the ancestors.[14]

Blacks did not leave the spiritual hierarchies of Africa behind when they were dragged from their homeland by slave traders. On the contrary, elements of the old religions survived in the American South. The most apparent of these were the lesser deities of the Fon, the Ewe, and the Yoruba who survived in the Latin area (see table 1). By the nineteenth century, however, these lesser deities had also taken over the role of magical helpers, which had been a separate class in Africa. In French-settled areas the gods of the Fon and Ewe speakers predominated. As in northern West Africa, the serpent god ruled the pantheon. Believers in the Fon-speaking kingdom of Dahomey had worshiped Da as a sacred python. Pythons were unobtainable in the American South, forcing substitutions of other snakes. African Americans continued to worship Da in the area around New Orleans, where he was known as Blanc Dani of Danny. In the United States the Voodoo "queens" kept the snakes of indeterminate species, bringing them out during major community rituals to signal the beginning of a period of praise to and possession by Blanc Dani. As with the supreme god of African beliefs, believers only occasionally utilized the serpent god in magic. He was too exalted a being.[15]

Other deities who survived in New Orleans had no compunctions about helping their devotees work magic. Legba, the second most powerful god of the Fon and Ewe, was always available to those who wished to call on him for conjure. Moreover, he retained his African role as the linguist of the gods, opening lines of communication to a variety of other beings. Early in major Voodoo ceremonies, believers called on Papa Lébat, Liba, or LaBas, the New Orleans forms of Legba, saying, "Bon jour Liba, ouvert la porte; Ouvert la porte, Bon jour ma cousin; Bon jour ma cousin, Bon Jour Liba" (Good day Liba, open the door; Open the door, Good day my cousin; Good day my cousin, Good day Liba).[16] Two of the gods to whom Lébat opened the door were Monsieur Assonquer and Monsieur Agoussou, the gods of good fortune and love, respectively. Because of their respective functions, these two were particularly popular among believers.[17]

The survival of African gods in New Orleans is well known, but they also persisted in other places as well. In Missouri the serpent god Da lived on in the form of Grandfather Rattlesnake, whom believers honored with dances. Florida's distinctive brand of syncretic religion, Nañigo, had a richer pantheon, drawn primarily from the gods of the Yoruba. Florida's blacks had no snake god, but they retained Obatala, greatest of the Yoruban gods. Obatala was the most powerful spirit, and unlike in the case of Blanc Dani, this power made him the best god to call upon for the performance of spells. Elegba, a trickster and phallic god among the Yoruba people, reportedly became an evil god in America. For this reason, he was especially useful in the performance of evil magic. Shango, god of thunder, and Yemaya, goddess of air and water, were two other prominent gods who survived from Yoruba belief. Nanga, an evil spirit in Nañigo, appears to have been a rare Kongo contribution to the pantheon. In Kongo belief, Nanga was a legendary hero who led his people on a great migration to the present-day home of the Kongo people. In contrast to their survival in the Latin areas, the lesser gods had largely died out in the English-settled lands by the nineteenth century. Occasional sacrifices to bring good weather or prosperity and praying to rivers before baptisms were two rare exceptions to the rule.[18]

What was different about the Anglo-influenced zones that made them less hospitable to such African traditional deities? Ultimately, a combination of black-to-white ratios, importation of slaves from the Caribbean, and European religious differences provide the answer. The territories around New Orleans and around the South Carolina and Georgia Sea Islands, both of which were major centers for hoodoo, had high black-to-white population ratios during antebellum times. This fact doubtless contributed to the persistence of magic in both Latin and Anglo zones. In addition, the concentration of African Americans made the continued celebration of large-scale religious rituals more viable. Black-to-white ratios alone, however, cannot explain the religious differences between the Latin and Anglo cultural areas. For instance, the Sea Islands, where blacks often outnumbered whites several times over, had a much higher percentage of blacks than did New Orleans, South Florida, or Missouri, all of which showed more African survivals during the nineteenth century.[19]

In addition to high black-to-white ratios, both the Latin area and English South Carolina had imported many of their slaves from the Caribbean islands.

TABLE 1. African Gods in America during the nineteenth and early twentieth centuries

AFRICAN AMERICAN NAME(S)	LOCATION OF WORSHIP	FUNCTION IN LATIN CULTURAL AREA	AFRICAN NAME(S)	TRIBAL ORIGIN	FUNCTION IN AFRICA
Bon Dieu and other names	Universal	Equivalent of Christian God, omnipotent and omniscient, creator	Olorun, Mawu-Lisa, Nzambi, and others	Yoruba, Fon, Ewe, Mande, Kongo, hand others	Equivalent of Christian God, omnipotent and omniscient, creator
Monsieur Danny, Blanc Dani, Grand Zombie, Voodoo Magnian	Louisiana and Florida	Chief god, worshiped in the form of a snake, god of discord, defeats enemies	Dañh-gbi, Da	Fon, Ewe	Chief earth god, python god, father of gods, early ruler of Dahomey
Papa Lébat, Liba, LaBas	Louisiana	Trickster, doorkeeper, evil	Legba	Fon, Ewe	Trickster, linguist of gods
Monsieur Assonquer	Louisiana	God of good fortune	Perhaps related to *asson*, meaning "rattle"	Fon	Used in religious rituals to summon gods
Monsieur Agoussou, Vert Agoussou	Louisiana	God of love	Agasu	Fon	Founder of the royal line of Abomey
Monsieur d'Embarass	Louisiana	God of death	Takes place of several African gods	Various	Death
Jean Macouloumba	Louisiana	Unknown	Unidentified	Probable Haitian	Unidentified
Dambarra Soutons	Louisiana	Perhaps identical with Danny	Dañh-gbi, Da	Fon, Ewe	Chief earth god, python god, father of gods, early ruler of Dahomey
Charlo	Louisiana	Child god	Unidentified	Unidentified	Unidentified
Vériquité (perhaps identical with Haitian Veleteke)	Louisiana	Important god with many roles, including causing illness	Unidentified	Unidentified	Unidentified
Yon Sue	Louisiana	Perhaps identical with Agoussou or Danny	Agasu or Dañh-gbi, Da	Fon, Ewe	Founder of the royal line of Abomey or chief earth god, python god, father of gods, early ruler of Dahomey

Name	Location	Local description	African name	African origin	African description
Joe Feraille	Louisiana	God of iron	Ogun	Yoruba	God of iron and war
Onzancaire	Louisiana	Perhaps identical with Assonquer	Unidentified	Unidentified	Powerful all-purpose being
Sanunga	Missouri	Called on when gathering mud	Gounja (?)	Khoisan (?)	Moon god
Abasi	Florida	Supreme being	Ubasi	Yoruba	Supreme Being
Obatala	Florida	Chief god, most powerful spirit	Obatala	Yoruba	Chief god
Elegba	Florida	Evil spirit	Elegba and Eshu	Yoruba	Trickster and phallic god
Shango	Florida	Spirit of good and evil, justice, and thunder	Shango	Yoruba	God of thunder
Yenaya	Florida	Spirit of the air and sea	Yemoja	Yoruba	Goddess of the Ogun River, wife of Ogun
Las Jimaguas	Florida	Twin spirits	Ibeji, Hoho, and others	Yoruba, Ewe, and others	Twin gods
Ecue	Florida	Son of Abasi, perhaps identical to Elegba	Legba	Fon, Ewe	Trickster, linguist of gods
Nanga	Florida	Chief spirit of evil	Nanga	Kongo	Early leader in Kongo migration from what is now Angola
Neque	Florida	Malevolent spirit	Unidentified	Unidentified	Unidentified
Mayunga	Florida	Malevolent spirit	Unidentified	Unidentified	Unidentified
Bilonga	Florida	Malevolent spirit	Perhaps related to *bilongo*, meaning "medicinal ingredients"	Kongo	Unidentified

Sources: Data from Brandon, *Santeria from Africa to the New World*, 77; Cable, "Creole Slave Songs"; Cable, "Dance in Place Congo"; Cable, *Grandissimes*, 99, 101, 135, 182, 184, 257, 272, 311, 447, 453–56, 468; Courlander, *Treasury of African Folklore*, 159–60, 187–88; Ellis, *Ewe-Speaking Peoples*, 13–90; Ellis, *Yoruba-Speaking Peoples*, 34–124; Hauptmann, "Spanish Folklore from Tampa Florida"; Jacobs and Kaslow, *Spiritual Churches of New Orleans*, 82–93; Kennedy, "Nañigo in Florida"; Long, *Spiritual Merchants*, 3–96; MacGaffey, *Religion and Society in Central Africa*, 53, 59, 79; Métraux, *Voodoo in Haiti*, 28, 31, 100–119, 129, 217; Murphy, *Santeria*, 77; Opoku, *West African Traditional Religion*, 54–90; Mary Alicia Owen, "Among the Voodoos," 238–42; Pitkin, *Angel by Brevet*, 185–213, 260–92; Rigaud, *Secrets of Voodoo*, 51–78; and Tallant, *Voodoo in New Orleans*, 175, 204.

Afro-European syncretic religions had developed there owing to an even more pronounced race imbalance and frequent negative population growth rates. Planters required continued importation of native Africans to support the profitable sugar trade on which the islands' economies relied. In the case of New Orleans, an influx of several thousand Haitian slaves from 1806 to 1810, following a successful slave-led revolution in the French colony, certainly spurred the growth of Voodoo in the area. Moreover, the Haitians' arrival in New Orleans took place at a time when 75 percent of American slaves were born in the United States. An even more pronounced case prevailed in Florida, where black Cubans began arriving in large numbers during the late nineteenth century to escape revolutions, persecution, and economic hardship. The Anglo coastal region had received no such sudden wave of immigrants. Even when combined with large black-to-white ratios, late Caribbean immigration cannot wholly account for the vitality of pre-Christian religion in the Latin zone. In New Orleans, Voodoo had been strong long before the large-scale arrival of Haitian refugees. For example, in the twenty years preceding 1800 Louisiana's European governors banned the importation of slaves from Martinique and Haiti, then known as Santo Domingo, for the express purpose of preventing the growth of Voodoo, already perceived as a social problem.[20]

A final factor in preserving the religious element of conjure was the Latin area's Catholicism, which allowed blacks to continue to worship their ancestral gods under the guise of saints, a common practice in Haiti, Cuba, and the other Caribbean islands from which the slaves hailed. Slaves adopted this subterfuge in the face of whites' antipathy to Voodoo and related religions, which the ruling class feared as witchcraft and a potential source of revolution. The practice of identifying gods with saints grew stronger once the blacks arrived in America, where they made up a smaller percentage of the total population, allowing whites to keep a much closer watch over them. For example, Papa Lébat, one of the chief Voodoo deities, was identical to the Catholic St. Peter. Likewise, St. Michael, the archangel, was the same as the Voodoo Magnian, another name for Blanc Dani, who was known for his serpentine form and his power over storms. Over time the rationale for the practice of hiding gods under the names of saints disappeared, and for all intents and purposes the gods and saints became the same. Adherents considered themselves Catholics, while continuing to serve the old gods. Unlike Latin Catholicism, English Protestantism had no saints, making it more difficult for blacks to preserve their old pantheon under new names.[21]

Though the combined lesser gods/magical helpers were the most readily recognizable survivals of African religions, they did not occupy the only tier of the African spiritual hierarchy to persist in the American South. Blacks also brought their conceptions of the supreme being as they entered lives of servitude. In the Latin area, the all-powerful Bon Dieu of New Orleans Voodoo filled the role of Mawu-Lisa of the Fon and Ewe. The absence of sacrifices and magic in the worship of Bon Dieu, illustrates the general African view of the supreme being as too lofty to need anything humans could offer. For the same reason, Bon Dieu was above helping his followers with magic. In Florida, Abasi, the Americanized version of Ubasi, the Yoruba supreme deity, likewise held sway over the universe. It was his son, Obatala, who helped conjurers in their magic.[22]

In Missouri and throughout the Anglo cultural zone the supreme being was the Christian God. While casual examiners might conclude that the absence of an overtly African name signaled another casualty of enslavement, such was not the case. On the contrary, many of the west-central Africans, who made up the largest group of the imports to the Anglo area and a significant proportion of those in the Latin area, had a Christian heritage in their homeland. Most notably, the Portuguese had brought Christianity to the kingdom of the Kongo in 1491. The new faith had spread rapidly, and converts included the king, the royal family, and many nobles by the early sixteenth century. Alfonso I, who ascended to the kingship of the Kongo in 1506, attempted to create a Christian state modeled on the monarchies of western Europe. Successive rulers followed his lead, though their dream never came to fruition. By the mid-sixteenth century the Portuguese had discovered the profitability of slave trading. To obtain captives, the Portuguese encouraged warfare between the various regions of the kingdom of the Kongo and with other groups. After holding back for a century, the kingdom finally declared war on the Portuguese, only to be dealt a death blow. By the late seventeenth century Christianity had largely disappeared. Nevertheless, the model of a religion with a single god was in place. Christianity had in effect become a traditional African religion, with which slaves from west-central Africa had already had experience, particularly during the colonial period.[23]

Just as important to African Americans' concept of God were the attributes they assigned to him. Many hoodooists from the Anglo zone called on the Christian God for aid in conjuring, thus violating the biblical teachings of orthodox Christianity, which is clear in its condemnation of the practice of divination and magic. Nor were they relying on a purely African world-view, in which supreme beings were usually considered too lofty to respond to the spells and charms of a mortal sorcerer. On the contrary, the God of nineteenth-century black hoodooists was, like the lesser gods of Voodoo, a creole combination of more than one tier of African spiritual hierarchies. In the Anglo zone and Missouri God was a magical helper who aided conjurers in their profession, an embodiment of the attributes of the lesser gods of Africa, and an omnipotent and omniscient being who was far above needing anything from his followers.[24]

This neither African nor European view of God was obvious in the practice of William Adams, a former slave from Texas. While Adams clearly believed in the Christian idea of God as an almighty creator of all, he claimed a special relationship with him. Adams's God fulfilled the role of a magical helper through acts of revelation, during which he showed the conjurer how to exercise his powers. Adams was far from unique. Ida Carter, an Alabamian conjure woman who went by the title Seven Sisters, worked within a similar conception of God. Asked by an interviewer to explain how she had learned to conjure, she stated that a spirit from the "Lord Jesus Christ" had taught her. While she had received her power from Jesus, her manner of referring to him as "Lord" indicates her conception of his lofty standing. Nevertheless, Seven Sisters claimed that God acted in accordance with her spells, much as the Voodoo gods of New Orleans responded to the offerings of their followers. Clearly, Seven Sisters's ideas were not wholly African. On the other hand, she relied on a God who did not fit well within orthodox Christianity. While she claimed to trick "in the name o' the Lord," her spells included ones intended to win male clients the sexual favors of women, give rivals bad luck, and kill women who had ensnared lovers by magic, all of which violated biblical teachings.[25]

Two other tiers of the West African spiritual hierarchy, ancestral and totemic animal and plant spirits, showed less persistence in the American South. The latter were virtually unknown, with almost their only representatives being taboos against eating certain animals by Anglo-area blacks and the animal names adopted by the likes of Dr. Buzzard. Ghosts, grave goods, and wakes were common throughout both the Anglo and Latin areas. Nevertheless, ancestral spirits' position in America was only a shadow of the position they had held in Africa.[26]

As far as conjure went, the ancestor's chief representative in the nineteenth century was the Kongo-derived goopher of the Anglo zone. Graveyard dirt, known as "goopher dust," was the most popular material for charms in the Anglo area, particularly along the Atlantic seaboard.[27] Goopher dust had a variety of uses, ranging from helping slaves escape their owners to aiding accused murderers in their trials. It could also be used to harm, frequently appearing in malevolent charms designed to cause sickness or death, powders to dissuade rivals in love, and even poisons to taint food and wells. Furthermore, conjurers chose the graves from which to take goopher dust based on what it was to be used for. For instance, to save the life of an accused murderer, friends of the prisoner would gather dirt from the grave of the murdered man, leaving three pennies in payment. The dead person, who had the best knowledge of the crime, could exonerate the wrongly accused. Even if the accused had committed the crime, the spirit might be persuaded by magic or payment to aid the guilty. In general, for malevolent work the grave would be that of an evil person, but for good magic, the goopher dust would be obtained from the grave of a child or good adult.[28]

The most well represented tiers of the African supernatural hierarchy were those occupying charms. The Mande speakers who contributed the term *gris-gris* were particularly influential in the Latin area. According to the eighteenth-century slave trader Nicholas Owen, the Mandingos' gregory bags were large leather pouches in which they carried religious items, including what European travelers were fond of referring to as "idols." Gregory bags' chief purpose, however, was protection from harm, thereby requiring their owners to carry them always. In the American South these pouches were smaller in size and formed only one of the many forms of gris-gris present in the Latin zone, but they continued to exist.[29]

The best examples of the Mandingo-derived bags were preserved in Missouri, where some African Americans carried linen bags containing luck balls. These luck balls, however, did more than communicate luck in the European sense; they also embodied the souls of their possessors. Their proprietors carried them always, fed them, and spoke to them, calling them by their own names. The loss of one was a dreadful occurrence, frequently sending its owner into a panic. The power of luck balls was illustrated by the words of King Alexander, a well-known conjurer interviewed by Mary Alicia Owen. Alexander called on God to empower a luck ball for Charles Leland, saying, "May this ball bring all good luck to Charles Leland. May it bind down all devils, may it bind down his enemies before him, may it bring them under his feet."[30] He went on to exhort God to imbue the luck ball with the power to bring Leland friends, honor, riches, happiness, success, and his "heart's desire." The physical portion of the luck ball was composed of knotted white yarn and silk thread, red clover blossoms, tinfoil, and dust. He imparted some of his own spirit to it by spitting on it. Then he named the ball "Charles Leland." For the spirit to remain strong, the human Leland would have to "feed" it with whiskey.[31]

The origin of Latin-area charms cannot be solely assigned to Mande gregory bags. Instead, they are a mixture of the beliefs of successive waves of imports into the area. Like American blacks, African peoples had a large variety of amulets and charms, occupied by indwelling spirits. Among Fon speakers these charms were called *gbo* and took the form of soaps, packets or bottles filled with mixtures of magical materials, rings, and numerous other items. They had a variety of uses, ranging from protection of crops, when tied to trees near fields, to binding evil spirits, when incorporating elements of knotting. In addition, these were usually "fed" with some form of alcohol, blood, or food, accomplished by soaking or covering the bundle with them.[32]

The influence of West African *gbo*-style charms is clear in the materials of the American South. Like their African counterparts, they often had specialized functions, designed to bring luck, love, financial success, and virtually any other desire. Moreover, they frequently required feeding, usually in the form of soaking the charm in an alcoholic beverage. In addition, while packets were the most common of African American charms, there were others, including powders and special bathing mixtures, both of which also appeared in Africa. For example, a slave named Henry Bibb once relied on a powder when seeking to avoid punishment from his master. Ewe priests and magicians used similar powders to force open locked doors, cause and heal madness, and blind enemies. Even gregory bag–style items incorporated elements from *gbo* charms. King Alexander's luck ball used knotting as a way to bind evil spirits, but he also specified that his charm's outer binding not be tied so that the charm's indwelling spirit would not be tied up. Similarly, he specified that it required feeding to remain strong.[33]

One of the most influential forms of African charms were the *minkisi* of the Kongo. Manufactured by magicians, *minkisi* were positive beings inhabiting charms designed to protect their owners from spirit-induced illness. Like gregory bags, *gbo,* and related northern West African charms, they frequently took the shape of packets. Unlike the charms of other areas, however, *minkisi* often incorporated the spirits of the ancestors in the form of dirt from graveyards, a material identical to the goopher dust of the Anglo zone. The pervasiveness of goopher dust alone speaks to the power of Kongo ancestry in the Anglo area, though unlike in the Kongo, American graveyard dust was as often used for evil as for good. For example, Roland Steiner, a Georgia observer, recorded the use of graveyard dust in charms designed to cause disease and kill, drive away enemies, and conjure wells. Steiner met one goopher doctor, Tom Franklin, who had a reputation for working all of his magic with graveyard dust. The more limited use of graveyard dust in the Latin area also bespoke the influence of *minkisi*. Other common forms of *minkisi* were roots, which likewise appeared in both cultural zones. According to Kongo belief, the first *nkisi* was the spirit Funza, who dwelt in twisted roots. John the Conqueror root, reputably one of the most powerful of all charms and found throughout the nineteenth-century South, was the American derivation of the African Funza. Kongos chewed and spat another kind of root, called *disisa* or *nsanga-lavu*, in order to drive off enemies and evil forces. This roughly corresponded to the chewing roots employed by African Americans. For instance, Henry Bibb chewed a root and spat its juice toward his master to prevent being punished. In later days such roots would be known as Chewing John, the most commonly used species of which was galangal, a member of the ginger family, as were the Kongo *disisa* or *nsanga-lavu*.[34]

Minkisi were but the benevolent side of Kongo magic. Alongside positive magic existed the evils of witchcraft. A common means by which witches harmed their victims was stealing their souls and imprisoning them inside a bottle. Similar practices persisted in conjure. Stopping bowels by sealing someone's excrement in a tree was one American derivation of such Kongo witchcraft. Another was the practice of placing materials representing particular people, such as names or fingernails, in bottles or packets that were then thrown in running water, buried in graves, turned upside down, or similarly manipulated in order to cause death.[35]

Other aims of African American charms and spells had their origins across the Atlantic. A black teacher who attended the Hampton Institute reported that as a teenager she had felt the effects of a "crazy spell," which had caused her to contemplate suicide and violence to others. To heal her, her mother took her to a root doctor. After a few days of taking a mixture of water and a mysterious liquid, she recovered. Such cases were well known in Africa, where evil magicians frequently and literally drove enemies mad. Among the Ewe they did so by throwing specially prepared powder on their enemies' footprints.[36]

The most feared maladies inflicted by nineteenth-century hoodooists were animal infestations of human bodies, usually taking the form of reptiles, amphibians, or insects inhabiting the internal organs or living under the skin of the victim. This dreaded distemper also originated in Africa. Throughout West Africa, witches were feared for their ability to harm others by placing both animate and inanimate items in their victims' bodies. According to the nineteenth-century traveler Mary Kingsley, this practice was particularly common among the Igbo and those speaking languages of the Bantu group, including the Kongo people. She reported examples of bodies infested with pieces of iron pots, bundles of palm leaves, and millipedes. An account she heard from two "very trustworthy" male witnesses impressed her more than the others. One of the men's mutual relatives had been bewitched. Following the administration of an emetic, a small animal emerged from the afflicted's body and grew rapidly in size. According to the men, it had the body of a lizard and wings like a bat. An hour after the reptile came to light, it flew away. Those present concluded that a witch had hidden the creature in some food that the victim had eaten. Had the victim not been treated, the creature would have continued to grow, eating away its host's body until he died.[37]

In many cases, even the items used to make up the various forms of African charms survived in America. Some materials common in African magical practices and later used in the United States had largely disappeared by the late nineteenth century and are now identifiable only from the archaeological record. One of the best examples was blue beads, which archaeologists have uncovered in several eighteenth- and nineteenth-century sites associated with African Americans. According to Linda France Stine, Melanie Cabak, and Mark Groover, these had most likely been parts of protective talismans. Throughout most of northern West and west-central Africa, blue beads had been part of benevolent charms for centuries. Their importance was such that along the Gold Coast certain types were worth their weight in gold.[38]

While blue beads faded in importance within a few generations of blacks' immigration to America, other such materials survived much longer. Throughout the South, cross marks (X) were powerful protective symbols. Archaeologists have discovered them on colonial pottery shards from South Carolina. Derived from a cruciform Kongo symbol for the cosmos and continuity of life, they have sometimes also adorned African American graves. In New Orleans, Voodooists drew similar marks on the tomb of Marie Laveau as a petition for her aid. In central Georgia, blacks traced cross marks in the earth and spat on them to avert bad luck. Anyone traveling on a path in which a cross mark was drawn who did not see it beforehand and walk around it would be cursed. Thus, tracing cross marks in the earth was an excellent way to dissuade trespassers and enemies. Hoodoo rituals performed at crossroads may hearken back to the same source.[39]

Red flannel, one of the favorite materials used in making conjure bags and other charms, likewise derived from African sources. Among the Kongo peoples red represented blood, birth, death, sunrise, and sunset. It was therefore a powerful color because of its sympathetic value. In addition, charms fashioned by the Fon people were usually red because the color was a favorite of the spirits.[40] Footprints were also often used in African American magic. Once again, the practice arose in blacks' ancestral home. In West Africa, treating footprints with magical materials could affect those who had made them. For instance, placing thorns in footprints injured their maker just as they would have had he or she stepped on them. Dirt from foot tracks could be incorporated into charms for similar ends.[41]

The use of animal and plant products in hoodoo most likely sprang from African roots. Red pepper, a common protective charm in the United States, served the same role in West Africa. The use of black cats' bones, thought to give invisibility to their possessors, also sprang from the same origins. One of the clearest examples of African magic surviving in the American South was the reputed protective powers of chickens. Newbell Niles Puckett proclaimed that black Americans considered a frizzly rooster a "veritable hoodoo watchdog," capable of scratching up any hidden malevolent conjures. In the Old World they could do the same. Moreover, chickens conferred luck when eaten and could destroy evil magic when they encountered it. In some areas they could even prevent fires in villages.[42]

In Africa a variety of human specialists dealt with the spirit world. Among the Kongolese, for example, village chiefs and elders were both governmental leaders and priests, communicating with and conducting worship of the ancestors. Localized spirits, however, were the province of priests. Chiefs, elders, and priests were public figures, but two types of private specialists also existed. The first were magicians who made benevolent charms for sale to clients. The second type, witches, were evil. Instead of helping others, they stole victims' souls, metaphysically "eating" those unfortunate enough to encounter them. They dealt chiefly with ghosts, the unhappy spirits of dead witches. Moreover, witches had no need to use charms themselves, though they might sell them to clients.[43]

In northern West Africa, functions were similarly divided. Among many peoples, tribal and village leaders such as chiefs and elders played spiritual roles. Among the Akan people, for instance, chiefs led the worship of national gods and ancestors, a common feature of northern West African cultures. Priests, like those of the Kongo, usually devoted themselves to particular lesser gods. Also, these societies recognized the existence of both good and evil magic, practiced by magicians or sorcerers and witches, respectively. Once again, witches preyed on the souls and property of humans, having no need of magical formulas or charms. Moreover, they could fly, take on the form of animals, become invisible, and "ride" their victims while they slept, gradually wearing them down in body and spirit. The Yoruba, the Fon, and other groups had a fifth type of specialist who performed divination. Some peoples had yet another category, typically known as a "witch doctor" or "witch hunter," whose sole purpose was to hunt down and destroy witches. Witch hunting was particularly popular in Ghana but eventually spread throughout much of the region. Though restrictions on the professions varied from society to society, spiritual specialists could usually be either male or female, with the exception of chiefs, who were almost always men.[44]

Like the tiers of African religious hierarchies, the categories of spiritual experts merged in the American South, but elements of each survived. For instance, both men and women could serve as magical and religious specialists. Moreover, in some places vestiges of the originally distinct roles of chiefs, elders, priests, magicians, witches, diviners, and witch hunters persisted. For example, Anglo-zone African Americans sometimes thought of witches, usually known as "hags," as separate from conjurers. Hags, like the witches of Africa, entered victims' homes under the cloak of invisibility, riding them during their sleep. The results were nightmares. In addition, they could change their forms, slipping out of their skin to appear as animals.[45]

Conjurers, meanwhile, usually combined the roles of diviners, magicians, and witch hunters. As such, they told the future, provided magical charms to their clients, and helped victims of witchcraft overcome their tormenters. This distinction did not always hold, though. Unlike the divinatory and magical specialists of Africa, conjurers were widely feared for their ability to work evil. For instance, South Carolina's Dr. Buzzard sold both positive and negative charms to his clients. The same was true of most nineteenth-century conjurers in both cultural areas. Even when a hoodooist eschewed evil work on moral grounds, public opinion continued to paint him or her as a dangerous individual who should be feared.[46]

Whatever the relation between hags and conjurers, African chiefs, elders, and priests largely disappeared in the Anglo South, with black preachers providing the closest approximation of their functions in religious worship. In the Latin area, where workers of magic also officiated over worship of African gods, the functions of chiefs, elders, and priests survived in the conglomerate office of Voodoo queens, kings, and doctors. Ironically, while more of the roles of African specialists survived in the Latin zone, they might all be manifested in a single individual.[47]

All living humans were also spiritual beings, regardless of their status as specialists. According to almost all African cultures, individuals were composed of multiple physical and nonphysical portions. In northern West Africa, in particular, the concept of multiple "souls" was strong. Among the Yoruba, human beings were considered to be primarily spiritual in makeup. Closely tied to the mortal body, or *ara*, was the *ojiji*, the shadow, which accompanied the body in life and ceased to exist upon death. In contrast, the *emi* gave life to the body and returned to God upon physical death but never itself died. The *okan*, or heart, was the center of thought and action. Like the *emi*, the *okan* never died; instead, it was reincarnated in the bodies of its physical descendants. Less closely tied to the physical body than were other parts of a human, the *okan* often wandered during sleep, exposing it to potential attack from another *okan*, especially if a witch was seeking prey. The *ori* was similar to the *okan* in that it preexisted the physical body with which it joined, but unlike the *okan*, it did not undergo the process of reincarnation. An *ori* was the most important part of an individual's personality and also acted as the guardian of the rest of a human's being. The final part of a human in Yoruba belief was the *iye*, or mental body, which was the conscious part of a person. Together the *ara*, the *ojiji*, the *emi*, the *okan*, the *ori*, and the *iye* worked together to create a unified being.[48]

The Kongo people also held that humans had a multipart spiritual existence. In addition to the physical body, the invisible part of a human was composed of a *life soul*, which gave vitality to the body; a *body soul*, acting as a person's eternal social identity; an *image soul*, which was one's mortal shadow or appearance; and a *death spirit*. From the last category sprang the inhabitants of the spirit world with whom the living communicated, including ancestors, ghosts, nature spirits, and inhabitants of charms.[49]

To be sure, the full complexity of African conceptions of human composition did not survive the crossing of the Atlantic. Nevertheless, conjurers, the most important representative of African survivals in America, sometimes held that multiple souls were part of what made them powerful magicians. A ninety-six-year-old Mississippi conjurer interviewed by Ruth Bass, called Divinity, believed that he had been marked as a conjurer from birth, as evidenced by his being born with a caul. The caul itself, however, was but a sign, indicating that he was a "double-sighter" with two spirits. One spirit remained in the body, but the other, like the *okan* of Yoruba belief, wandered about, allowing Divinity to see and talk to spiritual beings hidden from those not so gifted.[50]

In Georgia, Braziel Robinson also claimed to have two souls. Like Divinity, he said the reason for this unusual circumstance was his being born with a caul. Another similarity between Robinson and Divinity was that one of Robinson's spirits usually stayed put, while the other left the body. Once again, these two spirits caused their possessor to be able to see and communicate with spirits. In Robinson's experience, the spirits tended to be those of dead humans, linking his wandering spirit to the "death spirits" of the Kongo and other African peoples. One variation from African belief was that Robinson's two souls worked together to protect him from evil, as would the Yoruban *ori*. If he refused to listen to their guidance, both would desert him, and two evil spirits would take their place.[51]

Another important aspect of African culture was the so-called secret societies that served as combination religious, social, cultural, and governmental organizations. Though secrecy surrounded some aspects of these groups, they were much more than the term *secret societies* implies. They served a variety of functions, including providing moral regulation, care for the needy, diplomacy and trade between villages and tribes, and education for both men and women. For instance, among the Mande and related peoples of northern West Africa the Poro and Sande societies filled such roles.[52] The Poro and Sande organizations, for men and women, respectively, were open to all members of the culture. Moreover, one who did not enter a society upon puberty usually became a target of ostracism. After joining a society following a complex initiation ritual, members could advance within a pyramidal structure by a succession of further ceremonies. In addition to regulating life on a local level, the wide-ranging Poro and Sande societies also helped forge cultural and political unity among the many dispersed villages that made up the territories occupied by the Mande ethnic group. Other peoples had similar societies. For instance, the Krobo people of what is today Ghana had the Dipo society, which females joined upon entering womanhood.[53]

In the American South, African men's and women's societies truly became secret organizations, hiding many of their practices, and sometimes even their existence, from outsiders. They also largely abandoned their roles in economics and politics, becoming wholly religious and magical in purpose. As a result, evidence for the survival of African organizations in the South is sparse. What data exist, though, are convincing. Scattered references to sects involving "sacred spirits" suggest the minor presence of African-derived societies in the Anglo area. Like other aspects of African life, however, they were much more common in the Latin area. They were most easily recognizable in Florida, where the word *Nañigo* preserved the Cuban name for a society originally founded by the Efik people of the Niger River delta. In the United States, members of the Nañigo society/religion continued to practice traditional dances, parades, and other rituals well into the twentieth century. A few even remembered the society's African name, Carabali Apapa Abacua. The meanings of the three words referred to the origin and function of the organization: *Carabali*, a Cuban synonym for *Efik*, referred to its cultural origin, *Apapa* meant something "old" or "great," and *Abacua* meant "pledge." In short, the name roughly translated as "Pledge of the Old Efik."[54]

African societies existed in Missouri and Louisiana as well, though there they were generally confined to practitioners of magic and less clearly defined than in the former Spanish colony. In Missouri, conjurers formed a confederation known as the Circle, entered through a lengthy process of initiation and apprenticeship. Louisiana's hoodooists seem to have formed similar associations, as evidenced by secretive initiations and apprenticeships preceding entrance into the conjuring profession. The covert nature of Voodoo's rituals further indicates that its adherents may have seen themselves as members of some form of hidden organization.[55]

The form of the initiations into secret societies undergone by Latin-area hoodooists further emphasized their African origin. Zora Neale Hurston claimed to have undergone several initiations while studying hoodoo in Louisiana.[56] A conjurer named Samuel Thompson supervised one of the more complex of these rites. According to Hurston, her initiation began simply, with the wearing of a stocking on her right foot for nine nights. For these days she was to refrain from sexually defiling herself in mind or action. In preparation for the rest of the initiation, she paid Thompson an unspecified sum and purchased three snakeskins, one of a water moccasin, one of a kingsnake, and one of a rattlesnake. At the end of the nine days Hurston returned to Thompson, who prayed that the "Great One" would enter the skins. The water-moccasin skin was placed upon a couch draped in green, and Hurston lay nude and face down upon the couch. At her head was a jar of water for the serpent spirit. For three days Hurston lay thus in the belief that her soul was standing before the Great One, seeking favor.[57]

Her vigil ended at 11:00 A.M. on St. Joseph's Day, 19 March. At that time Thompson and two other men approached. After passing Hurston through running water, they painted a lightening bolt across her back, which indicated the Great One's method of speaking to her through storms; a sun on her forehead; and eyes on her cheeks. Then they dressed her in new clothes and a veil. Next, others entered the room and performed various rituals, after which they cut their fingers as well as one of Hurston's. They then mingled their blood with wine in a glass. Each person present drank some of the mixture. At 12:00 Thompson and his assistants sat Hurston before an altar bearing a communion candle, into which her name was set with sand. Copious amounts of food and various sacred items covered the rest of the altar's surface. After asking the Great One to accept Hurston, Thompson lifted her veil and placed a sacred crown upon her head. A ritual feast followed.[58]

The final act of the initiation took place outside at midnight. Its chief features included making a broom and sacrificing a sheep. As the sheep lay dying with its throat slit, those present thrust nine sheets of paper into its wound. On these papers they had written a petition from Hurston for power, repeated nine times on each sheet. This seemingly inhumane act was performed so that the sheep would cry out the petition to the Great One with its dying breath. As long as blood continued to flow from the sheep, one of those present dipped the broom into the blood and swept the ground. After the animal was dead, they dug the earth from beneath it and buried it, placing a white candle on its grave. From this point forward, Hurston had a special relationship to the Great One, who was doubtless identical with Voodoo Magnian and Blanc Dani, whom the previous century's devotees had worshiped in the form of a snake and who ruled over storms.[59]

Though designed primarily to give her the power to conjure, the rituals in which Hurston claimed to have participated appear to have constituted pared-down versions of the initiation ceremonies common to African societies. Like Hurston, prospective members of the Mande's Sande and the Krobo's Dipo societies lived in seclusion, having contact only with society officials during most of the initiation. Moreover, during this period both Hurston and the African novitiates were to keep themselves pure in mind and body and pay a fee to officiants. In addition, both the American and African initiations included a time during which those who hoped to enter the societies' ranks underwent a period of training. Among the Mande and the Krobo, they learned about topics as diverse as motherhood, respect for elders, physiology, and first aid, but in New Orleans Hurston learned only about magic. Both the African societies and Thompson's Voodoo initiation employed ritual clothing to signify the women's new state.[60]

Other elements of Hurston's initiation were specific to one or the other African society. Specifically Krobo elements were more prevalent than Mande ones. For example, one of the most important acts undertaken by Dipo initiates was the sacrifice of a goat. In Hurston's case, a sheep took its place, though the sacrifice remained. Also, both Hurston and her Krobo counterparts partook of communal feasts. Ritual cleansings followed by paintings on initiates' bodies by those officiating likewise appeared in the rituals of the Dipo society and Thompson. One of the last acts of both rituals was the "crowning" of the women with a specially made hat, originally intended to imitate Krobo priests' ceremonial headgear.[61]

Initiations in other parts of the Latin area likewise shared elements with those in African societies. For instance, initiates into the Sande and Poro societies took new names, a practice that Hurston encountered in other initiations. The custom was typical in Missouri conjure. Similarly, Missouri hoodooists learned dances as well as magic, a common feature in African men's and women's societies. Also, in both Missouri and Louisiana the initiations took on aspects of African priestly initiations, as evidenced by the novitiates' special relationship with particular gods or spirits.[62]

Despite the similarities between Mande and Krobo initiations and those of the American South, many features of the African rituals did not survive. Most notably, a man conducted Hurston's initiation, which would not have happened in Krobo or Mande lands. Also, particular items and sacred locations had disappeared by the time Hurston underwent her induction into hoodoo. Krobo women, for instance, had to climb a sacred rock called the Totroku before they could enter womanhood, an aspect of the ceremonies that had no part in the practices of the American South. Elephant hairs, with which Dipo initiates adorned their heads at the close of the initiations, shared a similar fate. Despite notable losses, however, these rituals remained largely African in form and function. Rather than deteriorating over time, they adapted to new circumstances, surviving for more than a century after the close of the international slave trade.[63]

African-derived initiations were but one way for prospective conjurers to gain their powers. Africa also provided the blueprint for those who gained them by other means. In the American South, hoodooists could also gain magical powers by inheriting them from their forebears or receiving them as a special gift from the spirits or the Christian God.[64] Throughout northern West Africa and the Kongo, priests and witches often acquired their abilities from parents, particularly mothers. Among the Tiv of Nigeria, for instance, magic was understood as a substance that grew in witches' livers, making it possible to pass it to children. Though no record of such liver disorders survives in the American South, many conjurers claimed to have inherited their powers from their parents. For instance, Dr. Buzzard supposedly acquired his ability from a line of ancestors stretching back to Africa. Others, including most of those interviewed by Hurston, also claimed to have acquired their abilities from ancestors.[65]

In other instances, African gods or spirits gifted those they wanted to serve them. Black American hoodooists also frequently attributed their abilities to a special relationship with God or other spirits. Most West African priests and priestesses received some form of call, usually indicated by possession by the being they were to serve. In the United States, however, gifting was more commonly indicated by peculiar birth circumstances, having a particularly significant number of siblings, or physical abnormalities. Africans had looked for similar signs when they considered whether a child would grow to be a worker of magic. For example, among the Fon, distinctive appearances, resulting from the likes of albinism, deformities, and melanism, indicated such gifts. Likewise, twins, infants delivered by breach births, and children born immediately after the death of siblings were often destined for spiritual careers.[66]

In Africa, gifting was not always a positive experience for the receiver. Evil spirits were apt to make victims of those they chose. According to Kofi Asare Opoku, demons sometimes forced people into witchcraft, coercing them, "even against their will, into casting evil on their neighbors."[67] Records of similar cases have appeared in the South. Unexplained deaths in one's presence or among one's associates were sometimes enough to convince observers that the survivor was working malevolent magic. Such supposed victims of the spirit world were frequently forced into conjuring because they had become outcasts from their communities; there was no other profession left open to them. Evil spirits, however, were often called on by West Africans to grant the power of witchcraft. In the United States, African Americans sometimes followed a similar path by offering their souls to Satan in exchange for the ability to conjure. Harry Middleton Hyatt recorded several instances of practitioners who had reportedly sold their souls. Zora Neale Hurston reported that she had personally done so during her study of hoodoo.[68]

Regardless of how a conjurer acquired his or her powers, he or she usually underwent a period of tutelage. Hurston studied with each of the practitioners with whom she underwent initiation. Even Ida Carter, who claimed her powers came directly from Christ, admitted to learning some of her abilities from "an old voodoo woman."[69] African workers of magic also underwent a process of learning. For members of the priesthood and sorcerers, it took place during initiations into their craft and periods of apprenticeship, during which they would learn herbal magic, sacred dances, taboos, and other aspects of their religion and magic. Witches alone had no need to learn how to perform magic, as was sometimes the case in the American South: they harmed the souls of their victims with their own souls.[70]

Nineteenth-century blacks shared much with their African ancestors. Their spiritual hierarchies, concepts of magical specialization and human spiritual makeup, and methods of gaining occult power demonstrate the truth of this assertion in respect to conjure. While much of African Americans' religious heritage was destroyed by the hardship inherent in slavery and by many blacks' willing conversion to Christianity, it retained a vital niche in their folk beliefs. Nevertheless, when old beliefs and customs disappeared, new traditions took their place. These innovations came not from Africa but from those peoples blacks encountered in their new homeland.

2

Witches and Medicine Men: European and Native American Building Blocks of Hoodoo

MOST AMERICANS, particularly whites, learn what they know of African American magical practices from television documentaries and print sources aimed at popular readerships. One recent documentary on Voodoo, entitled "The Evil Eye," appeared on the television program *History's Mysteries*. As with most recent productions of the sort, its central argument was that Voodoo was and is a valid religion, free from the demonic characteristics ascribed to it in popular belief. To this end, it stressed Voodoo's African roots, arguing that the vilification of the religion in past ages had been a result of racist assumptions. Other potential influences were summed up in a statement that Voodoo had been "enriched by contact with Catholicism."

The majority of recent books on conjure have followed the same formulation as the television programs. A. P. Antippas's *Brief History of Voodoo: Slavery and the Survival of the African Gods* is one such example. As its title suggests, this short book, published by a popular New Orleans tourist shop, emphasizes the role of African beliefs in Voodoo and conjure. Like "The Evil Eye," the book dismisses non-African influences with no more than brief acknowledgments that Catholic saints helped preserve the old gods and that Protestant worship styles reminded slaves of their traditional religious ceremonies. This presentation of conjure makes it appear to be an intact African religion; contributions from other cultures seem minimal or nonexistent. In a time when

New Age rejection of Western religion, pluralistic assertions of equality among faiths, and black cultural nationalism are central forces shaping interpretations of hoodoo, such an approach in popular media is to be expected.

Unfortunately for the study of hoodoo, the paucity of scholarly works on the subject has left the popular interpretation of conjure largely unchallenged. Without doubt, nineteenth-century blacks built conjure upon an African foundation. The structure they raised, however, incorporated elements from cultures far from their ancestral homeland. European and American Indian elements were as important in the practice of conjure as those originating in Africa. Moreover, conjure served as a cross section of the African American experience, demonstrating immigrant African origins coupled with an essentially American experience of assimilation of cultural differences.

In New Orleans, Voodoo survived as a religion in its own right, but in the Anglo South, Protestant Christianity succeeded in diminishing adherence to the older faiths. Even in the case of conjurers, it required accommodation to a monotheistic world-view, accounting for the gradual disappearance of full-fledged African religions. At the same time, contact with Europeans was far from simply a destructive force when it came to hoodoo. On the contrary, European contributions to nineteenth-century conjure rivaled those that survived from African. Though black Christians owed allegiance to a God distinct from those revered by their ancestors, they often felt no need to abandon their magical practices. European influence affected hoodoo in three distinct ways: erosion of African practices, reinforcement of African customs, and introduction of new ideas and practices.

Most sources, both popular and scholarly, are quick to point out the negative impact of European dominance on the survival of African beliefs. To most white slaveholders, Voodoo and conjure were at best offensive relics of paganism and at worst possible rallying points for slave rebellions. The result was often legal action. During the eighteenth century, governors of Louisiana banned slave imports from Martinique and Santo Domingo because of their predilection for Voodoo. Gris-gris practiced against whites could lead to imprisonment, as occurred in the case of a slave named Carlos, who died in prison after planning to use magic to kill his master, Francisco Bellile. Suppression of Voodoo and its related magical practices continued up to and beyond the Civil War, during which New Orleans authorities frequently broke up gatherings, fined believers, and arrested leaders. Outside New Orleans, conjure was likewise an object of attack, to the degree that blacks hid its practice from whites.

Even after emancipation, African Americans did not possess true spiritual freedom, with open practice of African religions being suppressed by force in at least one South Carolina case. By the late nineteenth century, white efforts to eliminate conjure had so stigmatized its practice that educated members of both races saw its survival as a major failing of the African American people. An editor of the *Southern Workman* went so far as to proclaim that accounts of conjure "throw light upon the mental condition of the masses of this people, and the kind of work that must be done among them if they are to be raised to civilization or even saved from extinction."[1] Public hostility, coupled with the rigors of a slave system that required supervised work from sunup to sundown, was enough to ensure that no African religion survived intact in the nineteenth-century South.

Despite overt opposition to African religious systems, much in European beliefs helped preserve the very African convictions that whites sought to destroy. First and foremost, Europe had its own brands of magic workers. During the centuries preceding the settlement of the New World, belief in witchcraft was widespread in the countries that would later supply America with its white settlers. By the time colonists had begun to cross the Atlantic, the church and general populace had firmly defined witchcraft as a form of heresy characterized by malevolent magic acquired through pacts with the devil, whom witches worshiped in groups called *covens*. Witches also reputedly sacrificed and ate children, changed their shape at will, and bent spirits to their service. They inspired such terror that Europeans executed at least sixty thousand on charges of witchcraft during the late Middle Ages and the early modern period.[2] Some estimates range above 1 million. Not until the eighteenth century did prosecution of witchcraft largely disappear from European legal systems.[3]

Witchcraft did not stay in the Old World. During the seventeenth and eighteenth centuries Anglo-American colonists accused at least 344 of their neighbors of witchcraft. About one in ten suffered execution. Ninety percent of the accused witches were New Englanders; other executions took place in the Middle Colonies, such as New York and Pennsylvania, with the last witch killing carried out by a Philadelphia mob in 1787. Rather than being a sign of witchcraft's absence from the South, however, the paucity of prosecutions reflected the region's more tolerant attitude in respect to religion and magic. For example, in Virginia, when allegations of witchcraft appeared before the courts, plaintiffs were likely to suffer fines for false accusation. Very few supposed witches suffered any punishment, and the death penalty was virtually unknown.[4]

Among the plain folk, particularly in the backwoods, witches were reportedly common and feared. While backwoods settlers killed no witches, they nevertheless regarded them as a malevolent force to be reckoned with. Among their evil acts, they would transform unwitting sleepers into horses and ride them, bewitch cattle to stop them from giving milk, and kill or injure victims by throwing witch balls, made of hair from cows or horses, at pictures of their victims. The most celebrated instance of southern witchcraft took place in Tennessee. In the first half of the nineteenth century a mysterious shape-shifting and often invisible being reportedly tormented John Bell and his family with apparitions, cursing from empty air, and physical attacks, eventually bringing about Bell's death and breaking up the family. Though suspicions focused on a woman by the name of Mrs. Batts, well known for practicing minor acts of magic, she was never formally accused.[5]

To prevent a situation from progressing to the seriousness of that faced by the Bells, one could call on professional "witchmasters" or witch hunters, who offered their services to drive out witches and cure the supernatural illnesses inflicted by them.[6] For less serious cases a variety of home remedies were readily available. For instance, a broom laid across a doorway prevented witches from entering. Likewise, sieves hung on the doors compelled witches to pass through each hole before going into a home, usually convincing them to look elsewhere. Despite whites' attempts to define blacks as superstitiously backward (and many blacks' ready acceptance of this proposition), whites were also strongly attached to supernaturalism.[7]

Popular beliefs about European witches did much to preserve African ideas about workers of magic. The European concept of witches' pacts with Satan reinforced existing African ideas about sorcerers, who often obtained their powers by deals with evil spirits. Moreover, as Zora Neale Hurston and Harry Middleton Hyatt discovered, at least some conjurers made the satanic pacts of which they were accused. European witches' supposed custom of meeting in groups helped preserve African concepts of witch societies. Moreover, the coven idea doubtless played a part in transforming Africa's pervasive men's and women's societies into true secret societies devoted to the practice of magic. Whites even had their own witchmasters, who operated in the same capacity as African witch doctors. This fact contributed to the survival of the notion of a conjure doctor, who cured those who had been harmed by hoodooists, though individuals usually practiced both malevolent and benevolent magic.[8]

The powers and practices of European witches likewise shared many features with those of African magic workers, good and evil. Most notably, European witches trafficked in the world of spirits, usually to harm their victims. In Africa, of course, witches were not the only ones who dealt with spirits; priests, chiefs, sorcerers, and members of other professions did so as well, with the major difference in their practices being the tier of the divine hierarchy that they addressed. The similar beliefs of the two cultures ensured that virtually all conjurers, regardless of the source of their powers, claimed to control supernatural entities, ranging from the exorcism of ghosts to the ability to imbue luck balls with indwelling spirits. Also, like European witches, African witches reputedly engaged in cannibalism, though their brand typically involved eating souls rather than flesh. Such beliefs were the basis for Braziel Robinson's concern that his two good spirits might be replaced by evil human spirits that he might inadvertently meet. African and European ideas of human sacrifice and cannibalism on the part of witches also supported a rumor that Latin-area Voodoo queens kept murdered children in their homes. Witches' shape-shifting abilities were also present in both cultures. In whites' belief, witches frequently transformed themselves into cats, rabbits, and other animals, while African witches had the power to become cats, owls, and bats. This ability, though not common, was nevertheless possessed by some conjurers, such as Railroad Bill, a legendary Alabamian outlaw and conjurer.[9]

Other European magical forms likewise reinforced African features of conjure. Most notably, charms and spells were easily obtainable from witches practicing benevolent magic. Today such individuals are known as "white" witches because their spells were meant to help others instead of harming them. In Great Britain they were commonly known as "cunning" men and women. They specialized in finding lost property, healing, fortunetelling, and making charms for luck, love, and protection. Like African American conjurers, they usually charged for their services. These magical specialists survived in the American South. Southern whites of all social classes had frequent recourse to fortunetellers, particularly astrologers. Others turned to cunning men and women to discover underground streams, remove curses, and perform a variety of feats traditionally ascribed to European white witches. A variety of homemade magical formulas were available to any who wanted to use them. For example, male Kentuckians believed that giving women water in which the paddle of a goose's foot had been boiled compelled them to love the ones who gave them the water. Other spells purportedly protected crops, improved the health of livestock, and otherwise bettered the lives of those who cast them.[10]

Even European science aided the survival of African magic. During the early colonial period many sciences had not yet developed as fields of study distinct from religion and what modern scholars call magic. Such eminent scientists as Isaac Newton were deeply interested in alchemy, chiefly known for its practitioners' attempts to transform base metals into gold. According to Keith Thomas, author of *Religion and the Decline of Magic*, the existence of certain types of what is now seen as magic was taken for granted by most intellectuals.[11]

At the heart of magic's believability was the idea that the universe was a living system peopled by a hierarchy of spirits and operating via a series of correspondences among different physical parts of the world. In this system each human was a microcosm of the universe. For this reason, intellectuals did not necessarily consider astrology and related fortunetelling practices magic. Instead, if studied carefully, the correspondence between the movements of stars and planets could conceivably become a science for the prediction of individuals' futures. Similarly, when based on correspondences, magic was an effective means of improving one's life or harming others. What seventeenth-century intellectuals described as science, modern folklorists and anthropologists define as a European form of sympathetic magic, so called because items sharing common properties could supposedly affect each other supernaturally.[12]

In the field of medicine, books of home remedies circulated throughout the colonial and antebellum periods. These ranged from works on traditional herbal treatments for ailments to treatises that purported to cure disease based on the magical properties of plants, animals, stones, and planets. One of the better known of the latter was *Pow-Wows, or Long Lost Friend*, by John George Hohman (whose real name was Johann Georg Hohman), which contained Pennsylvania Amish remedies for ills ranging from bleeding to swelling in cattle. One striking example of the magical nature of the cures in *Pow-Wows* was the remedy for fever, which prescribed writing "Potmat Sineat, Potmat Sineat, Potmat Sineat" on a piece of paper and then wrapping it in knotgrass. To complete the cure, one should tie the packet to the body of the afflicted. Most remedies followed the Doctrine of Signatures, the folk healing equivalent of seventeenth-century intellectuals' theory of correspondences or modern anthropology's sympathetic magic. According to this doctrine, materials within the natural world indicated their properties through their physical appearance.

For example, European herbalists believed that the wild pansy was a potent cardiac tonic owing to its heart-shaped leaves.[13]

How do we know that the two races interacted in the realm of the supernatural? First, whites often equated African American magic with European witchcraft. During the Salem witch scare at least three of the accused were black. In fact, it was the practice of Voodoo by a slave named Tituba that ignited the panic in the first place.[14] More important, the very presence of European charms and magical world-views helped ensure that African charms would survive, making whites potential clients for black conjurers. Furthermore, the universal principle of sympathy made blacks' magic all the more acceptable to the ruling class. As a consequence, several examples of white participation in conjure appear in nineteenth-century sources. European Americans commonly participated in Voodoo magical rituals. Charles D. Warner reported that several whites attended a New Orleans Voodoo ceremony that he witnessed. He was shocked to learn that one of them was a "pure white" Episcopalian from the American section of the city. Describing her as a "pretty, modest girl, very reticent, well-bred, polite, and civil," he lamented the "deep hold the superstition had upon her nature."[15] Whites also took part in African American magic in other locales. Aunt Zippy Tull, a famous Maryland conjure woman, served European American clients. In one instance she healed a white woman cursed by a romantic rival, another white female.[16]

Just as whites participated in African American magic, blacks took part in European American supernaturalism. For example, Byrl Anderson, a Tennessee slave, reported that his white master told fortunes using a Bible suspended on a string. According to Gladys-Marie Fry, slaveowners fostered respect for the supernatural in order to make it easier to control their slaves. Masters' virtually unchecked power over bondspersons was a strong incentive to obedience on its own. A slaveowner possessing occult abilities was even more fearsome. Participation in whites' supernaturalism was not always foisted upon blacks. African Americans frequently resorted to white conjurers in times of need. The first Dr. Buzzard, of Beaufort, South Carolina, served a primarily black clientele. The same was true of Dr. Harris, another white South Carolinian rootworker. A few literate blacks had access to printed magical treatises, which they used alongside African traditions. *Les secrets merveilleux de la magie naturelle du Petit Albert*, a French grimoire, is one example. It was long popular among black Louisianians, who knew it as the *'Tit Albert*.[17]

The Christian faith, which did much to undermine conjure, also helped to preserve it. Followers of Voodoo and Nañigo kept their African gods and goddesses alive within the realm of Catholic saints (see table 2). These were not simply African gods masked with saints' names, though. On the contrary, certain saints shared their personalities with African gods, effectively becoming a single entity worshiped in two different ways, depending on whether the Voodoo devotee was participating in a Voodoo dance or attending mass. In most cases the merging of the pairs originated in characteristics shared by both god and saint. For instance, Blanc Dani, the Voodoo snake god, shared an identity with St. Michael the Archangel, who was frequently depicted in religious iconography battling a serpentine Satan. Likewise, St. Peter, keeper of the keys of heaven, was identical to Papa Lébat, the linguist god who opened the door to other deities at the beginning of religious rituals. The Catholic practice of honoring saints with holidays and statues was similar to African practices, which frequently employed images of divinities and festivals in their honor. For example, St. John's Eve was a Catholic holiday characterized in Europe by bonfires and visits to holy bodies of water. Voodooists linked traditional African practices of ritual bathing, drumming, singing, and dancing to the occasion and made it the most important Voodoo celebration of the year.[18]

In the Anglo zone, where syncretic religions did not survive as long, God took on the attributes of Africa's lesser deities, becoming a powerful source of magical powers (see chapter 4). God's position within conjure mirrored his place in the religious life of blacks. He superseded all other spiritual forces. The mere presence of Christian belief in the supernatural helped African magic to survive by providing a foundation for its practice.[19]

European beliefs did more than just help African magic survive: they made their own unique contributions to conjure. The most readily apparent European influence was in the terminology of conjure. In the Latin zone African terms like *hoodoo* and *wanga* were more popular than European words for describing African American magic, but in the Anglo zone the situation was much different. There, practitioners were usually known as *conjurers*, an English term referring to those who used incantations to call up and control spirits, a concept adopted from Jewish Kabbala. Hoodooists' abilities to perform similar feats led them to adopt the title. The less common use of *witch* to signify African American sorcerers likewise arose from a situation in which blacks' reputed magical powers mirrored those of their European counterparts.

TABLE 2. Selected African American gods with Catholic equivalents in the Latin south

GOD NAME(S)	CATHOLIC EQUIVALENT	FUNCTION IN LATIN CULTURAL AREA	AREA OF WORSHIP
Bon Dieu	God	Omnipotent and omniscient, supreme being	Louisiana
Monsieur Danny, Blanc Dani, Grand Zombie, Voodoo Magnian	St. Michael	Chief god, worshiped in the form of a snake, god of discord, defeats enemies	Louisiana and Florida
Papa Lébat, Liba, LaBas	St. Peter	Trickster, doorkeeper, evil	Louisiana
Monsieur Agoussou, Vert Agoussou	St. Anthony	God of love	Louisiana
Abasi	God	Omnipotent and omniscient, supreme being	Florida
Obatala	Virgin of Mercy	Chief god, most powerful spirit	Florida
Elegba	The devil	Evil spirit	Florida
Shango	St. Barbara	Spirit of good and evil, justice, and thunder	Florida
Yemaya	Virgin of Regla	Spirit of the air and sea	Florida

Sources: Brandon, *Santeria from Africa to the New World*, 77; Cable, "Creole Slave Songs"; Cable, "Dance in Place Congo"; Cable, *Grandissimes*, 99, 101, 135, 182, 184, 257, 272, 311, 447, 453–56, 468; Hauptmann, "Spanish Folklore from Tampa Florida"; Jacobs and Kaslow, *Spiritual Churches of New Orleans*, 82–92; Long, *Spiritual Merchants*, 3–96; Métraux, *Voodoo in Haiti*, 28, 31, 100–119; Murphy, *Santería*, 77; Pitkin, *Angel by Brevet*, 185–213, 260–92.

Note: There is little information on the saint equivalents of African American Floridians' gods. As a result, the equivalents given here come from works on the closely related Cuban Santería. The exception is Elegba in Cuba, where Santería developed. There Elegba was much less sinister. Cubans identified him with the Holy Child of Atoche, an aspect of Jesus, or St. Anthony of Padua (see Brandon, Santeria from Africa to the New World, 77; and Murphy, Santería, 42–43).

Other synonyms for *conjurer* also replicated European words. For example, in Virginia and Maryland hoodooists were sometimes known as *high men, high women,* or *cunning doctors,* English terms that described white practitioners of benevolent magic. Another rare term, *pow-wow doctor,* hearkened back to the Pennsylvania German magical tradition, known as powwow. The best published representative of these folk customs was Hohman's *Pow-Wows.* Strange as it may seem, Amish remedies had spread throughout the Anglo South by the mid-1800s but were most common in Maryland and Virginia owing to these states' proximity to Pennsylvania.[20]

Europe contributed more than just words to hoodoo. In the Latin cultural area Roman Catholicism deeply affected the shape of hoodoo rituals. Charles D. Warner gave an account of a Voodoo ceremony that clearly demonstrated the impact of European Christianity. The most notable feature of the room in which the ritual took place was an altar surmounted by a statuette of the Virgin Mary and candles, all explicitly Catholic symbols. While altars were common in Africa, black Louisianians abandoned their traditional forms, which often took the shapes of the deities worshiped through their use, in favor of the rectangular one of Catholicism. Saint images, like the one seen by Warner, indicated the god/saint being honored by the offerings, effectively occupying the gap in African practice created by the changed shape of the altars.[21]

Often, in Voodoo and hoodoo ceremonies there were offerings of food for the saints/gods upon or surrounding the altar. In other cases, the altar held different forms of offerings, including money, alcohol, and other items favored by the deities being entreated. Perhaps the most common offerings, however, were candles. Long used in Catholic rituals honoring God and the saints, they were easily adapted to dealings with the deities of Latin-zone hoodoo. In African American magic, however, candles provided a way to please deities, usually by choosing colors favored by particular gods/saints. For instance, when seeking help in matters of finance one would burn a green candle, sympathetically linked to money by its color. Assonquer, the god of good fortune, would respond. If the candle sputtered, his aid was unlikely, but if the flame burned brightly, he had agreed to help. Black candles were the color of choice for dealing with enemies.[22]

In the Latin zone of the American South many of the beings honored with altars and candles were of European origin. Alongside deities with shared African European roots, such as Blanc Dani/St. Michael and Papa Lébat/St. Peter, were a variety of orthodox Catholic saints without any overt link to specific African gods and goddesses. For example, the Virgin Mary, whose statuette surmounted the altar observed by Warner, was widely honored in hoodoo rituals but apparently assigned no counterpart from the pantheon of Louisiana's Voodoo goddesses. Despite her important role in Catholic belief, she took a prominent position in several magical rituals. According to Helen Pitkin's account of another hoodoo ritual, the ceremony opened with a Hail Mary. There followed invocations to a variety of Voodoo gods, including Blanc Dani and Liba. Returning to Catholic antecedents, the ritual ended with the Litany of the Blessed Virgin.[23]

Other saints commonly appeared in rites designed to persuade them to serve the will of the conjurer. St. Rita, patron of desperate cases owing to her experience of abuse at the hands of a brutal husband, was popular among women. One of Hyatt's informants explained that St. Rita was bad luck to women with husbands but helped those without them. Men, however, need not seek her aid. As the informer put it, "She won't do anything for men at all because she don't like them."[24] Another informant told Hyatt that women could persuade the saint to grant wishes by placing a white candle, flowers, and money before her picture and then approaching the altar on nine consecutive mornings, asking that the wish be granted. At the end of the period St. Rita would do as she was asked. St. Raymond, St. Ann, St. Roc, and even Jesus himself were parties to conjurers' acts.[25]

One Christian contribution that reached beyond the Latin zone was the Bible. As a book from God, it became an important magical text throughout the South. According to Zora Neale Hurston, it was "the great conjure book in the world."[26] For William Adams, the Texan hoodooist, it was a manual for potential conjurers, teaching them to drive out evil spirits by prayer. Others used selections from the Bible in their spells.[27] Conjurers chose verses for their clients based on the verses' similarity to the result to be accomplished, keeping within the rules of sympathetic magic. For example, conjurers and their clients could successfully deal with unwilling tradesmen if they read Psalm 56 three times before bed and again before sunrise, both readings to be carried out while facing east. Psalm 56, one of David's prayers for deliverance while at the mercy of the Philistines, was an excellent choice in such situations. In other cases the power of the Bible went beyond its words. According to one of Hyatt's informants, a person could keen away "the law" by using nine needles to affix a page from the Bible over his or her door.[28]

Not all of the European features of conjure came from the Christian faith. Others came from European supernaturalism. Charms for protection and luck, which appeared throughout both cultural zones, were the most plentiful of this class. For example, one of the strongest protective charms among nineteenth-century blacks was the horseshoe. According to Elihu, a South Carolinian slave, a horseshoe hung over the entrance to a home thwarted witches' attempts to ride sleepers. This practice was a wholesale import from England. Reginald Scot's 1584 book, *The Discoverie of Witchcraft*, recorded that one of the chief methods of keeping witches out of homes was "to naille a horsse shoo at the inside of the outmost threshhold of your house."[29] Rabbits' feet were popular charms for luck and protection among nineteenth-century blacks. Like horseshoes, however, their use originated in Europe. In Britain those who carried the unfortunate creature's limb gained good luck and were safe from muscular cramps, colic, arthritis, and attacks by evil spirits.[30]

An evil charm that originated in Europe was the conjure bottle. Conjure bottles were glass containers filled with harmful magical items. They took the place of malevolent conjure bags in some areas, particularly those settled by the English. Bottles filled with magical materials had long been present in England, where they were known as "witch bottles." Archaeologists have also uncovered examples of Anglo-American witch bottles in Princess Anne County, Virginia, and Essington, Pennsylvania.[31]

Some items of European origin came to be tied almost wholly to blacks in the American South. For instance, cinquefoil, long recognized as a demon and witch repellent, came to be known as five finger grass among African Americans. Much more common among blacks than among whites, its possessors variously employed it as a protective device, a cure for conjure, and a charm for drawing money, the latter use inspired by its green color and handlike appearance. Even John the Conqueror, most famous of African American root charms, was at least partially European in origin. While the idea of John the Conqueror was a descendant of African concepts, like the Kongo *minkisi*, the roots used in Africa did not always grow in the United States. As a result, one of John the Conqueror's earliest American forms emerged from European herbalism. Mary Alicia Owen identified the nineteenth-century form that she called Conquer-John as Solomon's seal *(Polygonatum multiflorum)*, a plant long known in Europe for its medicinal properties.[32]

Blacks used European magic in more than making charms. For instance, playing cards were often used for fortunetelling and the diagnosis of magical illnesses, a practice common in Europe for centuries. Some blacks employed a divination system supposedly used by Napoleon Bonaparte that centered around the interpretation of self-made dots on a paper. Malevolent magic likewise found its way from Europe to African American hoodooists. A form of pillow magic practiced by Latin-area conjurers was one notable European contribution. German settlers, in particular, believed that witches hexed beds and pillows, causing wreathes or animal shapes to form in their feather stuffings. Once the figures were fully formed, those who slept in the bed would die. The African American form of pillow magic was identical to that practiced by German immigrants. European witches also bequeathed the power of the evil eye to their African American brethren. Blacks with the power of the evil eye could cause illness or otherwise harm people simply by looking at them. A surefire protection, however, was to carry the knucklebone of a pig in one's pocket.[33]

But how did blacks learn the magic of the white ruling class? Throughout the antebellum period whites and blacks came into frequent contact as masters and slaves. House servants, who typically lived in the homes of their owners, were in constant association with whites. This situation continued into the late nineteenth century. Observation alone would allow blacks to learn many of the ruling class's supernatural practices. Individuals of mixed European and African ancestry had an even greater opportunity to learn magic from white parents, and despite the racial assumptions of the period, miscegenation was far from uncommon. Slave masters throughout the South sometimes treated their female slaves as sexual objects. In New Orleans "quadroon balls" helped young white men to meet mixed-race women, often for the purpose of concubinage. The result was a large mulatto community in the city. Similar situations prevailed in Charleston and other large cities. Late-nineteenth-century whites' awareness of the secretive practices of black conjure testify to the permeability of the racial barrier.[34]

Whites and blacks sometimes intentionally taught each other their magic. White witches and conjurers, the latter of whom catered to a black clientele, constituted one means by which the races exchanged information. During the 1920s Newbell Niles Puckett, a white male, began to practice conjure in order to learn more about African American magic. Referring to his time as a hoodooist, he wrote, "Even conjurers are not without their professional spirit, and I found them quite willing to swap clinical knowledge and even materia medica with one, once they believed him to be a 'rale trick-doctor.'"[35] Doubtless, many black conjurers learned European magic through similar exchanges. Those African Americans who visited such white conjurers as the first Dr. Buzzard or Dr. Harris certainly gleaned tidbits of the magical art. However acquired, European practices had transformed conjure by the end of the century; hoodoo was no longer strictly an African practice.[36]

While popular authors and television producers have typically minimized European contributions, Native Americans' impact on conjure has rarely even been acknowledged. Nevertheless, blacks have interacted with American Indians almost as long as they have with Europeans. Whenever whites and blacks moved into a new area, they encountered aboriginal peoples. Furthermore, as two peoples persecuted by European immigrants, blacks and Indians often made common cause against their oppressors. The first to do so were black slaves who escaped from a Spanish expedition up the Carolina coast in 1526, living out their lives among the Guale people. When a neighboring people known as the Yamasee revolted against English South Carolina in 1715, runaway slaves fought at their side. Despite defeat, the Yamasee refused to surrender their black comrades. Creeks, Cherokees, and other Native American peoples likewise accepted black runaways into their society. Flight to the Indians remained a viable option for slaves well into the antebellum period.[37]

The best-known instance of mixing of blacks and Indians was that of Florida's Seminoles' welcoming African Americans as part of their tribe. Fugitive slaves were so numerous in Seminole territory that the United States began a series of three wars against them in July 1816 for the purpose of closing Florida off to runaways and recapturing those blacks already living among the Indians. At the same time, African Americans augmented the Seminoles' capacity to resist the American military. According to legend, an escaped African conjurer called Uncle Monday aided the Seminoles in their wars. Following a defeat on the shores of Lake Maitland, he refused to submit to slavery and escaped in the form of an alligator. Those not so gifted as Uncle Monday, however, submitted to the United States and resettled in the Indian Territory (modern Oklahoma). Even after the Seminoles' defeat blacks accompanied the tribe into exile, remaining there throughout the nineteenth century.[38]

Not all blacks who lived among American Indians were fugitives. Many were slaves to Indian masters. The nineteenth-century traveler Henry C. Benson reported that Choctaws turned to slavery as depleted hunting grounds forced them into agriculture. According to Benson, Choctaws despised manual labor to such a degree that "even very poor Indians will manage to get possession of one or two negroes to perform their heavy work."[39] Seminoles, Creeks, Cherokees, Chickasaws, and many other peoples likewise adopted slavery during the colonial and antebellum eras, taking their human chattel with them upon their removal to the Indian Territory.[40]

More important than black slaves' presence among American Indians, however, was the comparative freedom allowed them in Native American society as opposed to that of whites. Seminoles, who gave their slaves the greatest liberty, allowed bondsmen and bondswomen to live as they wished as long as they paid a portion of their agricultural produce each year to their masters. Henry Bibb attested to similarly benevolent treatment among the Cherokees of the

Indian Territory. Having been purchased by a wealthy Cherokee planter, one of his first tasks was to carry five hundred dollars of his new master's money on a lengthy journey with minimal supervision. Bibb further testified that overseers were unknown on Native American plantations. Whippings and other forms of punishment were rare, and when slaves resisted, their owners had no legal recourse. He concluded by saying, "I had by far, rather be a slave to an Indian, than to a white man, from the experience I have had with both."[41] Under such conditions cultural exchange with the ruling class was easy.

According to the nineteenth-century scholar James Mooney, a common misconception about Native Americans was that they knew "every plant of the field and forest, and that the medicine man outranks the white physician in his knowledge of the healing art."[42] Whether true or not, American Indians' reputed powers over disease and illness made knowledge of their abilities a useful marketing tool in the hands of black conjurers. For instance, the former slave Joseph William Carter reported that he had learned "Voodoo" from his cousin, a full-blooded Indian, who was so well known that both blacks and whites called on him for healing.[43]

Even better than knowledge, however, was Native American ancestry. Notable New Orleans conjurers, including Marie Laveau, could claim Native American forebears. The practice of claiming Indian blood reached its height in Missouri, however, where blacks easily mingled with the peoples on the borders of white settlement as well as with the Five Civilized Tribes, removed from the Deep South to the Indian Territory. Mary Alicia Owen spoke to many who claimed Native American ancestry, tracing their roots to such peoples as the Lenni Lenape, the Iowa, and the Fox. King Alexander, the greatest conjurer encountered by Owen, was reportedly half Cherokee and half "Guinea."[44]

While European beliefs often worked against African ideas, Native American religion did little to undermine blacks' ancestral practices. On the contrary, Indian religions strongly resembled those of West and west-central Africa. Among the aboriginal inhabitants of the American Southeast, belief in a supreme being who ruled the universe while remaining distant from humankind was common. Below the supreme god were a number of lesser gods or spirits. The Cherokee, the most widespread southern tribe, believed that the universe comprised three levels: the Upper World, This World, and the Under World. The inhabitants of the Upper World and the Under World mirrored the lesser gods of Africa. The greatest beings came from the Upper World, which was characterized by order, stability, and time past. Some of the most important of these were the sun, the moon, and thunders. The Under World, in contrast, contained monsters and ghosts, which, though fearsome and unpredictable, were responsible for innovation, fertility, and future time.[45]

Native Americans lived in This World. Under World creatures, including reptiles, amphibians, and fish, sometimes emerged from caves, rivers, and lakes to harm humans. For a time the beings of the Upper World lived in This World. As it became gradually less desirable, they returned to the Upper World, leaving behind images of themselves in the form of plants and animals. Birds continued to be associated with the Upper World, however, owing to their ability to fly. While plants befriended humans, animals became their enemies.[46]

Balance in the world and within individual humans required balancing elements from the Upper and Under worlds, for which the Cherokee turned to the living shadows of the divine. As in African and some European beliefs, each living thing (and sometimes inanimate objects or natural features) had a soul that gave it the power to help or harm those who dealt with it. Also, the use of animals and plants followed the principle of sympathy. For example, buzzards were symbolically linked to healing because of their ability to associate with dead creatures without ill effects. Because of their use and place on earth, animals and plants were analogous to the three lowest tiers of the northern West African spiritual hierarchy and the *minkisi* of the Kongo. Many Native Americans also worshiped their ancestors. For Cherokees this was a minor feature of their faith, expressed primarily in respectful treatment of the dead to avoid ghostly reprisals. Among other peoples the dead served as guardian spirits, intermediaries between humans and lesser gods, and manipulators of natural phenomena.[47]

Alongside Catholicism, late slave importation, and high black-to-white ratios, the proximity of Indians practicing traditional religions helped ensure that the western Latin cultural area would retain strong African religious elements. The best illustration of the interaction between Native American and African beliefs was the survival of the African snake god, Da. As was the case with Voodoo's gods/saints, Da's identity merged with that of Indian deities. Snake gods and spirits were plentiful in the beliefs of southeastern Indians. Chief among the beings of the Under World was a giant creature known as Uktena to the Cherokees. Combining physical elements resembling animals symbolic of the Under, Upper, and This worlds, it had a snakelike body, wings, and antlers. Living in enmity with the Upper World, it eventually fell to a hawklike deity called Tlanuwa.[48]

A variety of other serpentine creatures from the Under World also interacted with the human world. Indians set snakes apart from other animals because of their lack of appendages, crediting them with power over other animals, plants, and the elements. Mightiest of all was Rattlesnake. Once, he had saved humans from death at the hands of the sun, who had tried to wipe humankind out with disease. Thus, Rattlesnake was more powerful than Uktena, who had failed when he opposed the Upper World. In the Latin area the prevalence of snakes was a powerful force in preserving African serpent gods. Native American mythology validated Louisiana blacks' faith in Blanc Dani. Missouri hoodooists went so far as to specifically designate the rattlesnake as their most powerful spirit, whom they honored with dances. Moreover, they referred to him as Grandfather Rattlesnake. Several plains tribes conferred the same title on the guardian spirit of the Missouri River, known as Grandfather Snake. Though Da had lost his African name, he had gained others from those he encountered in his new home.[49]

The segmentation and organization of Native American magical specialists similarly mirrored African practices. For example, diviners chiefly concerned themselves with foretelling the course of individual lives, finding lost or stolen articles, and most important, diagnosing illness. Once diagnosed, clients turned to priests, more commonly known as "medicine men." Much of the medicine men's practice consisted in administering herbal remedies. They did not, however, rely simply on chemical properties of plants; illness was a spiritual condition, requiring magical cures. Brought on by an imbalance in nature, illness was usually a result of the actions of angry animal spirits who resented being killed by humans. Plants, as friends of humankind, were natural allies in the battle against ill health. In conjunction with herbalism, Indians used sacred dances, songs, and incantations to effect cures. Priests also used their medicine to bring about successful hunts, love, victory in war, and sometimes harm to their enemies. Furthermore, like African magical specialists, they received pay for their services and organized themselves into societies. These societies typically operated for specific purposes, ranging from promoting healing and agricultural fertility to honoring animals. Opposite the generally positive powers of diviners and medicine men was the evil art of witchcraft. Witches were wholly malevolent and could work evil simply by thinking it. They felt compelled to steal time from the lives of others in order to extend their own, which they did by inducing madness, illness, or death or by eating their victims. To facilitate their malicious designs, witches could fly and transform themselves into cats, wolves, owls, ravens, and balls of fire.[50]

American Indians' methods of gaining magical powers also strongly resembled African methods. For instance, like African and European sorcerers, Indian practitioners often underwent initiation ceremonies, during which they studied magic. Among the Creeks, small groups of prospective priests sought out older medicine men for induction and instruction. After secluding themselves from the rest of society, they fasted and ingested a large amount of "red root," inducing vomiting. Thereafter followed four days of instruction that concluded with a steam bath and washing in a cold stream. Five or six more of these four-day sessions would follow over the succeeding months. Prospective priests ended their instruction with two successive sessions of eight and twelve days, respectively. The initiation finished only after the old priest buried the inductees, allowing them to breathe through a tube. As the novitiates waited, symbolically entombed in the earth, the priest burned leaves atop the "grave." Also as in Africa, many Native American magical specialists were gifted with their powers. Diviners often gained their abilities in this way. For example, in several southeastern tribes the younger of a set of twins was thought to be a born diviner. Many witches were likewise born with their powers, being driven to evil by vermin that inhabited their bodies. Other witches fasted and drank concoctions of duck root *(Sagittaria latifolia)* over a seven-day period, which gave them the powers of flight and shape shifting.[51]

One of the more striking shared features of African and Native American beliefs was the concept of multiple souls. Southeastern Indians typically held to a two-soul model. One was the bodily soul, which gave a person life, mobility, and awareness. The other was the free soul, which wandered while its owner slept, as did the Yoruban *okan*. For example, the Seminoles believed that a person's free soul left the body through the anus and journeyed to the north while a person slept, resulting in dreams. Illness was the consequence when souls refused to return. A man or woman deserted by only one soul would not immediately die, however. Skilled priests could persuade it to return if contacted in time. Once four days had passed, the situation became desperate, because the bodily soul might leave the body. If it did, the afflicted was beyond help. Furthermore, while laymen and laywomen could do little to control the movements of their free soul, medicine men could send theirs wherever they desired. The influence of Indians' ideas of multiple souls is best illustrated by the cases of Braziel Robinson and Divinity. Both claimed to have two souls, one of which stayed put, while the other traveled. Their two-soul model more closely resembled the American Indian concept than the African, in which a person typically had four or five souls.[52]

Parallels likewise existed between the practice of Native American magic and that of African magic. One of the most fearsome powers of black conjurers was the ability to insert reptiles, amphibians, and insects into their victims' bodies, causing illness and eventual death. This practice, which was widespread in Africa, was just as common among the aboriginal Americans. Indian witches, who were themselves inhabited with vermin from the Under World, could harm others by transforming the food in their victims' stomachs into lizards or frogs. They also supposedly inserted nonliving objects, such as cloth, charcoal, and flint, into the bodies of their enemies. As with African American conjure, only a more powerful sorcerer could heal victims of infestation.[53]

A more benign power shared by blacks and Native Americans was the ability to make magical bundles. Indians' "medicine bundles" contained a variety of holy materials that were important in many communal and personal pursuits. For instance, Creek war chiefs carried medicine bundles when advancing against their enemies. The bundles' importance was so great that their carriers never allowed them to touch the ground, placing them on special pedestals instead. They were also important in religious ceremonies. The bundles used in wars and religious rituals were important to communities, but others were specific to individuals. Almost all North American Indians believed that each person had a guardian spirit whose physical representation was a personal medicine bundle. This idea closely resembled African explanations for the power of *minkisi, gbo,* and gregory bags. Most people obtained their guardian spirits by seeking them through fasting, prayer, and solitude, during which the spirits would instruct them in the manufacture of their medicine bundles. Some tribes allowed their members to buy the bundles and attendant spirits from priests or even laymen. However obtained, medicine bundles protected their owners and allowed them to call on the spirit world for aid in difficulty or danger. It is no coincidence that Mande-style gregory bags persisted the longest in Missouri, where blacks had close contact with Indian peoples who employed almost identical charms.[54]

Native American beliefs did much to preserve African ideas and practices, but they also enriched conjure with their own distinctive contributions. For example, a native African slave conjurer known to Roland Steiner declared

TABLE 3. Some materials common in or peculiar to conjure and their origins

ITEM WITH AFRICAN AMERICAN NAME	COMMON/ SCIENTIFIC NAME	USE IN CONJURE	CULTURAL ORIGIN(S)
Goopher dust	Graveyard dirt	Good and evil conjure	African
Horseshoes		Protection	European
Eggs		Divination and other uses	European and African
Playing cards		Divination	European
Rabbits' feet		Good luck	European
Parts of reptiles, amphibians, and insects		Numerous uses, but most commonly causing infestation of victims' bodies	Various
Salt		Protection	Particularly popular in Europe
Human bones, fingernails, hair, blood, and other parts or byproducts		Protection and to magically affect the person to whom they belong	Universal
Lodestones	Naturally magnetic stone	Protection and money drawing	European and American
Black cat bone		Invisibility, often for theft	African and European
Silver money		Protection from conjure	European
Needles and pins		Various, particularly causing harm	African and European
Bibles		Various uses, particularly powerful	European
Red flannel		To enclose charms, increasing their power	African
Devil's shoestring	Common plantain *(Plantago major)*, hobble bush *(Viburnum alnifolium)*, or goat's rue *(Trephrosia virginiana)*	Various	Native American and European
Asafetida	*Ferula foetida*	Protection from conjure and disease	European import from the Middle East
Devil's snuff box	Puffball mushrooms *(Lycoperdon perlatum, pyriforme,* and others)	Malevolent conjure	European and Native American
Pecune root, or puccoon root	Bloodroot *(Sanguinaria canadensis)* or hoary puccoon *(Lithospermum canescens)*	Good luck	Native American
Red pepper and Guinea pepper	*Capsicum minimum* and *Capsicum fastigiatum,* respectively	Protection	Native American and African

TABLE 3 *(continued)*

ITEM WITH AFRICAN AMERICAN NAME	COMMON/ SCIENTIFIC NAME	USE IN CONJURE	CULTURAL ORIGIN(S)
King of the Woods	Spikenard *(Aralia racemosa)*	Various, especially anything involving conquering	Native American
Snakeroot	Samson snakeroot *(Psoralea pedunculata)*	Various, including preventing snakebite	American origin
John the Conqueror, Conquer-John, or Conjure John	Various versions, including Solomon's seal *(Polygonatum multiflorum)*, Indian turnip *(Arum tripyhllum)*, St. John's wort *(Hypericum perforatum)*, and jalap *(Ipomea jalap and Convolvulus panduratus)*	Various, particularly powerful "king root of the forest"	African root concept, Native American and European medicinal plant substitutes
Chewing John the Conqueror	Galangal *(Alpinia officinarum)*	Protection from enemies	African root concept, related European import from Southeast Asia
Alligator body parts		Kills enemies	American substitute for African crocodile parts
Candles		Used to please particular spirits	European
Frizzly chickens		Protection from conjure	African
Brooms		Ceremonial, bad luck to be pointed at by it, and other uses	African and European
Conjure stone		Confers and heightens the power of conjure	Native American
Adam and Eve root	*Aplectrum hyemale*	Protection and to bring love, primarily	Native American
Five finger grass	Cinquefoil *(Potentilla reptans)* and related species	Money drawing, gambling, removing conjure, and other less common uses	European
Jimson burrs	Thorn apple *(Datura stramonium)*	Harms those who smell them	Various
Alanthus	Tree of Heaven *(Ailanthus glandulosa)*	Harms those who smell them	European import from Southeast Asia
Mayapple	American mandrake *(Podophyllum peltatum)*	Various	European and Native American concepts, Native American plant origin
Amaranth	*Amaranthus retroflexus* and *spinosus*	Various, particularly to bring love	Native American

Sources: Materials identified by consulting William Adams, interview by Sheldon F. Gauthier (Tarrant County, AL), in Rawick, *American Slave,* suppl. 2, 2:16–22; Bergen, *Animal and Plant Lore,* 78–79; Bibb, *Narrative of the Life,* 25–32; Breslaw, "Tituba's Confession," 539; Folk-Lore and Ethnology, *Southern Workman* 28 (1899): 112–13; Hearn, "New Orleans Superstitions"; Hurston, *Mules and Men,* 279; Hyatt, *Hoodoo—Conjuration—Witchcraft—Rootwork,* 923–24; Lampe, *Famous Voodoo Rituals and Spells,* 17; Neal, "Legalized Crime in Florida," 49; Mary Alicia Owen, "Among the Voodoos," 232, 247–48; Mary Alicia Owen, *Voodoo Tales,* 113; Pendleton, "Notes on Negro Folk-Lore and Witchcraft," 203; Pitkin, *Angel by Brevet,* 185–213, 260–92; Porteous, "Gri-gri Case," 51; Puckett, *Folk Beliefs of the Southern Negro,* 245–46; "Religious Life of the Negro Slave," 822; Steiner, "Observations," 177–80; Steiner, "Superstitions," 262, 269; and Yronwode, *Hoodoo Herb and Root Magic.*

Origins determined by consulting Bacon, "Conjuring and Conjure-Doctors," 209; Crellin and Philpott, *Reference Guide to Medicinal Plants,* 212–13; *Encyclopedia of American Popular Beliefs and Superstitions,* s.v. "Black Cat Bone"; Foster and Duke, *Field Guide to Medicinal Plants and Herbs,* 52–56, 63–64, 155, 244; Georgia Writers' Project, Savannah Unit, *Drums and Shadows,* 43, 61, 200, 206; Gomez, *Exchanging Our Country Marks,* 204–6; Grieve, *Modern Herbal,* 62–63, 101–3, 175–76, 316–17, 339–40, 640–42, 655–56, 707–8, 749–50, 802–7, 841–42; Hamel and Chiltoskey, *Cherokee Plants and Their Uses,* 23, 41, 46, 51; Hudson, *Southeastern Indians,* 166–69; Kingsley, *Travels in West Africa,* 446, 469; Long, *Spiritual Merchants,* 6–8, 15, 75, 102, 221–46; MacGaffey, *Religion and Society in Central Africa,* 52; Millspaugh, *American Medicinal Plants,* 488; Opie and Tatem, *Dictionary of Superstitions,* 135, 193–94; Opoku, *West African Traditional Religion,* 148; Mary Alicia Owen, "Among the Voodoos," 232; Mary Alicia Owen, *Voodoo Tales,* 113; Puckett, *Folk Beliefs of the Southern Negro,* 220, 290–91; Thompson, *Face of the Gods,* 49–50; Thompson, *Flash of the Spirit,* 108–31; and Vogel, *American Indian Medicine,* 224–25, 299, 326–28, 354–56.

Note: In general, those items listed above the two John the Conqueror roots were more common in the Anglo zone; those listed below them were more common in the Latin area; and the John the Conquerors were present in both areas.

that he had learned his art from Native Americans. Among the many powers he claimed were the abilities to control masters and overseers, compel runaway slaves to return to their owners, and guarantee his clients victory in games of chance. Unfortunately for later scholars, Steiner did not record how the hoodooists obtained such miraculous results.[55]

Indians' contributions were most obvious in hoodoo's magical herbalism, where many items can be traced to Native American medical practices. For instance, devil's snuff box, better known as the puffball mushroom (*Lycoperdon perlatum* and related species), was a common ingredient in Georgian conjure bags, particularly those designed with evil in mind. In American Indian belief it had the more beneficial qualities of stopping blood flow and keeping babies' skin healthy. Another plant used by both blacks and Native Americans was amaranth *(Amaranthus retroflexus* and *A. spinosus).* Missouri's African Americans believed that it had the power to win the love of whoever ate it when combined with pounded wheat, honey from a new hive, and a white dove's heart and baked into a cake. Indians valued it for its astringency and as a treatment of profuse menstruation. They also used it in magic associated with the Green Corn Ceremony. Although devil's snuff box and amaranth took on very different uses when transferred from Native Americans to African Americans, others retained their original uses. One of the best examples of such continuity was puccoon root (either *Sanguinaria canadensis* or *Lithospermum canescens*). Blacks believed that rubbing it on one's body brought luck. Native Americans had similar ideas. They rubbed it on their bodies for purposes ranging from creating success in love to preventing convulsions.[56]

In parts of the Latin area hoodooists spoke of stones or crystals that gave their owners the ability to conjure, regardless of whether they were favored by the spirit world and without the usual processes of initiation and instruction. Zora Neale Hurston wrote that Uncle Monday had a stone that was known as a "singing stone." According to Hurston's informants, it was a diamond and the most powerful charm in the world. Reportedly, such stones could only be obtained from magical serpents that lived in the depths of Lake Maitland. Each serpent had two stones, one imbedded in its head and one that it carried in its mouth. The only way to obtain one was to either kill the serpent or steal the stone that it carried in its mouth when the creature put it aside to eat. Mary Alicia Owen saw a "conjure stone" in the course of her investigations; she described it as black and shaped like a kidney. She wrote that if its strength lessened, it was readily restored by feeding it with whiskey or red pepper. Two of her informers estimated that there were only six in the United States. Though some conjurers told Owen that the stones came from Africa, they more likely originated with Native Americans.[57]

Most southeastern Indians believed that certain stones conferred magical powers on their possessors and enabled them to foresee the future. Among the Cherokees they were crystals, which reportedly came from the body of Uktena, the great Under World serpent. The most important of them was the Ulunsuti, a crest that projected from the head of the serpent. Trying to obtain one was of course very dangerous, but if the seeker succeeded, he would become "the greatest wonder worker of his tribe."[58] Even lesser crystals could attract game and members of the opposite sex, repel bullets, and bring favorable weather. Similarly Creek and Seminole sorcerers resorted to their own magic stones, called *sapiya*. Like the Cherokees' crystals, they brought success in hunting, love, and other pursuits. Like African Americans' conjure stones, they had to be fed; unlike blacks' stones, however, they turned on their owners if neglected. Even Plains Indians had their own sacred stones, which typically resembled animals.[59]

Conjure originated in Africa, but its transformation in the United States made it into a truly American practice. Contact with Europeans and Native Americans sometimes worked against African magic and religion, ensuring that they did not survive intact in the New World. At the same time, the blend of peoples worked to preserve other African beliefs and practices and even contributed many new ideas. In this respect, the transformation of African American magic followed a pattern similar to that of all immigrants to the United States: a tug of war between the desire to hold on to traditional beliefs and practices and the impossibility of recreating ancestral homelands in the New World. The result was a creolized hybrid of beliefs from all three cultures. Table 3, a compilation of materials common in nineteenth-century conjure and their cultural origins, demonstrates the extent of the mixing. Though not a scientific sampling, it shows that the current popular conception of hoodoo as an African import is misguided. Though it entered the colonies and the later United States as an immigrant belief, its development through resistance, acculturation, and accommodation resulted in a practice as American as anything brought from Europe.[60]

Some elements of conjure originated in America, without African, European, or Native American precedents. For instance, the term *rootwork*, common in English-settled South Carolina, was a creation of African Americans, used to express one of the conjurers' most obvious employments. Likewise, African Americans across the South considered Native American arrowheads and spearheads to have magical power. Archaeologists have uncovered them from African American sites as far apart as New Jersey and Texas. One twentieth-century conjurer explained that their power derived from the belief that God had made them out of thunder and lightning.[61]

The most striking example of black American creativity appeared in the gods of New Orleans Voodoo. In their magic and religious worship, hoodooists included a group of "saints" unfamiliar to both Catholic and African priests. The best known of these was St. Expedite, or St. Espidy, who first appeared among the Haitian forebears of Louisiana's slaves. Though the names derived from the name of an obscure Catholic saint named Expeditus, St. Expedite took on a uniquely important role in hoodoo. His devotees applied to him for luck, success in court cases, and money drawing. Hurston added that he was especially important in cases involving the need for speed. His identification is not surprising since the name apparently derives from a word referring to completing a task quickly. St. Marron is an example of a spirit who seems to have originated in the United States. During the antebellum period he was the patron of runaway slaves, who were sometimes known as "maroons." Other "saints" came from American history. The most important of these was Black

Hawk, a leader of the Sauk tribe in an 1832 war to preserve their territory against the encroachment of American settlers. Like African Americans, he had suffered at the hands of whites, but unlike many blacks, he had taken up arms, even winning a minor victory. Earning a reputation as a fierce, cunning, and merciful warrior in life, he retained this reputation as a hoodoo saint. While some turned to him for help in their problems, others stated that he was "one of the old evil saints," best called on to harm others.[62] The two faces of Black Hawk replicate his reputation among whites as a noble savage fighting to save his home and a killer who supposedly mutilated the bodies of his victims.[63]

By the decades preceding the Civil War the African, European, and Native American elements that composed conjure had blended into a seamless whole. Though regional variations persisted well into the twentieth century, hoodoo had become a presence wherever African Americans took up residence. When faced with hardship, whether in the form of cruel taskmasters, unrequited love, or simple bad luck, slaves and later free blacks had the option of turning to the supernatural for help. So many relied on conjure that it occupied a central position in black life and remained so throughout the nineteenth century.

3

The Conjurers' World: The Social Context of Hoodoo in Nineteenth-Century Black Life

ONE SPRING DAY in 1890 Samuel C. Taylor took a train that briefly stopped just south of Tuscumbia, Tennessee. There an unusual African American man boarded the train. His shaved head sported a fist-sized tuft just above the forehead. The stranger's clothes were equally bizarre, consisting most notably of three coats, each composed of a patchwork of materials and colors. Under his coats, numerous chains of brass, silver plate, and iron encircled his body from neck to waist. A peg in place of his right leg completed the odd picture. During his brief stay on the train the man conversed with numerous passengers, including a northern immigrant seeking political office, who asked the black man for his backing in the upcoming election. Throughout his conversations the stranger sipped from a bottle that Taylor initially believed contained gin. After a half-hour the man left the train. Taylor later learned from a black porter that the man he had just encountered was a hoodoo doctor. The bottle from which the conjurer drank contained a magical potion. Taylor also discovered, to his surprise, that the hoodooist was "by far the most influential man in [that] part of the state," a leader among members of his race.[1] Moreover, the hoodoo doctor had studied medicine and used his potion, along with a magical ring and incantations, to cure a variety of afflictions, with a purported success rate of 90 percent.[2]

As Samuel Taylor's encounter illustrates, nineteenth-century conjurers were often central figures in African American society. Taylor's conjurer was a potent political force among members of his race, to the extent that he undertook monthly tours of his constituency. Furthermore, as Taylor discovered, compared with most blacks of his day, the hoodoo doctor was a wealthy man, wearing a suit when off-duty and living in an expensive home just outside of town. Although he operated in the worldly realm of politics, he relied on the supernatural to cure sickness. Moreover, it was his occult knowledge that gave him social prestige.[3] In the nineteenth-century African American world, hoodoo doctors held a major stake in both the "natural" world of politics and economics and the shadowy world of the supernatural.

The key to conjurers' temporal power was the African American belief in the supernatural potency of hoodoo. How widespread were such convictions? Archaeological investigation in Virginia and Maryland has uncovered remains of conjuring "caches," the contents of bags, bottles, and the like that once held magical materials, in slave dwellings from as early as 1702. Occasionally the historical record also reveals examples of colonial conjuring. The best known of these was the event that set off the Salem witchcraft scare. The adolescent girls who initiated the accusations began their involvement with magic by practicing fortunetelling with the slave Tituba, who had learned some magic during an earlier period of enslavement in Barbados. In addition, references to slave "doctors" in colonial and early republican newspapers most likely refer to rootworkers rather than practitioners of scientific medicine. For instance, a 1792 article in the *Massachusetts Magazine* reported on a South Carolina slave named Cesar, who reportedly had discovered the cures for rattlesnake bites and for ingested poisons. The South Carolina Assembly was so grateful that it "purchased his freedom, and gave him an annuity of one hundred pounds."[4] While the assembly doubtless considered Cesar's cures to be scientifically based, blacks in the Atlantic coastal region often understood poisoning to be a result of malevolent spells.[5] A large number of blacks continued to believe in conjure on the eve of the Civil War, as demonstrated in the slave narratives collected by the WPA during the Great Depression. According to Sam Jordan, originally from Alabama, all slaves "wore a silver dime on a raw cotton thread around their ankles to keep from being voodooed."[6] Even if Jordan's estimate that all slaves believed in conjure was an exaggeration, the level of faith was high in the antebellum South.

Conjure was not the province of a single state or region. Long present on the Atlantic Coast and in Louisiana, hoodoo had spread throughout the South by 1860. During the 1850s Abbé Emmanuel Henri Dieudonné Domenech, a Catholic missionary, reported an encounter with hoodoo along the Texas-Mexico border. According to Domenech's report, a young European man went insane after refusing to marry a woman he had seduced. The man recovered only by following the advice of a black native of New Orleans, who told him that he was under the vengeful influence of Voodoo and that only marriage to his former sweetheart would cure him. Once the wedding had taken place, the man recovered.[7]

African Americans' faith in conjure remained strong following emancipation. Although most black and white educational reformers thought of hoodoo as "an absurd superstitious folly that should speedily be rooted out," they nevertheless recognized that it remained strong in the South, "where people are not so enlightened as they are in other parts of the country."[8] Some observers noted an increase in belief in hoodoo following emancipation. The historian Philip A. Bruce stated that freedom fostered conjure by removing blacks from close contact with whites, who had held slaves' natural emotionalism and intellectual predilections toward "superstition" in check. The writings of some planters identify an identical trend. James Sparkman, a South Carolina planter, reported that blacks relapsed into "fetishism" following emancipation. Of course, Bruce and Sparkman, as members of the white ruling class, are questionable sources of black folk belief. Bruce, in particular, was trying to use conjure to demonstrate that blacks had descended into savagery following the removal of the benefits of direct white oversight. The writings of the two authors do, however, demonstrate that whites who lived in close contact with blacks believed that conjure was a powerful force in blacks' lives. Nevertheless, exact figures for the extent of belief in hoodoo are unavailable for the postbellum period.[9]

Informants for Harry Middleton Hyatt's *Hoodoo—Conjuration—Witchcraft—Rootwork* provided several estimates of the prevalence of belief made by trick doctors practicing in the 1930s and 1940s. Moreover, many of them had learned their craft in the previous century. In addition to being more exact than Bruce and Sparkman, virtually all of Hyatt's interviewees were African American. These hoodoo doctors from areas as widely separated as Norfolk, Virginia, and New Orleans, Louisiana, agreed that more than half of African Americans believed in such magic. Undercover Man, of New Orleans, provided one of the lowest estimates, simply stating that a majority believed, but both Faith Doctor, of Little Rock, Arkansas, and Zorro the Mentalist, of Norfolk, Virginia, suggested figures as high as nine out of ten. These interviews, though carried out long after the demise of slavery, testify to the strength of

African Americans' beliefs despite decades of improved education and exposure to scientific principles following emancipation.[10]

Surprisingly, a number of Hyatt's informants argued that whites were also strong believers in hoodoo, with Faith Doctor maintaining that 50 percent believed in conjure and sometimes practiced it. Contemporary sources bear out this assertion. Whether learned from black "mammies," from personal encounters with conjurers, or by some other means, the fear of hoodoo was present in a significant portion of white southerners. For example, Martin Posey, a South Carolina planter, hired a root doctor, named Jeff, to keep his slaves healthy. Upon discovering that Jeff practiced magic, Posey offered to buy his freedom if he would kill Posey's wife. Jeff, however, apparently insisted on obtaining his freedom first and did not take part in the plot.[11] Similarly, according to Bertram Wyatt-Brown's *Southern Honor*, white Virginians feared conjurers because of their supposed ability to kill or seduce whites by using magic. In New Orleans, observers of Voodoo rites regularly reported white participation, and Louisiana's Creole elites were not above using black magic to their own ends.[12]

While whites' belief in the hoodoo of the supposedly inferior blacks may be surprising to some, it is less so when one bears in mind that the peoples of Europe and the American colonies had long believed in their own forms of witchcraft. The New England witch scares of the seventeenth century are cases in point. Backwoods southern whites continued to fear sorcery well into the twentieth century. Stories about witchcraft are told throughout Appalachia to this day. The few whites who practiced African American hoodoo as a profession illustrate the power of Euro-American supernaturalism. Mrs. Augustine Lombas Charpentier, of Franklin, Louisiana, is one particularly prominent example. According to one of her great-great-granddaughters, she was born in Madrid, Spain. When she was seventeen years old, sometime around the middle of the nineteenth century, she immigrated to the United States, where she built a reputation as a hoodooist that persisted for decades after her death in the early twentieth century. A daughter and granddaughter followed her into the profession. The best-known white practitioner, however, was doubtless the first Dr. Buzzard, of South Carolina, whose fame was such that a succession of black conjurers adopted his sobriquet.[13]

Did this widespread faith in hoodoo clash with Christianity? A few blacks accepted the biblical injunction, "There shall not be found among you *any one* that maketh his son or his daughter to pass through the fire, *or* that useth divination, *or* an observer of times, or an enchanter, or a witch, or a charmer, or a consulter with familiar spirits, or a wizard, or a necromancer."[14] One such was William Wells Brown, a former slave, who equated hoodoo with the service of the devil in his book *My Southern Home*. For average African Americans, however, Christianity and conjure were not mutually exclusive systems of belief. While most nineteenth-century black Americans considered themselves Christians, conjure nevertheless remained an important part of their understanding of the supernatural. The reason for this was that hoodoo filled a separate niche in their spiritual world. Unlike Christian ministers, conjurers performed rituals for the sake of controlling or manipulating supernatural powers, not for worship purposes. Thus, conjure was a form of utilitarian, pragmatic spirituality. Nevertheless, some Christian ministers also acted as hoodoo doctors. For instance, Mary Livermore, a northerner who spent three years on an antebellum plantation, recorded that she once encountered a conjurer-preacher known as Uncle Aaron, who exhorted believers to follow God from the pulpit, while raising evil spirits outside the walls of the church.[15]

The power of hoodoo translated into enormous influence within black society for successful conjurers. Traditionally, historians have depicted black preachers as the most important leaders to emerge from within African American communities. Although the influence of preachers was undeniable, they had powerful rivals in conjurers. While black preachers held sway over their congregations as teachers of God's word, bringing messages of righteousness, hope, and love, hoodooists had the power to harm and heal on a whim.[16] Some observers asserted that conjurers, not preachers, had the most power in black communities. Writing in 1889, Philip Bruce argued that hoodooists were the stronger influence of the two because their sway was based on fear. While Bruce was a white author who displayed the condescending racism of his time, black observers often agreed with his conclusions. In 1878 a person who signed him- or herself "S.," wrote to a former instructor at the Hampton Institute to report on his experience teaching black children in Virginia. The letter, which was later published in *Southern Workman*, stated that fear of *cunning*, an uncommon Virginia term for African American conjure, was pervasive. Moreover, though the author protested that he or she did not believe in conjure, the testimonies of so many eyewitnesses to its effects had persuaded him or her to write, "I have not said a word about cunning since, and never intend to; for they can poison you anyhow, for the devil seems to be at the helm.... They die here like sheep."[17]

Fear of conjure was a result of hoodooists' reputed ability to harm others through magic. Trick doctors typically cast their spells at the urging of a paying client, but many simply practiced their craft out of personal animus toward their victims. One of conjurers' most dreaded and most common means of inflicting death or serious illness on unwitting victims was causing one or more animals to inhabit the body of a person. For instance, according to several reports, snakes were frequently visible moving under the skin of the conjured, sometimes even peering from the victims' mouths.[18]

Other complaints common to people magically afflicted were "locked bowels" (a term denoting terminal constipation), "running crazy," and other illnesses causing death or permanent disability. While written accounts of locked bowels are uncommon in Victorian sources, they are common in later sources. Roland Steiner, a Georgia planter, offered a rare nineteenth-century formula for inducing constipation. Speaking from long experience with hoodoo and its victims, he stated that some stopped bowels by "getting the excrement of the person to be cunjered, boring a hole in a tree, and putting the excrement in the hole, and driving a plug in tight."[19] Only by finding, unplugging, and then burning the tree could the victim be healed. During his research in the 1930s Hyatt found cases throughout the South. One informant stated that stopping up a man or woman's excrement in a bottle and then throwing it in running water would cause the person's mind to drift, which would be followed by constipation, suffering, and ultimately death. Cases of insanity rumored to be magically induced were common in nineteenth-century writings. Reporting on a time just after the Civil War, a white man told Hyatt that his great-aunt had once been driven insane by conjure, brought on by a rival who had supposedly stolen some of her hair, bound it with a cord, and buried it under a brick beside the grave of the victim's brother. She had only discovered the cause of her mental problem by consulting the well-known Maryland conjurer Aunt Zippy Tull, who successfully cured her by locating the charm and instructing her to remove and burn the hair.[20]

Many acts of conjurers simply caused bad luck, discomfort, or other inconveniences. For instance, some antebellum hoodooists sold "hush water," which African American men gave to their wives to keep them quietly obedient. There were even some reports of hoodooists' stopping steamboats from reaching their destinations, halting their progress or turning them around through magic when it suited their purposes. Such was the case with Old Jule, an antebellum conjure woman, who supposedly killed so many slaves through supernatural means that her master determined to sell her. He did so and placed her on a steamboat for shipment. According to stories, Old Jule could not be so easily disposed of. When night fell, she caused the boat to run in reverse. The result was that she forced her master to keep her, allowing her to continue her depredations.[21] While these accounts and similar tales of the mighty deeds of conjurers were doubtless elaborated with fertile doses of imagination, they nevertheless testify to the fear associated with hoodooists' powers. To a believer, such fear was wise in light of the illnesses or death that were always potential consequences of incurring the wrath of someone with access to such awesome ability to harm.[22]

Negative evaluations of hoodooists were the norm in printed sources, virtually all of which were composed by scientifically educated whites and blacks, who did not respect and often opposed conjure. To believers, however, hoodoo also had a positive side. Although many blacks distrusted hoodooists for the evil they could perform, they also respected them as potential agents for good, providing hope where none existed otherwise. For example, while animals in the body and locked bowels were usually results of conjure, magic could also cure such maladies.[23] In fact, only wizardry could cure a victim of wicked hoodoo. In a letter to the *Southern Workman* a witness reported that in 1873 a conjurer had cured a female acquaintance of an unusual sickness that involved pains in her head and side, as well as the sensation that something was rising in her throat. After diagnosing her sickness through the use of cards, the conjurer revealed that she had been hoodooed through a cup of tea she had drunk at a wedding. To heal her, he mixed her a tea made from various roots and herbs. Five minutes after she drank the tea, a scorpion issued from the woman's mouth, apparently curing the victim. Often, conjure doctors banished illnesses simply by revealing how the affected person had been afflicted. Reporting on an event of the late nineteenth century, one of Hyatt's informants told of a young woman who had been cured of insanity when a hoodoo doctor helped her father locate an evil charm that had been buried at the corner of her home. Digging into the soil, her father discovered a barrel containing a silhouette of the woman cut from black cloth and pierced with pins and needles. Once he had uncovered and removed the source of the madness, the woman quickly recovered.[24]

Although scholars quickly dismiss magic as either cause or cure of maladies, hoodoo possessed some actual powers to harm. In rare cases conjurers may have used poison. Just as deadly, however, was the mind of the victim. Modern anthropology, psychology, and medicine address hoodoo as a question of psychosomatic illness. According to Walter B. Cannon's classic article, "Voodoo Death," curses harmed their victims in two "movements." The first of these was a process of social isolation, during which sufferers' friends and family withdrew in fear. At the same time, the afflicted rarely sought out communal support; instead, they usually followed the suggestions of their fellows, accepting their fate. In a second movement, the communities typically returned to the cursed persons just before they died in order to mourn. The movements heightened victims' dread, resulting in extreme psychological stress. Cannon concluded that the strain harmed the conjured by injecting heightened levels of adrenaline into the blood. The result was constricted blood vessels. Over a prolonged period, bodily organs would suffer from insufficient oxygen because of decreased blood flow.[25] Sufferers from conjure frequently experienced a lack of appetite as well, in which cases undernourishment and dehydration were constant dangers. In other cases fear could simply exacerbate existing psychological and physiological problems, leading to insanity, heart attacks, gastrointestinal problems, and other ailments. Once again, conjure worked through faith.[26]

While faith in hoodoo could harm, it could also heal. In the most basic sense, it offered hope of recovery, leading the afflicted to rally. Philip Bruce, no admirer of black folk beliefs, professed his astonishment at conjure's power to heal. In his own words, the idea that magic could offer a cure "causes a sudden revulsion of joy as soon as it is realized, and as the stages of recuperation advance towards a complete recovery, confidence takes the place of doubt and anxiety."[27]

When the ailment was a psychosomatic one, conjure was all the more useful. Modern medicine has provided many examples of its efficacy. For instance, in one twentieth-century case a man suffering from hallucinations that a friend was trying to kill him by conjure was admitted to a Hartford, Connecticut, hospital. When after five days of treatment with drugs he had not improved, the doctors reluctantly allowed him to leave the hospital in search of a root doctor after extracting a promise that he would return. He soon found a conjure woman, who gave him "medicine" to drink, prayed for him, and rubbed more medicine on his upper body. She then instructed him to bathe his head in the medicine once a day. The treatment cost him $150.00. Several days later the hospital released him, free of symptoms. Moreover, despite its magical elements, hoodoo has become a recognized medical concern. Health-related journals and books frequently contain material on conjure. Even the *Textbook of Black-Related Diseases* has a chapter titled "Voodoo Medicine."[28]

Some conjure doctors admitted the importance of faith to their art. William Adams, an ex-slave and conjurer interviewed by the WPA during the Great Depression, stressed the centrality of belief to the successful practice of hoodoo.

In response to an interviewer's question about the virtues of charms, he stated, "Dat am a question of faith. If deys have de true faith in sich, it wo'ks. Udderwise, 'twont."[29]

The medical powers of the hoodoo doctor extended beyond psychology, however. Many conjurers, acting as root doctors, offered herbal and other natural remedies to their clients. In *Hoodoo Medicine: Gullah Herbal Remedies* Faith Mitchell recorded more than fifty traditional remedies from the South Carolina Sea Islands, many of which have now been recognized by the scientific community for their medical efficacy. Many of these and similar treatments for illnesses were in use well before the Civil War. For instance, Harriet Barrett, a former slave and "doctor or midwife," stated that she used a combination of magical and herbal remedies in treating patients. Among them was a tea of red oak bark for fevers and a rabbit's foot tied around the neck for chills. Albert L. Robinson, a black man born as the Civil War drew to a close, claimed to be a "divine healer" who could stop the flow of blood with the touch of his hand and cure the most dire diseases through the laying on of hands, water, and prayer. He also admitted to using secret herbs to treat blood disorders. In antebellum days, when bleeding was an acceptable treatment, the herbal remedies of hoodoo, though originating in magical ideas, were at least as healthy as whites' medicine. While medicine continued to improve throughout the century, root doctors' methods retained their psychological and sometimes medical efficacy.[30]

Conjurers did more than simply treat afflictions. They often helped prevent recurrences of magical illnesses by identifying those who had caused them. In the case of the woman who was conjured by having her silhouette pierced with pins and needles, the hoodoo doctor traced a circle in the dirt around the house where she was staying and ordered the woman's father to sprinkle an unidentified white powder around the ring, stating that the family would then discover who was responsible for their daughter's suffering. Thirty minutes after these tasks were completed, the guilty party appeared and tried to enter the house, only to be prevented by the circle and powder. More commonly, hoodooists simply gave vague descriptions of the supposed culprits, allowing their clients to draw their own conclusions as to the guilty parties.[31]

In many cases hoodoo doctors went even further, turning spells back upon their originators. For instance, Zippy Tull offered her customers the option of reversing conjures. By turning the spell back, Tull was able to place the curse on the one who cast it, thus giving her clients revenge along with recovery. A. M. Bacon, author of "Conjuring and Conjure-Doctors," reported that such reversals of magic were usually part of conjurers' services.[32]

Hoodoo was not simply a system of alternative healthcare, however; it also empowered blacks. Conjure offered a means of protection first from the injustices inherent to slavery and then from the racist legal and social system of the late-nineteenth-century South. Under slavery, charms to prevent whippings and similar mistreatment were widespread. In the autobiography *Narrative of the Life and Adventures of Henry Bibb, an American Slave,* the author recorded some of his personal experiences with conjure. On one occasion Bibb feared a whipping as a result of fighting, presumably with a fellow slave. In order to avoid punishment, he visited a local conjurer, who provided him with a powder of alum, salt, and other substances and a bitter root. The conjurer then informed Bibb that to escape flogging, he should sprinkle the powder around his master. If this failed, he was to chew the root and spit its juice toward his owner. In this instance, whether through the workings of magic or otherwise, Bibb emerged unscathed. Unfortunately, he became such a fervent believer in hoodoo's power that shortly thereafter he "commenced talking saucy" to his master, believing that he was untouchable as long as he had the powder and the root. The result was a severe thrashing. Though this and other unpleasant experiences with conjure convinced Bibb that it was useless, he nevertheless admitted that "the great masses of southern slaves" continued to believe in its potency.[33]

Frederick Douglass, the most well known of slave authors, had his own experience with conjure. After suffering repeated abuse from a cruel professional "slave-breaker" named Covey, Douglass went to his friend Sandy Jenkins for help. Jenkins presented him with a root that he claimed would prevent Covey or any other white man from flogging him. When Covey attempted to do just that, Douglass resisted violently, fighting Covey to a draw. Douglass never received another whipping.[34]

When charms to prevent punishment failed or simply did not satisfy bondspersons, hoodoo provided other alternatives. The most well known of these were powders designed to aid runaways by throwing tracking dogs off their scent. John Barker provided one of the more detailed accounts of this form of hoodoo when interviewed by the WPA in 1937. Barker remembered that his grandfather would collect horned toads, dry them by the family fire, and grind them into powder. This powder was to be applied to the bottoms of shoes in order to throw dogs off the trail of escaped slaves. Barker recalled that it invariably worked on normal dogs, though "hell houn's" could overcome its influence.[35] If resistance failed, slaves could turn to magic to help them cope. For example, the same hush water that slave men gave to overly talkative wives was taken by bondspersons of both sexes to help them maintain enough patience and calm to stand up under the rigors of life as a chattel.[36]

After the Civil War, spells to better slaves' lives were no longer useful. Nevertheless, hoodoo's role as a protection from injustice continued. Inequity was apparent in the southern legal system, which was notoriously discriminatory toward blacks. As they had in the past, conjurers claimed to be able to thwart the law.[37] Some rootworkers reputedly prevented their clients from going to prison by breaking up trials with thunder and lightening. A more common means of affecting cases was "fixing" the courtroom. One of the more colorful figures to work on court cases was Stephaney Robinson, the second Dr. Buzzard. According to legend, Robinson could dissolve trials by sending flocks of magical buzzards to the courthouse.[38]

Whether used by bondspersons to subvert slavery or by freed blacks to fight racial inequality, conjure functioned as a means by which African Americans survived hardships and held on to the hope that they could better their condition. According to the archaeologist Laurie A. Wilkie, its ability to empower blacks was the central reason for its survival. Without doubt, it gave individual blacks and the African American community a means of subverting the pervasive racism and exploitation of the period. As such, it was a source of strength for a profoundly downtrodden people in the face of white oppression.[39]

In addition to its ability to empower blacks, hoodoo could ostensibly achieve a variety of personal aims. Some practitioners claimed to be able to locate treasure through the use of divining rods. All conjurers could provide charms with a variety of uses. They might perform such simple acts as bringing luck. Rabbits' feet were among the most popular. Though these were lucky with or without the aid of a conjurer, a skilled practitioner greatly increased their efficacy. In some areas, African Americans believed that the tip of a black cat's tail was even more powerful.[40]

Many lucky charms fulfilled specific functions. The most popular of these promised success in gambling or financial matters. One of the conjurer's most desired services was the production of love charms. For instance, reporting on a time about five years after the Civil War, Henry F. Pyles, a freedman, stated that he had bought a charm composed of a combination of pepper, wool, "Pammy Christy beans," and rusty iron in a bag tied with horsehair and wet with whisky. This bizarre concoction was designed to win the love of a woman with whom Pyles had become infatuated. Providing luck, messages about the future, and love were but a few of the conjurers' services. Any personal hope or problem meant a possible job for a hoodoo doctor.[41]

In addition to changing fortune, hoodoo doctors could also predict it. William Wells Brown reported that while a slave, he had once visited a fortuneteller called Uncle Frank. The soothsayer divined the future by gazing into a water-filled gourd and revealed that Brown would one day be a free man. Moreover, Brown stated that such experiences were far from unusual, since almost "every large plantation, with any considerable number of negroes, had at least one, who laid claim to be a fortune-teller."[42]

So how did the supernatural aptitude of the hoodooist translate into temporal power? On a basic level, fear of conjure had a profound effect on individual blacks. For instance, the suggestion that a person was the victim of hoodoo was enough to create panic in many blacks. If contemporary observers are to be believed, such fear could cause physical decline and death. Belief in the positive effects of conjure could lead to equally extraordinary events. As Philip Bruce maintained, rootworkers' magic could restore the health of the ill.[43]

More spectacular were those cases in which conjurers inspired individual antebellum blacks to resist the will of their masters. Hoodoo motivated both Frederick Douglass and Henry Bibb to oppose whites' control over their lives. Moreover, Douglass's experience helped him to become an influential black abolitionist. His battle with Covey, which marked the end of his whippings, was a direct result of his confidence in a magic root. As he later wrote, "It rekindled the few expiring embers of freedom, and revived within me a sense of my own manhood. It recalled the departed self-confidence, and inspired me again with a determination to be free."[44]

Likewise, William Wells Brown's visit to a fortuneteller notably influenced his course in life. For some time before his visit with Uncle Frank, Brown had been planning to escape slavery. As the time to carry out his plans approached, he paid a visit to the fortuneteller to find out whether he would succeed. Uncle Frank's assurance gave him the courage to go ahead with his plan. Within a matter of months Brown had escaped, going on to become a medical doctor and noted author. Simple faith in the power of conjure ensured that hoodoo doctors had the psychological power to bring illness or health, love or rejection, and freedom or slavery to nineteenth-century blacks.[45]

For successful conjurers, economic prosperity inevitably followed such influence. Even under slavery hoodoo doctors usually demanded payment for their work. Uncle Frank, for example, charged 25¢ per visit. Such an amount might seem small, but in a time when the vast majority of blacks were bondservants, it was a handsome sum. Following emancipation the price of hoodoo skyrocketed. Writing in the 1880s, Eugene V. Smalley recorded that one conjurer undertook to rid a Louisiana plantation of an unpopular overseer for $2.50. The magician had originally asked for $30.00 but had been willing to negotiate. Other conjurers refused to budge on high-priced spells. For instance, two letters to the editor of the *Southern Workman* in 1878 recorded prices of $25.00 for individual spells, one intended to rid the body of lizards and the other to win the love of a woman. The New Orleans hoodooist Jean Bayou reportedly sometimes charged $50.00 for mixtures of water and commonly available herbs.[46]

These high prices made successful hoodoo doctors wealthy. In contrast, following the Civil War the average southern black lived by tenant farming, the harshest form of which was sharecropping. Sharecroppers, like slaves, made no money directly. Their only cash income came from the sale of their share of the crops they produced on the property of their landlords. Many black tenant farmers made less than one hundred dollars annually. A conjurer, however, could gain several months' worth of wages in a single day. For instance, at the time of Jean Bayou's death he was supposedly worth about fifty thousand dollars. Even if a tenant farmer were able to save all of his or her hard-earned income, it would take five hundred years to raise such wealth. Aunt Caroline Dye, a famous Arkansan hoodoo doctor and fortuneteller who had been born a slave, reportedly owned eight farms at the time of her death.[47]

In some cases hoodooists could move into the realm of political leadership. Such was the case with the hoodoo doctor encountered by Samuel Taylor.[48] He was far from unique, though. Even before the abolition of slavery some conjurers rose to positions of community leadership. The most famous of these was Gullah Jack, Denmark Vesey's second-in-command in an 1822 conspiracy to overthrow slavery. More than a century earlier a conjurer had led a slave uprising in New York. According to another account, a Voodoo society secretly worked to overturn slavery in New Orleans during the Civil War. Hoodooists likewise fomented smaller rebellions in North Carolina, Mississippi, and Louisiana. Even Nat Turner's famed rebellion of 1831 was girded with elements of magic. Though Turner believed he had received a divine mandate from the Christian Holy Spirit to overthrow slavery and kill all whites, his followers could not help but understand his supposedly prophetic visions of black triumph over whites in light of their deep-seated faith in magic. Turner even felt it necessary to state to whites that he had not used conjure to build his following.[49]

The most unusual case of the power within the grasp of hoodoo practitioners, however, was the experience of Marie Laveau, the Voodoo Queen of New Orleans. During her life, stretching from the 1790s or early in the first decade of the nineteenth century to 1881, members of both races throughout Louisiana recognized her as a Voodoo priestess and powerful conjure woman. Neither her birth as a free woman of mixed race nor her reputed early employment as a hairdresser would have led one to expect the influence she later wielded. Nevertheless, by the mid-nineteenth century she was famed as a purveyor of magical charms and presided over New Orleans's most important Voodoo ritual, an annual dance on the shores of Lake Pontchartrain. According to legend, she could raise storms at will and kept a pet snake that she treated like a baby. Darker stories claimed that she spoke with the devil and sacrificed human victims.[50]

Following her death on 15 June 1881 the city's newspapers carried obituaries lauding her for her beauty, wisdom, charity, skill at healing, and ministry to condemned prisoners. One such obituary described her as "a most wonderful woman. Doing good for the sake of doing good alone, she obtained no reward, oft times meeting with prejudice and loathing, she was nevertheless contented and did not flag in her work."[51] Considering the rumors that circulated around her, it is not surprising that one irate reader angrily responded with a letter to the editor surmising that the authors of Laveau's obituaries were doubtless the victims of a practical joker who had fooled them into believing that Marie Laveau was a saint. Whatever contemporaries' opinions were, virtually everyone in New Orleans had one. Rare indeed was it for the death of a free black female to receive such attention.[52]

Laveau's deeds did not end with her death. Most authors agree that her daughter and perhaps her granddaughter took over her conjuring practice, and most of those who knew these later Marie Laveaus believed that they knew the original. Meanwhile, the grave of the first Marie Laveau became a pilgrimage destination for black and white believers, who made offerings to her spirit in return for favors. Some modern New Orleans Voodoo practitioners consider her a goddess, calling on her for healing, legal problems, protection, and matters of sex and love. As a member of a profoundly oppressed race during a time when slavery and lynchings were commonplace, Laveau rose from her position as a hairdresser to that of a goddess who continues to help those who believe in Voodoo and the magic associated with it. Without doubt, she was one of the most well known black women of the nineteenth century.[53]

The influence of nineteenth-century hoodoo was so great that many African American folk heroes were themselves conjurers. Railroad Bill, a legendary outlaw famed for evading capture by white sheriffs for years, supposedly did so by changing himself into animals in order to hide his identity. While Railroad Bill was an outsider, a killer, most folkloric conjurers were not so alien from the average black American. Stories of the slave known as Old John sometimes depict him as practicing conjure. For instance, Richard M. Dorson's *American Negro Folktales* includes a story of John's transformation contest with his master. Following a period in which his master whipped him frequently, John visited the local "mojo-man," who gave him a charm that enabled him to change shape. Unfortunately for John, he refused to pay top dollar, and what he got was inferior magic. His attempt to avoid a beating failed.[54]

Without doubt, the most famous folkloric conjurer was Rabbit, who frequently appears as a practitioner of magic. In *Gullah Folktales from the Georgia Coast* Charles Colcock Jones Jr. tells the story of how "Buh Rabbit" underwent a period of testing at the instruction of a conjurer who promised to teach him hoodoo. According to Missouri blacks, Rabbit learned conjure well. In addition to the usual overcoming of stronger animals through trickery, Rabbit also battled with rival hoodoo workers, most notably Woodpecker, another popular character in the folklore of nineteenth-century Missouri blacks. At one point Woodpecker stole Rabbit's powerful conjure bag, which contained a silver luck ball, but when he tried to take it away, it spoke to him, frightening him into returning it to its proper place. Conjure, already a powerful reality in African American life, grew in influence as men swapped stories of their favorite outlaws and mothers told their children animal stories.[55]

As was the case with Samuel Taylor's hoodoo doctor, wealth and power followed skilled practitioners of hoodoo. Even their names, such as *Uncle* Frank and *Aunt Zippy* Tull, testify to the respect they received in black society.[56] Doubtless, their deeds often had a negative effect on their clients, encouraging them to oppose masters without hope of success, to expect love from one who was uninterested, or to eschew medical treatment in favor of magic. Even if one assumes that their powers were wholly spurious, however, their reputed supernatural aptitude had powerful benefits for those who believed. They gave nineteenth-century blacks hope in lives over which they often had little control. Slavery and Jim Crow took away African Americans' economic, political, and often physical freedom. Hoodoo offered a means of asserting power over oneself and others, for good or evil. It is not surprising that conjurers rose to such prominence in their communities.

4
The Conjurers Themselves: Performing and Marketing Hoodoo

HOODOOISTS' TEMPORAL POWER rested upon the faith of the masses, who viewed conjure with a mixture of respect, fear, and hope. From the standpoint of the conjurers themselves, however, success rested upon a potent blend of manipulation of the supernatural world and effective marketing. Although notable regional distinctions defined hoodooists' practice, there were also surprising similarities in their practice throughout the South. This mix of difference and similarity that shaped the success of conjurers was most evident in four aspects of hoodooists' practice: the supernatural foundations of hoodoo, acquiring the ability to conjure, the theory and production of spells and charms, and the marketing of conjure.

One important regional distinction was the persistence in the Latin cultural zone of pre-Christian religious beliefs, which continued to play an important part in African American conjure into the late nineteenth century.[1] This role is best seen in the Voodoo practiced in the former French territory of Louisiana, with its center in New Orleans. *Voodoo*, though often used as a synonym for *hoodoo* or *conjure*, was more than simply magic. Drawing heavily from Haitian Vodou, it retained its pantheon of gods, who continued to be honored by the worship of their devotees. The most visible rituals of the religion were dances, the chief one of which took place along the shores of Lake Pontchartrain each St. John's Eve (23 June) in honor of Voodoo gods, including St. John, who was a powerful spirit in the religion. During the ceremony a Voodoo queen, the most famous of which was Marie Laveau, presided. In the early nineteenth century, kings also played major roles in the rituals, but by the second half of the century they appear to have declined in importance or disappeared altogether.[2]

Unfortunately for our knowledge of Louisiana Voodoo, most writers on the subject retold a sensationalized description of Haitian Vodou first published by Louis-Élise Moreau de Saint-Méry, a historian of colonial Haiti.[3] According to these accounts, the dances usually featured women and men dressed in an assembly of red handkerchiefs, and those presiding were girded with a blue cord. Women also wore headcloths, called "tignons," which they tied in seven knots sticking out above their heads. During the ceremonies, participants worshiped Voodoo Magnian or the Grand Zombie, the chief Voodoo god, in the form of a snake, held aloft and consulted by the queens. Various lesser gods would possess the queens, who, in a trance, issued instructions from the gods who controlled them. Following these pronouncements, individual worshipers would pray to the gods, petitioning them for help or guidance. Animal sacrifices, which pleased the Voodoo deities, were a necessary part of the ceremony. According to some writers, the dances frequently evolved into sexual orgies.[4]

Though such descriptions are questionable when applied to Louisiana Voodoo, they do contain elements of truth. For instance, one eyewitness of an early-nineteenth-century St. John's Eve ceremony, whose account is preserved in James W. Buel's late-nineteenth-century *Sunlight and Shadow of America's Great Cities*, confirmed the presence of a female queen or high priestess, a prominent male who assisted the queen, nude dancing, the use of a snake in the worship of Voodoo Magnian, and apparent spirit possession in the form of dances designed to resemble the writhing of snakes. In addition, before the dance, the participants shared in a grand feast. Voodoo ceremonies included more than just the St. John's Eve dance, however. Buel, for instance, reported that 19 July was the beginning of a major four-day festival for believers. Other large dances took place at midnight in Congo Square, inside New Orleans.[5]

Smaller ceremonies designed to honor the deities were also common in Voodoo. Charles D. Warner witnessed one of these. One Voodooist held weekly gatherings on Wednesday at noon, Warner observed. At the assembly he attended, a mixed group of whites and blacks, with women predominating, sat in a circle around an altar. A statue of the Virgin Mary with candles placed around it rested upon the altar. In front of it were dishes of fruit, candy, and other offerings brought by the participants. To open the ceremony, the presiding male Voodooist rapped on the floor three times. Then the group began to chant:

> Dansé Calinda, boudoum, boudoum!
> Dansé Calinda, boudoum, boudoum![6]

Chants of various sorts continued throughout most of the ritual. While the group was engaged in singing, the leader of the assembly poured libations of brandy on the floor. He next filled a bowl with the alcoholic beverage, which he thereupon set alight. Afterwards, he dipped the offerings from the altar in the flaming liquid. With his hands aflame, he tossed the offerings into the circle of observers, who were pleased if they were able to catch some. Next, the leader brought forward individual participants and covered their heads and faces with the burning liquid. All told, the ceremony lasted for about an hour and a half.[7]

Voodoo-like religions long survived in other places as well, the most important being part of northern Missouri. Among the religious rituals that survived were dances in honor of Grandfather Rattlesnake, the equivalent of New Orleans's Voodoo Magnian or Blanc Dani. Mary Alicia Owen, who studied Voodoo in North Missouri during the late 1800s, described this dance as being done in the nude and incorporating fasting beforehand, chanting, animal sacrifice, and communal feasting. Owen likewise recorded fire and moon dances. Believers performed the latter in a circle, revolving, at greater or lesser speeds, throughout the ritual. Unlike in New Orleans, self-styled "kings" presided over these dances.[8]

While Louisiana and nearby areas have long been recognized as the seat of Voodoo, pre-Christian beliefs also survived outside of the Mississippi Basin in the form of Florida's Nañigo. Nañigo evolved most directly from Santería, a Cuban folk religion.[9] Florida, only ninety miles from the island, has received Cuban immigrants throughout its history. They arrived in particularly large numbers during the late nineteenth and early twentieth centuries. The new arrivals blended their religious rituals with those of blacks already in the area and others who arrived from different parts of the Caribbean or the United States, including the Bahamas and Haiti. The result was a Voodoo-like faith.[10]

Like the Voodoo of the French-settled areas, Nañigo had its own pantheon of gods. We know even less about them, however, than we do about those worshiped in New Orleans. Most of the sources addressing the religion come from the early twentieth century, though they can plausibly be applied to earlier times. According to a report from the 1930s, African Americans in West Tampa performed ceremonies with drums. A "devil," armed with a knife and carrying a chicken, would appear and dance before the participants. Like most accounts of New Orleans Voodoo, this description of Nañigo was almost certainly sensationalized and misinterpreted by an unfamiliar investigator. Rather than a devil, the dancer more likely represented Shango, an aggressive deity popular in Santería and other Caribbean religions.[11]

During the same period, Felix Cannella collected a more credible account of Nañigo in Tampa while working for the FWP. According to Cannella, a usual Nañigo rite began with chanting, with participants seated in a circle surrounding a priestess known as a *mama-loi*. Those present then sacrificed a goat into which a human spirit had been magically transferred, and then they feasted on its raw flesh. During the rituals, the cry "Zombie!" was frequent. Next a priest, known as a *papa-loi*, would dance with two chickens, which he would then sacrifice, sprinkling their blood on the participants. Other investigators of Tampa's Nañigo documented the existence of several non-Christian gods, such as Yemaya, a spirit of the air, and Elegba, an evil god.[12]

Marie Cappick, writing in 1958, stated that what she variously called "Voodoo," "Nanigro," or "Obeah" survived in the Florida Keys until the early 1930s.[13] Among their activities were midnight processions in which participants carried torches and wore burlap bags and animal masks. Other practices of Key West's African Americans strongly resembled those of New Orleans Voodoo. According to Cappick, the "Voodooists" had a place of worship near South Beach, called the Congo Hall, where they gathered each St. John's Day. A queen presided over these and lesser ceremonies. A woman named Julia, who supposedly had come to Key West from Africa by way of the Bahamas, was the best known of these queens. In a St. John's Day ceremony witnessed by Cappick there were elements typical of Louisiana Voodoo, including dancing, drumming, and animal sacrifice. In this case a goat was the unfortunate victim. Participants drank its blood. Without doubt, these descriptions of Nañigo were embellished for the benefit of white readers, but they attest to the existence of a non-Christian faith among black Floridians.[14]

Unlike the Latin-settled regions, the Anglo zone had comparatively few pre-Christian beliefs that supported conjure. Of course, scattered elements of the old religions persisted. For example, until the early twentieth century African Americans along the Georgia coast prayed to rivers when undergoing baptism, asking the waters to wash away their sins. Although some elements of pre-Christian belief persisted, conjurers did not typically serve as religious leaders. Preachers who doubled as root doctors were, however, far from unknown. Nevertheless, some Atlantic Coast blacks believed that conjure was inimical to Christianity and attributed the rootworkers' power to evil forces, including the devil. Such was the case with the former slave Ank Bishop, of Livingston, Alabama, who announced, "But I'm a believer, and this here voodoo and hoodoo and spirits ain't nothing but a lot of folks outen Christ."[15]

Other notable regional distinctions in the practice of conjure were in the spiritual foundations from which practitioners derived their power. In the Latin cultural area these took the form of deities. Voodoo's pantheon of gods did not simply receive the worship of their devotees; the deities actively aided conjurers in their spells. Helen Pitkin's 1904 book *An Angel by Brevet* describes two New Orleans hoodoo rituals that incorporated petitions to and possession by a variety of gods, including Blanc Dani, Liba, and Vert Agoussou. George Washington Cable recorded similar spells in *The Grandissimes*. Hoodoo doctors decided which gods or goddesses to address based on the deities' particular qualities. For instance, according to Cable, in matters of the heart conjurers told their clients to call upon Monsieur Agoussou, god of love, and Assonquer, the deity of good luck, to ensure that the object of their affections would reciprocate. In order to persuade gods to accept tasks, supplicants were to make offerings and otherwise seek to please them. Those who sought the aid of Agoussou wore red, which was thought to be the favorite color of the deity. In matters of money supplicants could positively influence Assonquer by offerings of pound cake, cordial, and sugarcane syrup. To discover whether Assonquer had accepted the offerings, clients burned green candles set in tumblers filled with syrup. If the flame burned brightly, the god had accepted; if not, his help was doubtful. Areas outside New Orleans likewise called on such beings. For example, Missouri Voodooists called on Samunga when gathering mud, presumably for charms and spells.[16]

The Anglo cultural zone, in contrast, had no pantheon of deities to call on for magical purposes. Instead, hoodoo doctors in these areas were more likely to call on the Christian God for aid. Such was the case with William Adams. According to Adams, God supplied all of his powers, which he first came to experience as a small child before the Civil War. Elaborating, he explained that God chiefly gave him the power to cast out or keep away evil spirits and the devil. Adams exercised his sway over evil through the power of faith. He created physical expressions of his belief in the form of charms. A typical example was salt and pepper carried in a sack hanging from a person's neck, a sovereign mixture for repelling malevolent spirits.[17]

Attributing the power of conjure to God was common throughout the English-influenced areas. For instance, students at Virginia's Hampton Institute reported that conjurers usually cited God as the source of their abilities. One 1897 article made clear the pervasiveness of this view. The reporter observed that a particular conjure woman "said she had special revelations from God, as do all the conjure doctors I have ever heard of."[18]

Belief in the Christian God was typical in the Latin zone as well, even among believers in Voodoo, who knew him as Bon Dieu, meaning "Good God" in French. Surprisingly, calling on God for magical aid was rare in New Orleans Voodoo. While most recognized God as the supreme deity and prayed to him in the typical Catholic manner, most thought him too lofty and detached from the world to be called on in magic.[19] God was more prominent in magic on the border of the Latin cultural area.[20] Mary Alicia Owen, for instance, recorded that part of the preparation of a "luck-ball" required an incantation opening with the words "The God before me, God behind me, God be with me," and ending, "I call for it in the Name of God."[21]

While hoodooists in the Latin cultural zone typically attributed the power of conjure to pre-Christian deities, and most conjurers in the Anglo area preferred to credit God, a third source sometimes appeared throughout both regions: the devil of Christian belief. Many nonconjurers attributed all hoodoo to him. William Adams, who claimed his powers from God, affirmed that others gained their power from evil sources. Likewise, an anonymous contributor to the *Southern Workman* reported on a conjurer who supposedly had learned magic by consulting the devil. In some cases nineteenth-century hoodoo doctors agreed to pacts with the devil in exchange for supernatural power, though open admissions of alliances with Satan were rare. In the early twentieth century, Zora Neale Hurston discovered one such practitioner, whom she called Dr. Barnes. Before undertaking spells, Barnes would go to a fork in the road at midnight and pray to the devil for success in his spells. More typical than Dr. Barnes were those who accepted power from the hands of both God and the devil. Although Christian theology typically depicts the devil as the opposite of God, pragmatic conjurers believed that either could be relied on for aid. The nature of the work to be accomplished was the determining factor in hoodooists' choice of spiritual being. This practice was usual for Missouri hoodooists.

King Alexander claimed to be able to control the devil, using him in the making of "bad tricks." For charms designed to bring positive results he called on God for aid.[22]

The means of acquiring supernatural powers were as varied as their sources, but they fell into three categories.[23] First, some hoodoo doctors were specially gifted with the ability to conjure by God or spirits, as had been their African forebears. Such was the case with William Adams, who described his learning of conjure as follows: "Well, I's don' larn it. It come to me. We'n de Lawd gives sich powah to a person, it jus' comes to 'em."[24] Though such blessings happened throughout the South, they were most common in the English-influenced lands, where Protestant Christianity stressed familiarity with the Bible. To justify his occult practices, Adams relied on the Bible, specifically citing Mark 3:14–15. In the King James Version the verses read, "And he ordained twelve, that they should be with him, and that he might send them forth to preach, And to have power to heal sicknesses, and to cast out devils." For Adams, who claimed that his abilities were a spiritual gift to drive out evil spirits, these verses provided scriptural proof of their existence.[25] Other biblical teachings likewise favored the view that ability to conjure was an unsought blessing from God. One such reference is 1 Corinthians 12, which describes such spiritual gifts as healing, prophecy, tongues, and discerning of spirits as the manifestations of the indwelling Holy Spirit, who gives them to individuals in order to make them productive servants of God. Within a world-view that credited God or other supernatural beings with the ability to confer magical aptitude on humans, people did not need to seek out the divine. It found them.

The signs that indicated hoodoo doctors-to-be were numerous. For instance, unusual sequences of birth could indicate that one possessed inherent powers of conjuration. Being a twin, the next born after twins, or the seventh son of a seventh son designated many as trick doctors. Strange circumstances in the birth itself were another way for blacks to recognize a potential conjurer. Being delivered feet first or with a caul over one's face were two of the most commonly recognized of these signs. Other conjurers were readily identifiable by unusual physical features, such as light-colored eyes or eyes of different colors, red eyes, albinism, serious deformities or disabilities, strange birthmarks, or perhaps the best-known peculiarity, blue gums. Not all divinely gifted hoodooists were so from birth, however. For example, in *Conjuring Culture* Theophus H. Smith wrote that Sojourner Truth, the famous antebellum black activist and religious leader, was a conjurer given prophetic powers as a gift from God through divine visions. Smith's interpretation matched William Adams's understanding of God's magical role in the world.[26]

As had also been the case among their African ancestors, while most American blacks welcomed divine gifts of magical powers, a few did not, particularly when they came from beings other than God. One example of an unwilling tool of the supernatural was Robert Williams, who was driven to conjure after three people with whom he had recently had contact sickened and died. Accusing him of possessing evil powers, the black community of Grovetown, Georgia, his home, refused to associate with him further. The result was that he had to move outside the town and earn a living through the practice of magic. A particularly powerful story of one who tried to flee his assigned role as a hoodooist was that of Donis, a late-nineteenth- or early-twentieth-century conjurer. Having no aspirations to practice hoodoo, he unsuspectingly

> picked up a hat that had been blown from another negro's head in a whirlwind. He handed the hat back to the man. A few hours later the owner of the hat stooped to untangle the traces from his black mule's leg. He was laughing. The mule became frightened and kicked the man to death. He had died laughing aloud, and his death was attributed to Donis who had taken the hat from the devil in the whirlwind. Men would no longer work around him. He could not get a place to stay or to eat. Eventually he was forced to live away from his fellows . . . and follow conjuring as a trade.[27]

Fortunately for nineteenth-century African Americans, the experiences of Williams and Donis were unusual, and the temporal rewards of hoodoo were often enough to persuade even the reluctant to embrace their position.[28]

Inheritance of supernatural abilities from forebears was a second means of obtaining the ability to conjure. Before the Civil War, slaves generally held that native Africans possessed supernatural powers by virtue of the land of their birth. In New Orleans Dr. Jean Bayou claimed to be the child of a Senegalese prince. Without doubt, he was a native African, as witnessed by ceremonial scarring on his temples and cheeks. His ancestry helped him build a reputation as a mighty Voodoo sorcerer that warranted an obituary in *Harper's Weekly* upon his death in 1885. Belief in the magical aptitude of native Africans was not confined to the Latin cultural area, however. The Georgia Writers' Project, under the aegis of the WPA, found that belief in their supernatural abilities was widespread among the state's coastal blacks as late as the 1930s.

Charles Hunter, an African American resident of Harrington, Georgia, told of a conjurer he knew as a boy. The conjurer, one Alexander, was African-born, a circumstance that he claimed gave him the ability to harm others, cure all diseases, and even fly. The latter, Alexander maintained, was an ability possessed by his entire African family. Georgia blacks also attributed the powers of invisibility, to make others invisible, and to boil water without fire to those of African birth.[29]

More important than birthplace, however, were immediate ancestors who were conjurers. The best-known cases of parent-to-child inheritance were the daughter and granddaughter of Marie Laveau, who reportedly took over the practice of the original. Whether the stories of the multiple Laveaus were true or not, kinship to Marie Laveau, genuine or fictional, was of great benefit to New Orleans hoodooists. When Zora Neale Hurston interviewed many of the city's conjurers during the 1920s and 1930s, at least two of them claimed to be grandnephews of the great Voodoo queen. Moreover, the importance of a hoodooist parent was not limited to Louisiana. Second in fame only to Marie Laveau, Stephaney Robinson, better known as Dr. Buzzard of Beaufort, South Carolina, claimed to be the son of a conjurer. Following his death in the mid-twentieth century, his son-in-law took over the family business, adopting the name Dr. Buzzard for his own, though he was more affectionately known as Buzzy. Aunt Mymee Whitehead, a conjure woman who served as the childhood nurse of Mary Alicia Owen, was doubly blessed as the child of an African sorceress who gave birth to her shortly after arriving in America. According to Mymee, her mother's power had been so great that she had fled her native land on board a slave ship to escape the wrath of her fellow countrymen, who both hated and feared her.[30]

Although most conjurers would prefer to be gifted with or inherit supernatural power, those who were not could overcome this misfortune through ritual initiations, which were far more common in the Latin cultural zone. Unfortunately, few accounts of these exist from the nineteenth century. The easiest way to overcome the misfortunes of birth or divine favor was also the most sinister: a pact with the devil. One of the few to speak from firsthand knowledge of this was Zora Neale Hurston. During the course of her investigations, Hurston supposedly underwent initiations by various hoodoo doctors, the most simple of which involved a trip made by her and Dr. Barnes to a fork in the road at midnight, where they prayed to the devil. While Hurston considered this to be "no real initiation ceremony,"[31] it strongly resembled several rituals of selling one's soul recorded by Harry Middleton Hyatt. Like Hurston's experience, Hyatt's accounts typically described praying to the devil at the fork in a road or a crossroads, sometimes with the added feature that the pacts must be contracted at midnight.[32]

More rigorous but lacking the indebtedness to Satan were the rituals by which Latin-area Voodooists gained their powers. Hurston wrote that she had participated in several during the early twentieth century.[33] The most reliable account of nineteenth-century Voodoo initiations comes from Missouri. One of those recorded by Mary Alicia Owen consisted in walking backward, with head and feet bare, into a fallow field at midnight. There, the initiate would pull up a weed from behind his or her back and then take the weed home to keep it under the bed until morning. Upon waking, the initiate would strip off the leaves and make them into a packet, to be worn under the right arm for nine days. At the end of the specified period the leaves were to be removed and scattered in each of the four directions by throwing them over the right shoulder.[34]

Although most initiations took place in the Latin area, they sometimes occurred elsewhere. For instance, George Foss, of Virginia, told stories of Jim Royal, a slave, who gained magical powers by undergoing an initiation that involved being locked in an outhouse into which a variety of frightening creatures entered to test his mettle. While Foss's stories were folkloric, Carl Carmer recorded a rare factual account of an Anglo-area initiation in *Stars Fell on Alabama*. According to Carmer, Ida Carter began her self-initiation when she was seven years old by burning seven candles all night on the first of May.[35] She did so each night for the next six days. Each May for seven years, she repeated the process. By the time she reached her fourteenth year she had become a conjure woman known as Seven Sisters. Unlike New Orleans Voodooists, who offered themselves to a particular god, Carter entered into a special relationship with Jesus Christ, who revealed whatever she needed to know.[36]

Regardless of the manner in which conjurers gained their supernatural abilities, virtually all underwent a period of training. In the area settled by the French and the Spanish the learning process often took the form of apprenticeship to master conjurers. In her study of Missouri hoodooists, Owen discovered that following initiation, conjurers-to-be underwent periods of study under members of the opposite sex. If a teacher of the proper sex was unavailable, students and teachers took turns playing the role of the missing gender. Moreover, throughout the course of the initiation novices would adopt a secret name, which they would use when performing spells. The first objective was to learn "luck numbers" that would appear in charms and spells to ensure their success. Second, apprentices studied the various materials used to make charms, learning their virtues, propitious harvest times, and other secrets about them. Tutelage in the manufacture of such charms followed. The next step in the process of apprenticeship was learning the lore of Grandfather Rattlesnake, the Voodoo Magnian of New Orleans Voodoo. Finally, novices participated in two dances: a snake dance in honor of Grandfather Rattlesnake that supposedly gave them strength of mind and a fire dance to gain strength of body. Only after completing these steps did potential conjurers enter the ranks of the Circle, a decentralized Missouri hoodoo society.[37]

If Hurston's later reports can be applied to the nineteenth century, a similar process of apprenticeship prevailed in New Orleans. Under Father Simms, "the Frizzly Rooster," she began her course of study by helping her master in the more mundane tasks of hoodoo, including spreading magical powders around clients' homes and other tasks requiring only superficial knowledge. During this time Simms never told her the purpose of what she was doing. After two weeks Simms initiated her in a manner similar to what she experienced at the hands of Samuel Thompson, giving her the title Boss of Candles. Following this ceremony, she began to hold meetings with clients. During this time she consulted Simms about what steps should be taken in particular circumstances, learning his greatest magical formulas in the process.[38]

Those from the Anglo area, who usually relied on God for divine inspiration, also studied magic. Seven Sisters, who maintained that "a spirit from the Lord Jesus Christ" told her how to perform magic, admitted that there had been an "old voodoo woman lived next my mammy's cabin. She tol' me how to trick."[39] Ironically, she went on to define Voodoo as evil, while proclaiming her magic as good. Even William Adams, who professed that he did not need to learn magic because God revealed all he needed to know, stated that he had learned some of the "signs dat de Lawd uses to reveal His laws" from his mother and other people during his days as a slave child. As in so many professions, both innate ability and a period of learning gave conjurers the tools they needed to operate in nineteenth-century America.[40]

Conjurers throughout the South usually exerted their power in the manufacture of powders, washes, and charms, each with its own indwelling spirit. Charms, the most popular form of hoodooists' manufactures, were commonly known as "hands," "jacks," "tobies," "mojos," or "luck balls" when employed for benevolent ends and "tricks," "wanga bags," or "conjure bags" when used to harm someone.⁴¹ In the manufacture of these items spirits other than the hoodoo doctors' ultimate source of power played a role. These spirits were of two sorts. The first were animistic spirits, which some claimed dwelt in every natural and manufactured item, from animals to trees to household items like needles and buttons. Ruth Bass argued persuasively in "Mojo: The Strange Magic That Works in the South To-day" regarding the tenacity of the belief in animistic spirits among southern blacks. Bass recorded that conjurers of her acquaintance spoke to pots when they refused to boil, fish hooks when they failed to catch fish, and trees when they wished to learn wisdom. Divinity, a Mississippi conjurer, explained the virtues of herbs by stating that their indwelling spirits healed various ailments by driving them away. In order to prove his point, he offered to take Bass to a spring that was haunted by the ghost of a bucket. Paraphrasing Divinity, Bass wrote, "Now if that bucket didn't have a spirit where did its ghost come from?"⁴²

By the late nineteenth century, explicit recognition of charms' spirits had begun to fade, but though disappearing from blacks' personal theologies, this recognition remained strong in the practice of magic. For example, according to the former slave Henry F. Pyles, a hand designed to attract women to its possessor must be soaked in whiskey. The act was designed to win the favor of the charm's indwelling spirit. This practice of feeding the hand played a role in the manufacture of a charm created by King Alexander, who combined several items in a luck ball upon which he spat whiskey. When he gave the charm to Mary Alicia Owen, he instructed her to wet it once a week in order to keep its spirit strong.⁴³

A second type of spirits was human spirits. Most frequently, conjurers used them in the form of dirt collected from graves, called "goopher dust" in the Anglo zone, or by burying items in graves. A onetime Florida slave, Samuel Simeon Andrews, called on the power of the dead when he anointed his feet with goopher dust to elude slave-tracking dogs. At times hoodoo doctors used body parts, though these were more difficult to come by. One star-crossed lover reported that during the late 1800s a rival stole his wife from him by using a bone from a dead preacher. In rare cases the human spirit did not have to be that of a dead person. For example, when King Alexander spat whiskey on charms, he claimed that part of his spirit was entering them along with his saliva.⁴⁴

While they offered spells and charms for virtually any desired result, hoodoo doctors had three basic types of clients. One type simply wanted to employ conjurers' powers of divination, most commonly to foresee the future. This type of magic was easily accomplished through the use of playing cards, coffee grounds, water-filled gourds, eggs broken in water, or a variety of other means. Those who hoped to purchase charms to bring about specific results, ranging from the prevention of disease to success in love, formed a second type of clients. Like fortunetelling, this type of magic was usually simple, consisting in casting spells and/or making charms in accordance with customers' requests. Examples of this type of conjure are the cases of former slaves like Frederick Douglass and Henry Bibb, who obtained charms designed for the express purpose of averting punishment by cruel masters.[45]

The customers who received the greatest proportion of the hoodooists' attention, however, were those who believed themselves to have been conjured. Such cases required a process divided into three phases: diagnosis, curing, and turning back.[46] In the first phase, diagnosis, hoodoo doctors had to determine, first, whether victims' afflictions were the result of magic, and in what form, and, second, who was to blame. Both steps often involved some form of divination similar to that used in fortunetelling. Following diagnosis, hoodooists cured the problem, again in two steps. The first and more important step was to eliminate the source of the malevolent magic, which was often some form of a physical conjure bag or trick, located by divination. The second step was to remove the symptoms of conjuration from the victim. The final phase, of only one step, involved turning the spell back on the one who had cast it.[47]

Several examples of curing conjure exist from the nineteenth century. Daniel Webster Davis recorded a composite account of this three-phase cure in an 1898 article for the *Southern Workman*. According to Davis, a typical case of counterconjure consisted in the doctor's—in this account the doctor was a male—identifying the presence of conjure. Davis used the example of a victim whose body was infested by snakes and whose hair was falling out. Unless the victim was treated speedily, she would die. The conjurer announced that his female client had an enemy who was in love with her husband, but he remained vague as to the person's identity. Next, he discovered the location of a harmful charm by sprinkling the blood of a chicken into his left hand and then striking it with the forefinger of the other hand. The direction in which the most blood flew was that in which the immediate source of the evil magic lay. Following the blood, the hoodooist dug in the earth until he uncovered a bottle containing various articles ranging from a dead snake to bent needles. With the source of the malady removed, the conjurer easily cured the symptoms by application of a variety of unidentified home remedies. His last act was to turn the spell back on the one who had cast it.[48]

While the account given by Davis illustrates the classic process of diagnosis and cure, not all cases employed the full five-step process. One of the cases treated by Zippy Tull provides an example. At about the time of the outbreak of the Civil War a man named George from Princess Ann County, Maryland, went to see Tull in order to have his fortune told. What he got was much more. After using cards to foresee his future, Tull revealed that she had also found that he was the victim of conjure brought about by a "big dark woman." The mysterious woman, she said, hated George's parents and had already killed his dog. Next, instead of simply leaving the identification of the guilty party to a brief description, she used magic to compel the secret enemy to approach George's mother and reveal her deeds. Tull skipped the first phase of curing, however, not bothering to look for a hidden charm. Furthermore, Tull combined the curing and turning-back phases into one, instructing George to fill a bottle with new pins and needles, his own urine, and several other unnamed materials and then to bury the bottle upside down in his fireplace and cover it with a brick. As the liquid leaked from the bottle, the enemy would pine away. Once it was gone, she would be dead, and his ailment would leave him. When his enemy died, from suffocation in this case, the first step of the curing phase was also accomplished, owing to the elimination of the origin of the malevolent magic.[49]

The choice of items and actions used in making charms and performing spells rested with the conjurer but relied on the universal magical principles of *contagion* and *sympathy* and on appeals to spirits. Contagion is the idea that objects once in contact continue to influence each other. On the other hand, as mentioned briefly in earlier chapters, the principle of sympathy holds that objects that possess characteristics similar to spells' intended results can bring them into being. The best materials for contagious magic were portions of conjure victims' bodies or their by-products, such as hair, fingernail clippings, sweat, or excrement. When these materials were difficult or impossible to obtain, objects that had merely touched the body would do. In some cases the items used needed only to have been in metaphysical contact with the person to be conjured. Written names sometimes substituted for physical contact; that was particularly common in spells designed to influence court cases during the late nineteenth and early twentieth centuries.[50]

The principle of sympathy, in contrast, was not specific to the individuals to be conjured. For instance, by sprinkling dried and powdered reptiles, amphibians, or other creatures in the food of victims, hoodoo doctors could reportedly cause them to enter the bodies of the victims after they had eaten the food.

Other forms of sympathy were not so blatant. Pillow magic, in which hoodooists caused feathers inside pillows to form shapes that would then harm sleepers, was one such example. In one case a woman whose husband had taken ill consulted a conjurer, who told her to open his pillow. Inside she found "half a dozen or more tiny conglomerations of feathers, closely resembling the plumes on a hearse."[51] After she removed and destroyed them, the man recovered. Time and spatial orientation also frequently appeared in sympathetic magic. Night was the typical time for performing malevolent magic because of its association with mystery and evil. Likewise, inversion of objects was one means of reversing the effects of magic. In practice, the principles of contagion and sympathy operated in conjunction to bring about desired results.[52]

A Mrs. Williams, of Baltimore, Maryland, encountered one of the clearest examples of the interplay between contagion and sympathy. In this case a woman named Harriet Henderson conjured Williams's grandmother, who had once been her friend, by secretly cutting a coffin-shaped piece of cloth from her underwear as it lay drying on a bush. Williams's grandmother sewed the hole shut without realizing its cause. Henderson then returned or sent an agent, stealing the repaired underwear. After doing so, she took a stick and measured a track left by the victim's bare foot. She then wrapped the stick in the stolen garment and buried it at the foot of the newest grave in a cemetery. Only timely intervention by a more powerful conjurer saved Williams's grandmother, who had rapidly lost the power of speech and the ability to walk.[53]

In Williams's account the principle of contagion was represented by two of the items used in the spell, the underwear and the stick. The garment, which had once been in intimate contact with the victim's body, provided a means by which Henderson could harm her from a distance. The stick likewise represented Williams's grandmother. By being used to measure a footprint made by the bare foot of the victim, the stick came to represent the everyday activities of William's grandmother. Henderson's possession of the underwear and the stick, however, was not enough to bring about the death of her onetime friend: she had to employ sympathetic magic to bring about the desired result. This was likewise undertaken in more than one step, each of which centered around images of death. When Henderson cut the coffin-shaped piece out of the underwear, she set up a situation in which the victim would most likely sew it up. By doing so, Williams's grandmother unwittingly "closed" her own coffin. By burying the underwear and stick in a grave, Henderson reinforced the sympathetic power of death.[54]

Mrs. Williams's account exemplifies but one combination of contagion and sympathy used by conjurers. Common variations were those in which charms were prepared without utilizing contagion, but contagion nevertheless played a role in affecting victims. In such cases conjurers contrived a means to bring their charms into contact with the person to be affected, often by burying them along a route commonly taken by that person. Whatever the spell or charm, contagion and sympathy always played a part in successful hoodoo.[55]

While the laws of contagion and sympathy were the primary aspects of the performance of individual acts of conjure, some items had spirits whose alleged power extended beyond these principles. In the Latin cultural zone, Voodoo conjurers relied heavily on their gods. They built altars, burned candles, and made sacrifices to them based on the deities' personalities. In places settled by the English, hoodooists called on God for similar purposes, while sacrifices were uncommon but far from unknown. More commonly used, particularly in the Anglo lands, were powerful spirits that inhabited certain items, regardless of their sympathetic value. The best known of these was High John the Conqueror root, called the "king root of the forest" by blacks. Hoodoo doctors used it for a wide variety of purposes, ranging from winning love to curing diseases.[56] One author maintained that its power was so respected that believers "quake when they see a bit of it in the hand of anyone."[57]

Exceptionally strong spiritual power also resided in certain bones from black cats, which could only be obtained by boiling the unfortunate felines alive. Once the flesh fell from the bones, the bones possessing magical power would rise to the surface of the water. By placing one of these in his or her mouth, a conjurer could supposedly become invisible. Goopher dust, which sympathetically possessed the power to cause death, could also be employed for virtually any use owing to the spirits of the dead who dwelt within it. Samuel Simeon Andrews, who used it to escape slavery, is but one example of a man who looked beyond its sympathetic value.[58]

Closely related to these spirits were lucky or unlucky days and numbers, which also possessed magical properties for reasons independent of contagion and sympathy. For instance, some North Carolina conjurers believed that Friday was a bad day to begin new work. Likewise, Missouri hoodoo doctors specified certain numbers to be used in spells and charms, which would help insure their success. According to King Alexander, three and seven were good numbers to conjure with, nine and five were better, but the best number for hoodooing was four times four or four times four times four. In contrast,

Alexander said, ten was an unlucky number, and Missouri's conjurers carefully avoided it. Like lucky numbers, the color red carried special weight in the spirit world. Conjurers throughout the South relied on it in the manufacture of charms for both good and evil results.[59]

Though the theory and practice of hoodoo were very similar in both cultural zones, differences sometimes arose, most notably in the choices of magical elements used in the manufacture of charms. For instance, New Orleans hoodooists' use of altars, statues of saints, and offerings to appeal to gods was atypical outside of the Latin area. Meanwhile, goopher dust was used far more frequently in the area of English influence. Other items were also rare outside of one or the other cultural area. Two such were beef tongues, which New Orleans conjurers often employed in court-case spells, and conjure bottles, which often took the place of conjure bags in the Anglo zone. Nevertheless, many items were popular in both cultural areas. The best examples of such materials were High John the Conqueror root and black cat bones, whose powers were respected throughout the South by the end of the nineteenth century.[60]

Whatever a conjurer's relationship to the divine or the depth of his or her knowledge, no conjurer would be successful without a reputation. Throughout the American South, African Americans viewed hoodoo doctors with great trepidation, springing from their fear of conjurers' ability to lay "tricks" or "hexes" against their victims. It was this very dread, though, that won hoodooists many of their clients. For example, when struck with unusual illnesses, many African Americans believed that enemy hoodooists were to blame. The remedy was to consult conjurers whose power surpassed that of those who had wrought the initial maladies. Likewise, hoodooists were sometimes able to overcome cruel slave masters or employers. Power that could defeat evil magicians and undermine the strength of the white ruling class was to be feared. At the same time, it held the hope of creating positive circumstances, most commonly in matters of love or money.

Ultimately, this blend of fear and hope did not spring fully formed from the supernatural sources of conjurers' power. Instead, it developed primarily by word of mouth. Failure to build a reputation could result in situations similar to one described by Cornelia Robinson, a former Alabama slave. Speaking of her old plantation, she said, "Us had a ol' quack herb doctor on de place. Some bad boys went up to his house one night an' poured a whole lot of de medicine down him. An honey, dat ol' man died de next day."[61] At the very least, conjurers would lose business and thus temporal power. On the other hand, highly respected hoodooists could hope for a career like that of another Alabamian conjurer, Monroe King, whose reputation was so great that he did not have to work at all. In fact, those who lived in his vicinity "useta give him chickens an' things so's he wouldn't conjure 'em."[62]

For a conjurer, there was no substitute for successful displays of his or her reputed powers. Gaining a thorough knowledge of the properties of herbs was one way to increase one's chances of success, especially when physical illness was involved. Another way was to give common-sense advice to those who sought aid. According to Newbell Niles Puckett, who studied conjure in the early twentieth century, practitioners frequently supplemented their magic with useful counsel. Advice was especially helpful in matters of the heart. One New Orleans hoodooist sold a powder to a lovelorn male client, instructing him to sprinkle it upon everything he gave to the woman with whom he was infatuated. The objects upon which he was to sprinkle the powder, however, were to be frequent gifts of the woman's favorite things. Throughout the courtship, the man was to never quarrel with her or show jealousy. The two were married within a few months. Puckett gave other examples. A conjure woman from Algiers, Louisiana, had a client who wanted to stop her husband from arguing with her. The hoodooist gave her a bottle of "medicine" with which she was to fill her mouth whenever her husband showed signs of anger. Moreover, she was to hold the formula in her mouth until he calmed down, upon which she should swallow it and kiss her husband. Puckett claimed that this spell worked so well that many other women soon applied for the same formula.[63]

Even when hoodoo failed, a clever doctor could blame its failure on the client, asserting that he or she had not obeyed instructions. Such was the case in one story told about John, the antebellum black folk hero. According to the story, John approached a conjure man in order to buy a charm that would allow him to "cuss his master."[64] The hoodooist gave him a charm to carry in his pocket, telling him to keep his hand on it. John tested the charm, only to receive a severe whipping from the overseer. When he complained to the conjurer, the hoodooist replied, "I gi' you a runnin' han'. Why didn't yer run?"[65] Another readily applicable way of turning back blame for failure was to accuse the client of lacking the necessary faith in the conjurer's powers. On the other hand, with each successful application of magic, people's confidence in individual conjurers would grow, increasing the likelihood that their treatments would succeed in the minds of their clients.[66]

Even though a conjurer's reputation depended heavily on the effectiveness of his or her spells and charms, he or she also had to compete with other conjurers. The most successful practitioners convinced potential clients that their abilities were somehow greater than those of other hoodooists. To build their customer base, they played on their clients' intertwined fears and hopes. Once again, though, there were regional differences and commonalities. In Latin areas, the reputations of hoodooists who were also religious leaders were frequently guaranteed. Marie Laveau and the other Voodoo queens, who dealt directly with the divine, ranked highly among pious folk. To the average believer, such a person had a much better chance of performing successful magic than a mere layperson.[67]

Conjurers from the Anglo zone lacked a specifically African American faith from which to obtain temporal power. Nevertheless, some of them used their status as Christian ministers to enhance their image. Like the Voodoo queens, they relied on their reputation for having a closer than average relationship with the divine to spur their business. Such was the case of Uncle Aaron, the African American preacher from Virginia. In addition to teaching his congregation from the pulpit, he was feared as a conjurer throughout his community. Even in places where Voodoo prevailed among conjurers, hoodoo doctors sometimes filled the role of Christian ministers. A Missouri conjurer named Alexander, encountered by Mary Alicia Owen, claimed to be the "king" of the African Methodist Church of which he was a member.[68]

A hoodooist who failed to obtain a religious office had to turn to other methods of building a reputation. One of the easiest was to create a title designed to impress potential clients. Male hoodooists, in particular, were fond of this method. Owen's Alexander, for example, insisted on being called *King Alexander*. Others used names bearing a specifically religious connotation even when they held no office to warrant them. One example of this practice was "the Rev. Mr. H.," who served a Virginian clientele during the mid- to late nineteenth century. By far the most commonly used sobriquet was *doctor*, adopted by hoodooists throughout the South. One of the first to do so was one Doctor Hercules, an eighteenth-century Georgia slave. Another early practitioner who called himself a doctor was Dr. Jean Bayou, of New Orleans. By the late nineteenth century the practice was widespread. In 1898 Daniel Webster Davis, of Virginia, wrote of a "doctor" who used the initials "h.p." after his name, which he intended as an abbreviation for *homeopath*.[69]

Conjurers living in the English cultural area frequently added the name of a totemic animal to their titles, a practice that was particularly common in the Sea Islands. Moreover, the animals chosen were usually birds or insects, picked for the feeling of power or dread they inspired. Dr. Buzzard of Beaufort, South Carolina, was, without doubt, the most famous to do so. An event was his inspiration. Sometime around the turn of the century a group of fishermen had died at sea. When the boat in which they had set out was eventually found, their bodies were still inside, being eaten by a group of buzzards. Another well-known Sea Island conjurer went by the name Dr. Bug, but in reputation he remained a distant second to the fearsome Dr. Buzzard. Not all who used titles were men. Ida Carter, better known as Seven Sisters, is an example. Still, the practice was unusual among women, who typically kept their birth names, without exalted sobriquets. Marie Laveau and other Voodoo queens, such as Sanité Dédé, Marie Saloppé, and Malvina Latour, and Aunt Zippy Tull of Maryland are but a few examples of highly successful conjure women who saw no need to resort to titles.[70]

Another means of fostering fearful awe was setting oneself apart from the rest of the black community, creating an air of mystery. Hoodooists in the Anglo zone frequently used this tactic. They rarely mingled with their fellow African Americans and actively took steps to dissuade others from approaching them without reason. One common way of doing so was to adopt bizarre dress. Most accounts of nineteenth-century Anglo-area conjurers describe their unusual raiment. Dr. Buzzard reportedly limited his strange dress to a pair of purple-shaded eyeglasses. In contrast, one of the more elaborate dressers was the Tennessee conjurer described by Samuel Taylor, who arrayed himself in multicolored coats and chains.[71] The Reverend Mr. H., of Virginia, "had his hair braided like a woman, and rings in his ears."[72]

In the lands around New Orleans, where Voodoo queens and doctors were key figures in the religious life of slaves and later free blacks, they felt no need for unusual everyday dress. Their dealings with the gods made them mysterious enough. Nevertheless, before the Civil War, major figures in New Orleans Voodoo were invariably free people of color, effectively setting them apart from the average African American. A tendency for conjurers to be free was present to a lesser degree throughout the Latin antebellum South. Aunt Mymee Whitehead, of Missouri, for example, was a free woman of color who was also a powerful conjurer.[73]

In Anglo lands, conjurers were less likely to be free. During slave days, each large plantation usually had a resident hoodooist or two. Following emancipation, however, conjurers actively sought isolation from their communities. Patrons could only reach the island home of Dr. Buzzard by boat. Moreover, his efforts at generating fear were so successful that some believed that the necessary conveyance would appear on its own, rowed by buzzards. If someone other than the one for whom it was intended got on board, the buzzards would drown the interloper. Other conjurers simply traveled through different communities. This practice had the added benefits of increasing their potential clientele and limiting the impact of failure. According to an anonymous contributor to the *Southern Workman,* traveling conjurers were the norm in the postwar years. During the 1890s Samuel Taylor's conjurer combined monthly tours with bizarre dress to spread his influence over a substantial portion of his home state. Even conjurers in the Latin zone sometimes chose to travel. King Alexander did so, as Owen stated, to make "his movements as mysterious as possible."[74]

Even without the benefits of religious office, fancy titles, and personal mystery, conjurers throughout the South could build their reputation through cleverly handled interactions with clients. In a time when hoodoo doctors relied on word of mouth, such interactions could make or break careers. Successful conjurers used their dealings with clients to further exalt their fame. A few conjurers did so by knowing the names of clients who approached them before they spoke. Those who remembered Zippy Tull frequently cited her ability to do so.[75]

It was particularly easy to create fear during the diagnosis phase, however. In a typical case described by Daniel Webster Davis, a woman feeling physical pains she had not felt before called on a conjure doctor when ordinary remedies failed. The conjurer, seeking to convince the sufferer of the supernatural source of the disorder, arrived at night. After examining the patient for a few moments, the hoodooist pronounced, "Yes hunny, youse bin tricked. . . . Youse got er in'my."[76] Further explanation revealed that the enemy was a rival for her husband's affections and was using magic to kill her. The only remedy was stronger magic, which the conjurer could of course supply. In cases like the one described by Davis, believers feared for their lives. Even those with a more scientific inclination might decide that it was better to be safe than sorry. Furthermore, the strength of faith generated by such dire pronouncements made it more likely that victims would either believe themselves cured following treatment or accept that their enemies' magic was simply too strong or had gone too long untreated in cases of failure.[77]

The fear and hope associated with conjurers could be further heightened during the curing phase. One way of doing so was to find the tricks, whose presence conjurers could easily assure by sleight of hand or a previous visit to the spot where the charm was to be found. Likewise, when the diagnosis was that reptiles or other living creatures were inhabiting the afflicted, hoodoo doctors frequently produced the culprits, again presumably by trickery. In one case a man claimed that following the ministrations of a hoodoo doctor, his sick aunt was cured when she succeeded in drawing a lizard from her leg and a spool of thread from her right arm.[78]

Even by claiming that a turned-back spell would kill the one who cast it, conjurers could enlarge their reputations. If someone in the locality happened to die shortly after a conjurer announced the doom of a vaguely described enemy, he or she would automatically become a suspect in the affliction of the client. If no one died nearby, observers could assume that the antagonist must have been from outside the immediate vicinity.

Conjurers throughout the South were both mystical and pragmatic. Despite notable regional distinctions, a mixture of supernaturalism and marketing was constantly in evidence. Still, while building reputations relied heavily upon manipulating the perceptions of potential clients and frequently descended into outright deception, one must not conclude that conjure was mere chicanery. Some conjurers were doubtless frauds. For most, though, their craft was genuine. Belief in their own powers was more important than the presence or absence of the spiritual forces that reputedly served as the foundations of their skills, taught them to conjure, and operated in the making of charms and the casting of spells. As William Adams put it, "Thar 'tis 'gain, faith. Dat am w'at counts."[79] Just as it gave conjurers temporal power in the black community, so it gave them the ability to perform miraculous cures, lay curses on enemies, foretell the future, and otherwise fulfill the wishes of their clients.

Believers tenaciously held to their faith in the awe-inspiring powers of the conjurers. As the nineteenth century drew to a close, conjure not only survived; it prospered. In the rapidly approaching twentieth century hoodoo would find new opportunities in mass media and commodity culture, participation in which had been denied slaves and those left in blinding poverty following their emancipation. In the new century, however, conjurers would increasingly fade in importance, being replaced by mail-order companies and hoodoo shops.

5
Conjure Shops and Manufacturing: Changes in Hoodoo into the Twentieth Century

THROUGHOUT MOST of the nineteenth century conjure was a personal affair conducted between hoodoo doctors and their clients. While it was practiced throughout the South, regional and local variations were common. By the early twentieth century, however, hoodoo was undergoing profound changes. First, the differences between the Anglo and Latin cultural areas were becoming less pronounced. Likewise, African American migrants carried conjure to areas of the country where it had been rare in the preceding centuries. Much more important, however, was the process by which hoodoo became an increasingly impersonal affair. As Carolyn Morrow Long put it, hoodoo was undergoing "commodification."[1] Old-fashioned conjurers who performed spells and made charms at the request of local clients were becoming rare. Twentieth-century practitioners were more likely to operate shops selling ready-made magical products shipped from hundreds or thousands of miles away. In some cases large-scale manufacturers replaced conjurers altogether. Advertising their products through agents and in local and national newspapers, they operated as mail-order companies.

One of the most readily identifiable changes in hoodoo was the fading importance of regional distinctions. Of course, some differences between the Latin and Anglo areas persisted. For instance, as Zora Neale Hurston learned, initiations continued to take place in New Orleans as late as the 1930s. They were rare outside of the area. Similarly, conjurers in the Atlantic coastal region were as attached to graveyard dust as their predecessors had been. Also, along the Mississippi River and the Gulf of Mexico unique gregory bag–style charms persisted. Known as "nation sacks," they were worn by women under their clothes against their waists.[2] Men were forbidden to touch them. Unlike Missouri conjure balls and bags, nation sacks were filled with whatever magical materials women needed at a given moment. For example, dried egg yolks were supposed to keep husbands and boyfriends from leaving, and peels of red onions brought general good luck. During the 1930s, nation sacks could sometimes be found in New Orleans and Mobile, Alabama, and they were common in Memphis, Tennessee. In the region initially settled by the English, however, they were unknown.[3]

New Orleans's reputation for Voodoo also survived the passage of time. It remained so strong that the author Henry C. Castellanos asked his readers, "Who has not heard, in connection with the local history of New Orleans, of that mysterious and religious sect of fanatics, imported from the jungles of Africa and implanted into our midst, so well known under the appellation of *Voudous?*"[4] The city's reputation for magic survives to the present.[5]

Ironically, while Voodoo's fame was at its height its practice was undergoing a decline. Both Voodoo and Nañigo had lost much of their specifically religious character by the turn of the twentieth century, bringing them in line with conjure in the rest of the nation. In part, this transformation was due to active suppression by the authorities. During the Civil War the Union forces occupying New Orleans broke up gatherings of Voodooists, usually arresting the participants. After the Yankees departed, the New Orleans police took over. Unlawful assembly and nudity were the usual charges, but the aim was to wipe out what Castellanos referred to as "this disgusting organization or order, with its stupid creed and bestial rites."[6] In 1873 the *Daily Picayune* reported that Voodoo ceremonies no longer took place within the city limits. The only ritual still practiced was the annual St. John's Eve gathering on the shores of Lake Pontchartrain. After 1876 even this ceremony occurred sporadically. When it was held, its organizers geared it toward white spectators, who paid entrance fees and additional sums for charms, the right to witness "secret" rituals, and the services of prostitutes.[7]

Nañigo met with a similar fate. Though the religion continued to be practiced in the Tampa area and in Key West, its popularity had peaked during the 1880s and 1890s. Following the murder of a Cuban immigrant during a Nañigo street festival, the faith's reputation suffered, and its adherents fell away. According to Stetson Kennedy, the last Nañigo dance was a 1923 reenactment by a young nonbeliever. As in New Orleans, the later ceremonies were often moneymaking endeavors. Ganda, one leader of the Key West branch of the religion, continued to dance for visiting sailors well into the twentieth century, charging them a dime per performance. Once Voodoo and Nañigo had lost their distinctive religious characters, the hoodoo of the Latin area increasingly resembled the conjure practiced in the rest of the nation.[8]

New Orleans's Voodoo was fading, but its magical practices remained the most well known form of African American sorcery. As a result, its terminology spread beyond the confines of the areas settled by the French and the Spanish. English terms for magic workers, such as *cunning doctor* and *high man*, were virtually extinct. *Rootwork, goopher,* and *two head* survived in the Anglo cultural zone. By the early twentieth century, however, *hoodoo* had spread beyond the Latin area. When Harry Middleton Hyatt carried out his interviews during the 1930s and 1940s, he found that *hoodoo* was used throughout the South. One of his informants described a Newport News, Virginia, sorcerer as both a "cunjure man" and a "hoodoo man." A Georgia interviewee stated the case more directly, saying, "Some of us call it *rootworkin,*' some of us call it *witchcraft* an' some of us call it *hoodoo,* but it's all run into de same thing."[9] The words had become synonyms. Nevertheless, some acknowledged the term's newness. One former Florida slave told Hyatt that *hoodoo* had not come into use until after emancipation. Despite its novelty, it became so popular that it partially displaced *conjure* as the favored designation for African American magic. Zora Neale Hurston, who studied African American magic in Louisiana, Florida, and Alabama, stated that "Veaudeau is the European term for African magic practices and beliefs, but it is unknown to the American Negro. His own name for his practices is hoodoo."[10] She went on to recognize that the words *conjure* and *roots* remained popular.[11]

The two cultural zones had ceased to be major factors by the time Hyatt and Hurston carried out their investigations. Despite the spread of Latin terminology, hoodooists throughout the South had fallen into the form of conjure first practiced along the Atlantic seaboard. Its practitioners were no longer priests of a distinctly African American syncretic faith. Instead they had become professional sorcerers whose primary motivation was personal financial betterment.

Conjure had also spread beyond the bounds of the South. Beginning in the second decade of the twentieth century, hundreds of thousands of African

Americans left the South's rural poverty for urban life in the North, taking their magical traditions with them. The migration continued for many years, peaking during World War II. By the middle of the twentieth century conjure was no longer solely the province of the South. Folklorist Elon Kulii has recorded recent instances of hoodoo in northern Indiana, including cases of lizards in human bodies and the use of women's menstrual blood to win men's affections. Healthcare professionals throughout the United States encountered patients suffering from hoodoo-related illness. For example, Renaldo J. Maduro treated six cases involving conjure during approximately four years of postdoctoral training in clinical psychology and psychiatry in San Francisco. Ronald R. Wintrob, a medical doctor, likewise encountered several cases of rootwork in his practice in Connecticut.[12]

Though the dissolving of regional distinctions and the geographic expansion of hoodoo changed the face of African American magic, conjure was undergoing an even greater change by the turn of the century. Hoodoo was traditionally a practice in which conjurers, operating out of their homes, made charms and performed spells at the request of individual clients. Any materials needed were gathered from nature. As the twentieth century approached, such practices were becoming rare. By the 1930s and 1940s a form of conjure without conjurers had developed. Consumers, no longer clients, could purchase manufactured magical goods from shops or by mail, and by the 1990s they could order them online. No hoodooist was necessary. Like so much else in American life, African American magic was becoming an impersonal industry.

The first step toward consumer conjure was the opening of "conjure shops," now more commonly known as "spiritual supply stores." The beginnings of such shops went undocumented, but evidence suggests that their precursors developed among urban free blacks before the Civil War. For instance, according to Robert Tallant, Marie Laveau kept an office for consultations in her home and a separate house for her more secretive Voodoo rites. George Washington Cable hinted at the existence of full-fledged antebellum conjure shops in his novel *The Grandissimes*. In one incident, a wealthy African American mistakes a pharmacy for a conjure shop. Upon entering an apothecary owned by Joseph Frowenfeld, he requests a "ouangan," a variation of *wanga*. Despite Frowenfeld's protestations of ignorance, his client believes that his request has simply been rejected. Similar mistakes recur throughout the book. A logical inference is that such shops did exist. Though Cable's work is fiction, he intended it as a realistic portrayal and critique of the racial attitudes of New

Orleans's Creoles. Just as important, he was a native of New Orleans. Born in 1844, he was in an excellent position to observe the practice of antebellum African American magic.[13]

Whether Cable's account is trustworthy or not, conjure shops became an established feature of African American society in the decades following emancipation. During the period immediately after the Civil War many hoodooists traveled a wide area in search of clients. Some, like King Alexander, continued to do so until near the turn of the century; others settled in particular locales, opening offices or small shops. Archaeologists recently discovered evidence of this trend in the remains of the Levi Jordan Plantation, which once occupied a part of Texas's coastal plain. While excavating slave cabins, they uncovered one littered with the remains of magical paraphernalia. They determined that it had been the home of a conjurer. Before 1865 the cabin had been a simple one-room affair. Sometime after the Civil War its occupant had added a second room. According to the archaeologists, the "added space served as 'office' or ritual room."[14] It was not yet a conjure shop in the fullest sense of the word, but it was an important step along the way.

The earliest description of a full-fledged late-nineteenth-century conjure shop came from the pen of Daniel Webster Davis. Above the door was a sign reading "j. t. sheltun, h. p.," advertising its occupant's employment as a homeopath. Inside were jars filled with preserved snakes that he had reputedly taken from the bodies of conjure victims. Mr. Sheltun also displayed a variety of dried herbs and ready-made charms designed to prevent conjuration. Davis further described such shops as generally dark, the better to unnerve clients. Though Davis did not record the year of his visit to the shop, he wrote in 1898 that it had occurred "many years ago."[15]

By the 1930s and 1940s shops like the one owned by J. T. Sheltun were common in urban areas. While working for the Federal Writers' Project, Zora Neale Hurston discovered one in Jacksonville, Florida. She described it as permeated with the smell of incense. Its shelves were filled with boxes and bottles of roots, herbs, oils, powders, and other charms. Unlike J. T. Sheltun, its owner did not emphasize the frightening aspects of conjure, stressing the benefits instead. Above the shop's door hung a sign reading, "Through the Days of Labor and Nights of Rest, The Charms of Fairy Stones will Keep you Blest."[16] The business, located in the 400 block of Broad Street, was in the heart of the city's African American section. It reportedly earned its owner thousands of dollars each year, a remarkable sum since Hurston visited it during the Great

Depression.[17] Other conjure shops opened during this period, many doubling as drugstores. The Cracker Jack Drug Store in New Orleans was the most well known. Founded in 1897 as a pharmacy, it had become a hoodoo supply store by the time Hyatt interviewed area blacks.[18]

Some of the conjure shops that developed during the nineteenth and twentieth centuries remain a prominent part of many African American communities today. For many years Bishop Master F. L. Robinson, DD, has offered his services as a "spiritual adviser" to the people of Micanopy, Florida, from his shop, Robinson Hall. Rondo's Temple Sales, of Atlanta, Georgia, has supplied its customers' magical needs since 1940. The Stanley Drug Company, of Houston, Texas, a combination spiritual supply store and pharmacy, has been in operation since 1923. Not all conjure shops are survivals from an earlier era. For instance, Thomas "Pop" Williams and three business partners opened the Eye of the Cat, in Columbia, South Carolina, in 1985. Like those of the conjure shops of the 1930s and 1940s, its shelves are packed with herbs, oils, and many other magical items. Williams performs consultations from his office in the back of the store. Customers who have to wait to speak with Williams can take advantage of the waiting room adjacent to his office, where a television keeps them entertained.[19]

Many shops simply provided a way for conjurers to make their charms and spells more readily available, thereby increasing their income. On the other hand, one did not have to be a practitioner to open a hoodoo store. Donald Miller and his nephew Richard, of Atlanta, Georgia, are an excellent example. Donald Miller opened a pharmacy, now known as Miller's Rexall, in 1960. Miller is not an African American. On the contrary, his ancestors were Russian Jews who immigrated to America in the early 1900s to escape service in the czar's armies. Miller opened his business as a pharmacy serving Atlanta's African American community. He gradually turned to spiritual goods in the face of high customer demand. Though the elder Miller would study clients' problems, pray, and prepare charms for their remedy, his nephew does not believe in the power of hoodoo. Felix Figueroa, owner of the F and F Botanica and Candle Shop of New Orleans, likewise expresses skepticism about conjure's effectiveness. Though many of his customers call the business a "hoodoo shop," he maintains that it is open to all religions. Figueroa, however, is a Baptist, who describes his store as "a business to make a living."[20]

While conjure shops were springing up in many southern cities, an even newer form of conjure arose in the form of large-scale manufacturers who sold magical supplies by mail. Hoodooists and conjure shops provided the impetus. Traditionally, root doctors gathered their materials from nature. By the early twentieth century, however, many purchased their herbs and other botanical goods from mail-order companies geared toward the home-remedy market. They likewise ascribed magical power to some preexisting manufactured goods. Jockey Club Cologne is the best example. Though it originated as a personal-hygiene product, by the 1920s it had become a magical tool that believers expected to bring them love and work.[21]

Conjurers and their shops further demonstrated the viability of postal sales by operating their own mail-order businesses. One of the earliest practitioners known to do so was Julius P. Caesar, of New Orleans. Specializing in matters of love, he eventually ran afoul of a city ordinance forbidding the sale of charms. By the 1920s Dr. Buzzard was also involved in mail-order conjure. James McTeer, a white sheriff who was pursuing the conjurer for dispensing medicine without a license, reported that Dr. Buzzard once destroyed fifteen hundred dollars' worth of postal money orders when he discovered that they could be used in evidence against him in a criminal case. Pierre McGowan, son of a rural mail carrier who served the area in which Dr. Buzzard lived, confirmed that much of the latter's income came from mail-order customers. Perhaps Dr. Buzzard was himself a patron of mail-order hoodoo. P. H. Washington, of Beaufort, South Carolina, better known as Dr. Eagle, claimed that Dr. Buzzard "sent to me for all the high priced roots."[22] Carolyn Morrow Long has compiled further cases of mail-order conjurers throughout the United States, including Virginia, Alabama, Illinois, and New York. Today, many of them have their own Web sites, making it even easier for customers to obtain needed spiritual supplies.[23]

With commercial organic and manufactured goods already entering the hoodoo market and the feasibility of mail-order conjure established, it was only a matter of time before existing companies incorporated hoodoo into their product lines. The first known manufacturer of black-oriented spiritual supplies was DeLaurence, Scott and Company, now known as the L. W. DeLaurence Company. Lauren William DeLaurence, the founder, began his career as a Chicago-based hypnotist and self-proclaimed adept at Eastern mysticism in the late nineteenth century. His early products included several books on European magic, Jewish Kabbala, Far Eastern occultism, and hypnotism. By the first decades of the twentieth century he had moved into the African American market, selling herbs, amulets, candles, charms, and books to blacks throughout the United States. For other manufacturers the occult accounted for only a part of their products. Two companies founded in the 1920s, the Valmor Company, of Chicago, Illinois, and Keystone Laboratories, of Memphis, Tennessee, sold hoodoo supplies, as well as laxatives, cosmetics, and other personal-hygiene products. Unlike DeLaurence, these two companies began as businesses aimed at an African American market. Several similar companies appeared in succeeding years. In 1991 Martin Mayer founded Indio Products, currently the world's largest manufacturer and supplier of spiritual supplies.[24]

Manufactured conjure differed widely from traditional hoodoo. Most notably, few of those involved were part of African American culture. Carolyn Morrow Long undertook an exhaustive study of spiritual supply stores for her book *Spiritual Merchants*. Of the twenty-three companies she investigated, she was able to identify the founders of eighteen of them by race. Only two were black. Many founders of both manufacturing companies and conjure shops were recent Jewish immigrants who had fled Europe in the face of rising anti-Semitism. In America they encountered a less virulent form of prejudice that nevertheless pushed them toward African American society as a source of income. Catherine Yronwode, owner of the Lucky Mojo Curio Company, reports that a cousin had such a history. Leaving Germany in the days before World War II, he arrived in the United States with the intention of practicing pharmacy. He opened a shop in a black community, where, because of high demand, he soon began selling spiritual supplies.[25]

As might be expected from whites using African American "superstition" to make a living, most manufacturers paid little attention to the materials used in traditional charms. For example, nineteenth-century conjurers predominantly worked with a variety of roots, animal parts, and other naturally occurring materials. Mail-order manufacturers introduced new forms of magical products. Incense, magical soaps, and a vast array of oils took their place alongside old-fashioned conjure bags, goopher dust, and powders. More recently, aerosol sprays have promised supernatural benefits to their users. Many of these items, however, do not employ traditional magical materials. According to a 1951 article in *Ebony*, New Orleans "fast luck water" was nothing more than water colored with Easter egg dye. "Black Cat oil" was motor oil, with soot sometimes added for color. "Love oil" was perfumed olive oil. Recent products follow similar rules. A can of Quick Money aerosol spray obtained by the author appears to be a cheap air freshener transformed into a spiritual product by its label. Even when mail-order companies have sold supposedly traditional favorites, they often differed from their earlier versions. For instance, whereas nineteenth-century African Americans recognized John the Conqueror as the plant more commonly known as Solomon's seal, twentieth-century manufacturers have usually substituted the roots of the jalap plant, a native of Mexico.[26]

Many mail-order manufacturers also entered the publishing industry. Since the Civil War, African American literacy had been on the rise, and manufacturers were quick to take advantage of this fact. The result was books aimed at those interested in practicing hoodoo. One of the first occult books specifically marketed to black Americans was *Aunt Sally's Policy Players' Dream Book*, which first appeared in 1889. It consisted primarily of a list of dream subjects, each of which was assigned particular lucky numbers for gambling purposes. Players of bolita, a popular game of chance that originated in Cuba, were particularly fond of such books. A researcher for the Federal Writers' Project reported that stores "in Negro neighborhoods are filled with books on the subject; even two books alleged to have been writings of Moses inadvertently left out of his compilation of the works in the Bible are included."[27] Not all such works focused on gambling. *The Life and Works of Marie Laveau*, which was in existence by the 1920s, includes a variety of spells, including ones to "uncross" the cursed, to secure financial success, and to win love. The writer professed to be Marie Laveau herself, though this was almost certainly false. Nevertheless, its authorial claims guaranteed its popularity in New Orleans. By the time Zora Neale Hurston investigated hoodoo in the city, many practitioners reportedly recited spells from the book as if they had learned them from the great Voodoo queen herself.[28]

In some cases mail-order companies' goods introduced new influences into African American conjure. On a national level, they helped break down regional distinctions by providing standardized products across the United States. Sonny Boy Products, based originally in Miami, Florida, and later in Birmingham, Alabama, has long sold its goods to customers as far away as California. Similarly, Robinson Hall, of Micanopy, Florida, stocks a selection of Indio Products oils, which are manufactured in Los Angeles, California.[29]

Books played an even greater role in dissolving local idiosyncrasies. For instance, while the use of candles in conjure was usually confined to areas settled by the Catholic French and Spanish, it has now spread throughout the South. This diffusion has been largely the result of books like Henri Gamache's *The Master Book of Candle Burning*, an instruction book explaining methods of burning candles to achieve a variety of personal aims. First published in New

York in 1942, it was sold throughout the United States and remains in print today. Books like *The Life and Times of Marie Laveau* and the more recent *Famous Voodoo Rituals and Spells*, by H. U. Lampe, have similarly spread the lore of New Orleans Voodoo across the nation. Other books combined hoodoo traditions from throughout the South into a single work, further undermining regional distinctions. *Papa Jim Magical Herb Book* is a recent work in this tradition. Among the more than two hundred botanical products that fill its pages are Adam and Eve root, formerly popular in the Latin cultural area; Guinea pepper, usually found in areas settled by the English; and John the Conqueror, common in both areas. Older works in the same vein are Henri Gamache's *The Magic of Herbs*, first published in the 1940s, and Lewis de Claremont's *Legends of Incense, Herb and Oil Magic*, which appeared in 1938.[30]

Mail-order companies also introduced influences from outside the United States into African American hoodoo. Books most clearly demonstrated these new elements. Catherine Yronwode, a contemporary rootworker, has compiled a list of books sold by King Novelty, a sister company of Valmor, in 1942. Among those listed were Godfrey Selig's *Secrets of the Psalms* and *The Sixth and Seventh Books of Moses*. The former was a Kabbalistic text first published in seventeenth-century Pennsylvania. Its formulas rested on the belief that properly invoking God, angels, or demons would bring about the will of petitioners. *The Sixth and Seventh Books of Moses*, the most popular conjure text during the 1930s and 1940s, was a similar collection of incantations, accompanied by a selection of magical seals.[31]

More than just Kabbala entered the field of hoodoo in the early twentieth century. The Orient, long defined by white Americans and Europeans as exotic and magical, came into vogue.[32] For instance, Lauren William DeLaurence published *The Great Book of Magical Art, Hindu Magic, and East Indian Occultism* in 1902. The book contains a photograph of DeLaurence dressed as a Hindu mystic. Lewis de Claremont's *Legends of Incense, Herb and Oil Magic*, has a similar picture, an "artist's conception" of the book's author, depicting him in a turban and colonial military uniform. Incense burns at his right hand, and behind him stands a spirit guide. Claremont's work did not disappoint, discussing Far Eastern incenses alongside European spells and herbs from African American hoodoo.[33]

Following the advent of the hoodoo manufacturer, conjure shops often evolved into retailers of the products of the larger companies, only occasionally producing their own goods. Dr. Eagle, who operated his own conjure shop during the middle years of the twentieth century, stated, "We buy straight from the factory in Baltimore now. They have direct contact with Egypt and the Orient."³⁴ Dr. Eagles's suppliers probably deceived him about their products' origins. More than likely, they manufactured them on their premises. In any case, his statement illustrates the rapidity with which conjure shops turned to mail-order manufacturers to stock their businesses. Though many continued to carry such traditional goods as conjure bags and roots, by the mid-twentieth century most of their inventory typically consisted of manufactured goods. In an article on Voodoo for *Ebony* Edward T. Clayton accompanied his text with several photographs, one of which depicts spiritual supplies available at New Orleans's hoodoo drugstores. Of the eight items shown, at least four were manufactured. In 1967 and 1968 David J. Winslow visited the Calvary Religious and Occult Store in Philadelphia, Pennsylvania. Like many of its ilk, the shop had a distinctive odor, "sandalwood and other exotic incenses" in this case.³⁵ Its proprietor, Bishop E. E. Everett, BS, a native of North Carolina, was pastor of the Calvary Spiritual Temple, which Winslow identified as affiliated with the Apostolic Church of Christ in God. Though Bishop Everett called himself a "spiritual advisor," his business differed little from the conjure shops of Florida, Louisiana, or South Carolina. Commercially bottled "graveyard dust," human figures made of wax, and various oils, bath salts, and aerosol sprays graced the shelves. Among his bestselling items were candles and *The Sixth and Seventh Books of Moses*.³⁶

In the nineteenth century, conjurers' reputations had spread by word of mouth. Success, or at least a reputation for it, was a prerequisite. For manufacturers and some conjure shops, however, word of mouth was not enough to ensure financial prosperity. They needed a new marketing strategy. Their most basic form of promotion was the catalog. Most manufacturers and many conjure shops produced them, and they could be picked up at the business or requested by mail or phone. They did more than just list the items available by mail. Like most sales catalogs, they also promoted the goods. For example, in a recent Miller's Rexall catalog an advertisement for Root of Life Oil, New Orleans Class reads, in part, "ROOT OF LIFE OIL is said to have been used by CONJURE MEN, VOODOOS, and SPIRITUALISTS for anointing their bodies and LUCK CHARMS. They believe that the oil would drive away EVIL SPIRITS and bring GOOD LUCK, LOVE and SUCCESS."³⁷ Such advertisements were usual for hoodoo catalogs. A few have been more creative. Sonny Boy Products currently sells a spellbook that doubles as a catalog. A representative selection is spell number eight, a ritual designed to keep husbands, wives, and lovers from adulterous affairs. The first step is to write Psalm 37 on a piece of white unlined paper. It must then be moistened with Glory Water, a Sonny Boy product. Next, the person casting the spell should bathe for seven days in the company's Love Drawing Bath. Success remained uncertain, however, unless the customer wore Sonny Boy's Strong Love Cologne when with his or her loved one.[38]

Many manufacturers also employed agents to ply their wares. Black-oriented cosmetic companies had earlier proven the success of this technique. Because many mail-order companies incorporated both beauty merchandise and conjure supplies into their product lines, their owners were well aware of the concept's profitability. Among the manufacturers employing local dealers were Valmor and Keystone. The latter recruited its agents through the Church God in Christ and newspaper advertisements. Local dealers served a second purpose by providing their employers with information on local beliefs and product demand.[39]

Manufacturers frequently took marketing cues from the proprietary medicines industry. Proprietary medicines, also know as patent medicines, were extremely popular in the late nineteenth and early twentieth centuries. In some ways, patent medicine resembled both traditional and manufactured conjure. For instance, both conjurers and vendors of patent medicine adopted the title *doctor* regardless of their qualifications. Titles sold products. Likewise, makers of patent medicines and hoodoo supply companies frequently credited God with their products' efficacy. For example, Dr. Muncy, maker of a kidney cure, reported that God had revealed the formula to him. Others quoted Bible verses on their products' packaging. Most important, both hoodoo manufacturers and proprietary medicine companies sold products without any scientifically proven beneficial qualities. The application of their techniques to the spiritual supply industry was a natural development.[40]

Spiritual supply manufacturers and conjure shops adopted two marketing techniques from the purveyors of patent medicines. Like black-oriented cosmetic companies, owners of patent medicines used agents to promote their nostrums. Since colonial days these agents or even the proprietors themselves had traveled the nation providing public spectacles. These might take the form of plays, juggling acts, musical performances, or a variety of other attention-getting devices. All incorporated a demonstration of the medicines being sold. At least two of the conjurers interviewed by Harry Middleton Hyatt had at one time participated in such shows before turning to the profession of hoodoo. Most hoodoo agents did not employ large-scale spectacles, choosing low-key agents instead. Nevertheless, there were exceptions. When Hyatt interviewed Herman Henry, he learned of a man calling himself Dr. Buzzard who performed feats of magic before crowds of hundreds before selling magical goods to them. Hyatt commented that such traveling magicians were common a generation before his interviews. Similarly, "Black Herman" Rucker, an African American stage magician, published a book on hoodoo, slight of hand, and other forms of supernaturalism and sold his own line of patent medicines. His acts, performed across the United States, helped promote his products.[41]

The influence of patent medicines is much clearer in mass-media marketing. Beginning in the early eighteenth century, advertisements for proprietary medicines appeared in periodicals. By the late nineteenth century virtually every newspaper carried them. A typical example was a notice for Warner's Safe Kidney and Liver Cure that appeared in the *Key West Democrat* in 1882. Below a drawing depicting an African gathering herbs, the text proclaimed that "95 Per Cent of all diseases arise from deranged kidneys and liver." It went on to promise that for "the innumerable troubles caused by unhealthy Kidneys, Liver and Urinary Organs; for the distressing Disorders of Women; for Malaria, and for physical derangements generally, this great remedy has no equal."[42] Black-oriented periodicals carried similar sales pitches. For instance, during the 1920s the *Chicago Defender*, a nationally distributed African American newspaper, printed advertisements for Professor J. H. Swayne's Lone Star Tea, which claimed to be even more indispensable to good health than was Warner's Safe Kidney and Liver Cure. A money-back guarantee supported its proprietors' claims that it was a "remarkable remedy for Rheumatism, Liver, Kidney, Bladder, Stomach Troubles and Lost Manhood."[43] A line drawing of a healthy, muscular man drove the point home. Such claims were no more fantastic than the properties attributed to spiritual products.[44]

By the end of the nineteenth century, pitches for magical products had taken their place alongside advertisements for patent medicines in African American newspapers. One of the first appeared in the 11 March 1898 issue of the *Alabama Time-Piece*. It was a simple notice that M. P. Fowler had rods for detecting gold and silver for sale. Over time the impact of patent medicines began to grow more evident. By the early decades of the twentieth century the *Chicago Defender* was publishing several magic-oriented advertisements in each issue.[45] For instance, on 17 January 1920, Lucky Star, a hoodoo manufacturer, pitched its incense. According to the advertisement, the practice of burning incense "has never been without beneficial results . . . the disinfecting, deodorizing and perfumizing vapors thus produced are, and always were, highly conducive to health and happiness."[46] One of the best illustrations of the link between patent medicine and consumer hoodoo is the case of the Last Chance Medicine Company, which advertised in the *Chicago Defender* in 1921. Despite proclaiming that its products were medical and eschewing any mention of luck, magic, or the like, it nevertheless advertised "a full line of John the Conqueror Root, Eve and Adam Root, Five Finger Grass, Orris or Love Root, Samson Snake Root, Sacred Powder, and Holy Sandalwood and hundreds of others."[47] Though rare before 1920, such advertisements were plentiful by the end of the decade.

In time, many advertisements appeared touting specific practitioners' supernatural gifts and abilities to help those in need. For instance, a 1923 advertisement by Madam Ida B. Jefferson, of Longview, Texas, proclaimed that she could "reach any disease you were not born with." Furthermore, her abilities allowed her to cure illnesses without any information from patrons. All that she needed from customers was twenty-five dollars.[48] In 1974 a supposed son of Dr. Buzzard used the pages of the *Miami Times* to proclaim that he was the "World's Greatest Spiritualist" and "King of the Blessing."[49] Similar advertisements continue today.

The spiritual products industry also learned from the failures of the patent medicine companies. In the first few years of the twentieth century proprietary medicines remained free of government regulation. Since the late nineteenth century, however, they had been under attack by social activists for their questionable value. According to muckraker journalists, such as Samuel Hopkins Adams and E. W. Kemble, makers of proprietary medicine were perpetrating fraud by selling useless or even dangerous nostrums to unsuspecting customers who believed their fantastic claims. Beginning with the 1906 Pure Food and Drug Act, the federal government required companies to print their products' ingredients on their labels. A major loophole was that the law only applied to ingredients listed in the official *United States Pharmacopoeia or National Formulary*. Not until a patent medicine named Elixir Sulfanilamide claimed more than one hundred lives in 1937 did the federal government take a more aggressive stance. In 1938 Congress passed the Federal Food, Drug, and Cosmetic Act. Among its provisions was one placing all medicines under government oversight, requiring proprietors to prove the safety of their products, and allowing the government to stop false claims by makers of patent medicines without proving fraud. Many proprietary medicine companies, unable or unwilling to comply with the new law, closed down. Gone were the days when nostrums like Warner's Safe Kidney and Liver Cure and Professor J. H. Swayne's Lone Star Tea could claim to cure virtually any ailment.[50]

The Federal Food, Drug, and Cosmetic Act may have dealt a serious blow to patent medicines, but hoodoo manufacturers and retailers found a way around the law. They had long faced the threat of prosecution under charges of mail fraud and medical malpractice and under a variety of local laws forbidding the sale of charms. The easiest way to avoid legal trouble was simply to avoid making any claims for their products. But this made continuing to attract customers a vexing problem. The solution was to describe products' "alleged" powers, a practice occasionally employed even before the passage of the 1938 law. For example, Hyatt reported that he encountered circulars sold by two hoodoo manufacturers carrying the disclaimer, "We make no preternatural claims on any of these products and sell them all merely for curios."[51] Others incorporated the disclaimer into their product descriptions. The folklorist Loudell Snow's "Mail Order Magic" includes an undated reproduction of an advertisement for the Glowing Black Cat Talisman, produced by an Indiana spiritual manufacturer. In its product description it reported that the "alleged BLACK CAT BONE is said to be very magnetic and powerful," and for a mere thirty-five dollars customers could obtain a "REPLICA OF THE ALLEGED BLACK CAT BONE WITH SECRET INFORMATION NEVER BEFORE PUBLISHED IN BOOKLET FORM."[52] Manufacturers and conjure shops continue the practice today. In the year 2000 Rondo's Temple Sales Company published a catalog with the disclaimer, "The publishers of this book wish to have it understood that the statements made are not to be accepted as facts, but only as things people do and believe. We make no claim to these rituals being of help to anyone."[53] The company nevertheless offers a list of products and their uses, sometimes backing them with testimonials.[54]

Despite the decline in traditional conjure, it would be wrong to assume that commodification was necessarily a negative development. As George Ritzer has pointed out in *The McDonaldization of Society*, consumerism brings important advantages to producers and buyers. First, spiritual products guaranteed increased efficiency for both parties. Neither had to undertake lengthy rituals or spend time searching for herbs in the forest. Conjurers and customers alike could simply order ready-made magical items straight from manufacturers. Individuals in need of a quick fix need only step into the nearest spiritual supply store to gain instant gratification. Just as important, the availability of similar oils, floor washes, candles, and other items throughout the United States helped standardize conjure, making costs easily calculable and products more uniform. By the early decades of the twentieth century, buyers could reasonably expect to receive consistent levels of quality and quantity when they made a purchase, regardless of where they lived and whether they visited a conjure shop or ordered from a catalog.[55]

While gaining efficiency and uniformity, conjure lost its personal nature. Shops selling ready-made charms eliminated customers' need to individually interact with conjurers. At any rate, shops frequently did not always employ practitioners. Consumers, however, did not even need to enter a shop. They could order through the mail, buying products that had never come in contact with a professional hoodooist. With mass advertising, even the importance of reputation declined. In some cases manufacturers went so far as to discount the effectiveness of their products in efforts to avoid legal troubles. An impersonal form of conjure without conjurers had developed.

Although conjure shops and manufacturers permanently transformed African American supernaturalism, some elements remained constant. First, spiritual products performed the same motivational function as they did for their traditional forebears. During the nineteenth century someone like Henry Bibb might visit a conjurer to purchase a root harvested from the forest to prevent beatings by an unjust master. In the twentieth century an African American was more likely to consult a catalog and order a Job Kit of manufactured items to help him or her keep or get a good job. Both individuals were concerned with improving their employment, but the situation and products had changed. Similarly, during the late nineteenth century Henry F. Pyles thought he had to purchase a mixture of pepper, wool, "Pammy Christy beans," and rusty iron in a bag tied with horsehair and soaked in whisky to win a woman's love. Had he lived in the late twentieth century, he could have simply sent for a love pentacle, an amulet from the ancient Kabbalistic *Key of Solomon the King*. Mail-order companies in no way decreased the versatility of hoodoo. Luck, love, money, protection, and revenge could all be had with manufactured magic.[56]

Magical commodities also continued to follow the same rules as traditional charms and spells. The principle of contagion was often evident. For instance, according to the *Sonny Boy Blue Book Guide to Success© Power©*, customers could keep unwanted people out of their cars by using Cast Off Evil incense and bath, thereby preventing theft and driving away undesirable passengers. Buyers should sprinkle the incense on the floor mats and apply the bath to the steering wheel using a white cloth. These uses of Cast Off Evil items were examples of contagion because of their power as repellents against those who might approach one's automobile unbidden. Several other spells from the *Sonny Boy Blue Book Guide* used written names, images "captured" in mirrors, and objects once in contact with customers' or their enemies' bodies for their contagious properties.[57]

Likewise, the principle of sympathy remained an important part of manufactured magic. Around half of the *Sonny Boy Blue Book Guide*'s spells employ biblical passages, especially the Lord's Prayer and Psalm 23, both of which focus on God's protection and guidance. Biblical passages were not the only forms that sympathy could take. For example, a spell from Marie Laveau's *Original Black and White Magic* entitled "The Lady Who Has an Empty House" recommended the use of Magnetic Sand in conjunction with Easy Life Oil, Compelling Oil, Nine Lucky Mixture, and other magical items to bring men and riches to one's door. Because of its ability to attract metal to itself, Magnetic Sand was a powerful sympathetic charm for drawing both men and money.[58]

Easy Life Oil, Compelling Oil, and Nine Lucky Mixture illustrate a form of sympathy that first appeared in the spiritual products industry. Since most manufacturers used few traditional materials in their goods, they relied on their products' physical characteristics, packaging, and names to express their alleged magical qualities. A modern example is Indio Products's Holy Oil. According to Bishop Master F. L. Robinson, it clears the thoughts when used in conjunction with Bible reading. Composed of Duoprime 70 and fragrance, it has nothing to recommend it beyond an agreeable odor and a clear appearance, a label showing crosses and flowers, and self-proclaimed holiness. These very qualities, however, make it effective in the eyes of customers. Its pleasant smell and clarity indicate its purity and beneficial qualities. The label emphasizes its holy properties through its name and the crosses. Flowers, which adorn the bases of the crosses, both allude to herbal medicine and further emphasize the formula's reputed positive powers.[59] Other manufactured products employ the principle of sympathy as well. Seven Sisters of New Orleans brand Court Case Just Judge Incense uses blue as the primary color of its label and of the incense itself. The label also sports a line drawing of a judge dwarfed by a colorful flower-bearing root. Blue was long associated with protection. Moreover, the judge-and-root motif hearkened back to protective items like the herb chewing John the Conqueror, which had once offered protection from slave masters and enemies. Some manufacturers have used Indians, who symbolized healing and occult aptitude, to further their products' claims. A contemporary example is Sonny Boy Old Indian 3-Day Quick Money aerosol spray, which is adorned with a drawing of a Native American, labeled "Chief Tar," flanked by two green hands grasping money. Hindu and other Oriental themes have also been popular in product names and on labels, a practice common in patent medicine since the nineteenth century.[60]

As during the nineteenth century, some items had power beyond their sympathetic values. In the past, John the Conqueror root was widespread and popular, and now Sonny Boy Products offers High John Conqueror in seven different forms: candle, oil, incense, bath, salt/sand, soap, and spray. While most of Sonny Boy's items have specific uses, John the Conqueror is good for anything. An advertising blurb in the company's *Blue Book Guide* reads, "Works only for you. Also add to any product. Conquers all."[61] Alleged black cat bones have also remained similarly powerful, having a variety of uses, from bringing good luck to winning love to guaranteeing rebirth after death. The Bible and other Christian religious objects have also continued to fulfill their versatile roles. During the twentieth century they were joined by statues of Buddha, which can reputedly bring luck in a variety of pursuits.[62]

Without doubt, the survival of the conjurer was the most important carryover from the nineteenth century to the twentieth. Seven Sisters of Hogansville, Alabama, continued to serve her community well into the twentieth century. The same was true of the redoubtable Dr. Buzzard, who did not pass away until 1947. Not all hoodooists were holdovers from the nineteenth century. James Spurgeon Jordan, of North Carolina, did not gain a reputation as a rootworker until the early twentieth century, though he had been dabbling in hoodoo since the 1890s. Likewise, after the death of Dr. Buzzard, his son-in-law took over and continued to practice until his death in 1997.[63]

Despite the presence of impersonal, easily obtainable mail-order products, conjurers remained powerful forces in their communities. Furthermore, the decline of traditional conjure in the face of the spiritual products industry generated a crisis of supply, leading to greater demand for hoodooists' services. In keeping with classical economics, prices skyrocketed. Whereas Dr. Jean Bayou, of New Orleans, reportedly left behind real estate worth $50,000 at his death in 1885, several modern hoodooists approached or surpassed such riches. When Julius P. Caesar died in the early twentieth century, he was worth approximately $150,000. According to a price list compiled by employees of the Federal Writers' Project, New Orleans hoodooists charged prices ranging from $5 for love spells to $500 for spells to kill enemies or drive them insane. Wealthy conjurers also lived outside New Orleans. Nancy Rhett, a native of the South Carolina low country, reported that she once had a striking experience while visiting a bank. In front of her in line was an unusual man. His clothing was covered with what appeared to be diamonds, and he was depositing a stack of checks more than an inch thick. Upon asking the teller, she learned that he was a well-known rootworker.[64] Likewise, observers reported that James Jordan earned an average of at least $3,000 a month from 1940 to 1960. He sometimes made this amount in a single week. He used the money he made from conjure to purchase several other businesses, including farms, a logging company, and a baseball team. In the twenty-five years following 1937 he made about $2 million from his various pursuits.[65]

Twentieth-century hoodooists, like their nineteenth-century counterparts, possessed more than just economic power. Dr. Buzzard was held in respectful awe by those who had heard of his powers. During the 1920s High Sheriff James McTeer, of Beaufort County, South Carolina, pursued a medical malpractice investigation against the dreaded sorcerer, but he found it extremely difficult to collect evidence. The reason for this dilemma was that witnesses were unwilling to testify against or even discuss his doings. After much difficulty, the sheriff convinced a prisoner who was also a client of Dr. Buzzard's that he could protect him through his own magical powers. The prisoner, who had recently purchased some "medicine" from the root doctor, agreed to face Dr. Buzzard and confirm that he had sold him the nostrum. His resolve did not last long. When brought before the conjurer, he began to groan and "beat himself as if he were covered with stinging ants."[66] After a few moments, the prisoner collapsed and began foaming at the mouth. Fear had eliminated McTeer's best hope for a successful prosecution.[67]

Not all hoodoo doctors were objects of fear. Aunt Caroline Dye, of Newport, Arkansas, built herself a near-mythical reputation for helping those in need. According to John Quincy Wolf, "If a circle were drawn four hundred miles in diameter and centering in Newport, it is almost certain that the majority of adults living within that circle in 1918 [the year of her death] would have heard of her: it is doubtful that even the name of President Wilson was more generally known."[68]

Many hoodooists even became community leaders. The most impressive example of conjurers' leadership role was James Jordan. During the middle decades of the twentieth century a settlement of several hundred grew around his practice, becoming known as Jordansville. The community was composed, as his biographer put it, of "his legal children; off children; grandchildren; waifs snuggling beneath his protective wings; men and women in his employ and their families; the multitudes bridled with economic obligations or professional services." He provided for the physical needs of those who lived there and expected obedience in return. Government officials and law-enforcement personnel found it easier to work through Jordan than to assert their jurisdiction. Even the fearsome Dr. Buzzard lent positive leadership in his community, paying for the rebuilding of a church destroyed by fire in 1937.[69]

A few conjurers' fame spread far beyond the boundaries of their communities, rivaling the reach of spiritual products companies. For example, James Jordan operated a brisk mail-order business throughout the country. It was also not uncommon to find cars from New York, Pennsylvania, and other northern states parked outside Jordan's office. Dr. Buzzard, though, was the most well known conjurer of the twentieth century. He was a living legend in South Carolina, where conjurers were plentiful. Mamie Garvin Fields, who began teaching school on John's Island, South Carolina, in 1909, testified to Dr. Buzzard's reputation. According to Fields, a local hoodoo doctor, Jimmy Brisbane, was "what you could call a higher type of witchdoctor, because he knew how to drive all the way to Beaufort, which was noted for this: a witchdoctor of witchdoctors lived there, a Dr. Buzzard." He was also known much further afield. Federal Writers' Project employees discovered that his fame had spread to coastal Georgia by the 1930s, Harry Middleton Hyatt found that informants recognized his name as far away as Louisiana, Florida, and Virginia.[70]

A few conjurers ignored the spiritual products industry, continuing to practice the traditional magic of their ancestors. One example was Aunt Jenny Dailey. Aunt Jenny, a former slave, lived alone near Burnt Corn, Alabama, during the first few decades of the twentieth century. Both blacks and whites feared her. During the late 1930s a young white girl named Eugenia Brown had an unnerving encounter with the conjurer. One day she and her friends were playing on her front lawn when they spotted Aunt Jenny approaching. As she passed by Eugenia and her companions she halted, drew a cross in the dirt, and spat on it. Having done so, she moved on. Eugenia feared she had been cursed. Drawing a cross in the dirt, however, had been a common protective ritual during the nineteenth century and may have remained so in the next. Eugenia also related that Aunt Jenny carried roots and other traditional magical materials with her wherever she went. Conjurers like Aunt Jenny were far from extinct, but they were not as common as they once had been.[71]

Most conjurers changed with the times, learning from their competitors in the spiritual products industry. They quickly grasped the benefits of advertising. One of the earliest to do so was the second Marie Laveau, who distributed cards describing her business. By the early twentieth century, individual conjurers were also placing advertisements is newspapers, alongside advertisements for manufacturers and spiritual supply stores.[72]

Hoodooists adopted much more than marketing techniques from their manufacturing competitors. First, many began to use manufactured hoodoo in their practice. Beginning around 1927, James Jordan studied many of the books produced by spiritual supply companies, including Gamache's *Master Book of Candle Burning*, *The Sixth and Seventh Books of Moses*, and Selig's *Secrets of the Psalms*. He went even further, buying roots, patent medicines, and ready-made conjure bags from mail-order companies for resale in his shop. Before this time he had gathered most of his materials from nearby forests, but once he discovered the ease of buying wholesale, he largely gave up this practice. Jordan was not alone. Bishop Master Robinson likewise sells manufactured spiritual products. His aid is still needed, however, because he alone knows the biblical passages to use with each item. The root doctor Pop Williams, who also retails manufactured products, shares Robinson's philosophy. He says that his knowledge of spiritual products' uses sets him apart from the average salesman.[73]

As part of their adaptation to competition with the spiritual products industry, hoodooists have also sought to change their image. One way has been to adopt the Orientalism promoted by many spiritual products companies. For example, when Julius P. Caesar performed his spells, he usually wore a black robe and a green turban. More recently, an African American resident of St. Petersburg, Florida, practiced under the name Prophet Warkiee Sarheed. When he worked, he donned a "seeing and hearing hat," which resembled an orange turban.[74]

More common than Oriental trappings were concerted efforts by magic workers to distance themselves from evil magic. Published literature had gone far to excoriate African American magic. Whites, in particular, strongly associated blacks' supernaturalism with Satanism. As a result, most African American sorcerers abandoned words like *hoodoo*, *Voodoo*, *witchcraft*, and *rootwork* and began to refer to themselves as *mediums, spiritual advisers, reverends, psychics,* and *healers.* Many twentieth-century practitioners have designated hoodoo and Voodoo as evil, while proclaiming their own God-given abilities for good. Bishop Master Robinson draws a further distinction between hoodoo and what he calls "spiritual advising." Hoodoo or Voodoo, he argues, is a lower form of supernaturalism designed to compel others to do the will of the practitioner. Spiritual advising, however, deals with Christ, making it hoodoo's more powerful and more benevolent counterpart. Pop Williams also argues that hoodoo is a lower form of supernatural power, adding that those who practice it have little knowledge of the materials they use.[75]

Some titles, such as *spiritual adviser* and *reverend,* had an added benefit in that they linked hoodoo to religion. Such terms filled roles analogous to manufacturers' disclaimers. Hoodoo "doctors" were open to prosecution for practicing medicine without a license; ministers performing religious rituals were protected by the U.S. Constitution. By the second half of the twentieth century conjure "doctors" were rare.[76]

For most of the twentieth century conjure's future was in doubt. Throughout the nation conjurers' charms were giving way to commodities. Despite coming to be more in line with white Americans' beliefs and practices, however, both hoodooists and mail-order manufacturers remained liable for prosecution if they continued to practice their art. In part, this was because of white Americans' genuine concern for the physical welfare of those ingesting hoodooists' concoctions or being duped by unscrupulous frauds. More important, conjure was not yet an acceptable tradition in the eyes of a people who had long linked blackness with inferiority and supernaturalism with backwardness. In addition, some shops and manufacturers have experienced declining sales over the past few decades. Several venerable conjure shops and manufacturing companies disappeared in the second half of the twentieth century. Among them were Valmor, which was bought out by a competitor uninterested in its spiritual products, and all of New Orleans's older hoodoo drugstores. Most of the great traditional conjurers also passed away. James Jordan, one of the last root doctors to exert near-absolute power over a large, national following, died in 1962.[77]

On the other hand, plenty of hoodooists and spiritual products manufacturers and retailers continued to survive. Many entered the business in the second half of the century. Pop Williams is a prime example. Indio is another business that opened in recent years.[78] In part, these new hoodooists and businesses were responses to forces that began to affect the United States during the 1950s. In the closing decades of the twentieth century and the opening years of the present century, hoodoo has gained a new life and relevance through an ongoing struggle between old notions of hoodoo as at best suspect and at worst diabolic and a reevaluation of African American conjure as an alternative "religion."

6

The Magic Continues:
Hoodoo at the Turn of the Twenty-first Century

REVEREND CLAUDIA WILLIAMS owns Starling Magickal Books and Crafts in New Orleans. In addition to books, she sells a small selection of black-oriented spiritual supplies and a variety of European magical materials. She also practices Voodoo. Williams's background gave little indication of her future career. She was born to white Episcopalian parents in Manhattan. When she was a small child, psychic experiences sparked her interest in the occult. Williams never believed in the faith of her parents, who urged her to seek out her own path. Today she is an ordained minister of ancient ways, with specialization in Lakota Native American beliefs, Yoruba-based religions, witchcraft, and some ceremonial magic.[1]

Clearly, Reverend Claudia Williams is not a traditional conjurer. Her race, religious beliefs, and regional origin mark her as a member of a new brand of practitioners that arose in the late twentieth century. In the nineteenth century magical practices originating in Africa survived by drawing on European and Native American beliefs. In the early twentieth century individual conjurers and large companies turned to shops, mail order, and mass media to distribute their products to a broader area. Hoodoo developed further in the second half of the twentieth century, when conjure interacted with new features in American society, most noticeably scientific investigations of hoodoo, the rise of New Age ideology, and increased immigration from Latin America. It not only survived but adapted and prospered despite the changing situation. The result has been a growing acceptance of hoodoo even beyond the borders of black society.[2]

By the late twentieth century old-fashioned conjurers who gathered their materials from nature were becoming increasingly rare. In one sense traditional hoodoo was a rapidly fading practice. On the other hand, consumer conjure had itself become a tradition. Manufacturers had existed since the late nineteenth century. Even companies like Valmor and Keystone Laboratories were serving second- and third-generation customers. Spiritual supply stores had been around since at least the 1880s and probably earlier. To put this in perspective, other traditional features of black life had pedigrees dating from the same period. In music, blues and ragtime, the precursors of jazz, evolved in the late nineteenth century. The same was also true of legal segregation, which whites imposed on African Americans during the post-Reconstruction Redeemer period.[3]

Another product of the nineteenth century was "tourist Voodoo," and like the manufactured form, it has also become a tradition. In New Orleans, Voodoo designed for the tourist trade can be traced to the later St. John's Eve dances, to which spectators were admitted for a fee. During the mid-1870s the Pontchartrain Railroad made late-night trips to the nearby lake for those who hoped to witness the rituals. By 1885 at least one guidebook featured a chapter on Voodoo, describing the St. John's Eve rites for visitors to the city. At times the crowds of sightseers numbered in the thousands. Key West, Florida, had its own "tourist Ñañigo" by the turn of the century, personified by one of the religion's former leaders, Ganda, who danced for a fee.[4]

In recent years Voodoo-oriented tourism has become a substantial industry, particularly in New Orleans. Visitors can purchase Voodoo dolls in many French Quarter shops.[5] Robert Tallant's *Voodoo in New Orleans* and *The Voodoo Queen*, which are easily obtainable from most of the city's bookstores, provide entertaining blends of folklore and fact to curious readers. A few shops sell nothing but tourist-oriented hoodoo materials. Marie Laveau's House of Voodoo and Reverend Zombie's Voodoo Shop are on and just off Bourbon Street, respectively. Their goods range from traditional conjure formulas to T-shirts. Another store, Voodoo Authentica, is on North Peters Street, which runs alongside the Mississippi River. In addition to souvenirs, it "provides authentic ritual entertainment" for business functions and social events.[6] Those who are interested in more than just souvenirs can take one of the city's many Voodoo tours. Guides take visitors to see such sites as the grave of Marie Laveau, Congo Square, and the offices of current practitioners. There is even a New Orleans

Historic Voodoo Museum, which displays artifacts from Haiti and Louisiana.[7]

Louisiana is not the only place where one can experience African American magical practices from a tourist's perspective. Excursions offered by Gullah Tours of Charleston, South Carolina, include tales of Dr. Buzzard. Moreover, one need not leave home to get a taste of hoodoo. Information on Voodoo is readily available to cybertourists courtesy of Web sites provided by the New Orleans Historic Voodoo Museum, Voodoo Authentica, and other tourist attractions. While touring or visiting an Internet site, one can quench one's thirst with a bottle of Voodoo Rain fruit drink, which comes in such flavors as "Black Magic," "Mojo Luv," and "Lucky Devil." Each bottle is complete with a list of the flavor's herbal ingredients, along with their reputed benefits. The drink's magical image is complete with a logo in which the *V* in *Voodoo* is formed by two pins, doubtless designed to inspire thoughts of Voodoo dolls.[8]

Many owners of tourist businesses are believers in hoodoo or at least respectful of it. At the same time, however, they follow the example of Voodoo Rain, relying on traditional stereotypes of Voodoo and hoodoo to attract their primarily white clientele. For example, the front cover of a brochure issued by the New Orleans Historic Voodoo Museum announces its goal as "Proclaiming Multicultural Understanding." The text proposes that those who visit will "marvel as history and mystery unfolds from the lips of your knowledgeable guide." While there, patrons will hear "authentic sounds of ritual drumming and chanting" as they "view our permanent collection of bizarre and rare historic displays—some belonging to the Great Marie Laveau herself!" The words are illustrated by intentionally grotesque drawings of dolls resembling skeletons, idols with protruding tongues, and scantily clad women dancing with snakes. Similarly, Marie Laveau's House of Voodoo employs actual hoodoo practitioners and sells many old-fashioned herbal goods. At the same time, its location on Bourbon Street guarantees that most visitors are tourists, uninterested in Voodoo beyond its value as a source of mystery and entertainment. In short, while visiting conjure shops and ordering spiritual supplies by mail are longstanding African American customs, Voodoo tourism is a distinctly white tradition.[9]

During most of the twentieth century, participation in hoodoo has remained outside the mainstream American experience. Whites have usually viewed it as backward or even satanic. For instance, in a 1927 article for the *New Republic* Lyle Saxon compared New Orleans Voodoo to the "black masses" of European witchcraft. Most middle-class African Americans also denigrated conjure. A 1951 article in *Ebony* described Voodoo as "a snake-worshiping cult" that had developed into a "lucrative racket." After describing the respect that modern believers held for Marie Laveau, the author concluded, "Like her present-day contemporaries, Marie Laveau, too, was a charlatan of the worst sort." A similar article, "Would You *Believe* It . . . Superstition Lives!" appeared in a 1976 issue of *Ebony*.[10]

Three major developments have helped conjure begin to escape its negative image. First, many blacks have embraced scientific explanations for hoodoo, usually drawing from the fields of psychology and psychiatry. While interviewing African Americans for a doctoral dissertation in 1977, Elon Ali Kulii discovered that a number of believers interpreted hoodoo as a scientific, not a supernatural, practice. As one informant put it, "Well, hoodoo had its beginnings back in the late seventeenth and eighteenth centuries, among the slave plantations. The people of poor economic status. Therefore, it substituted very much for what we use psychiatry for today." Elaborating, he described the practice of conjure as the workings of "mind over matter." Another, when asked about other names for conjure, replied, "Mainly science, the study of science. . . . But many stupid people or uninformed people call it voodoo or hoodoo."[11]

Many modern hoodooists practice with the understanding that they are providing valuable, scientifically sound services. One of the first explicitly to profess this belief was the white witch doctor James McTeer, who advocated the incorporation of rootwork into medicine and psychiatry as a means of calming the minds of those who believed themselves to be under the influence of evil conjure.[12] Today Pop Williams describes himself as "a salesman with good advice." He maintains that most of his clients' problems are the results of troubled minds and that his job is to relieve their emotional distress. To do so, he often prescribes spiritual products. Nevertheless, he argues that these lack any power outside of his clients' beliefs.[13]

The primary reason for African Americans' scientific approach to hoodoo is that modern science itself has taken a more positive view of conjure than in years past. Anthropologists were the first to examine the effectiveness of magic, typically through the idea of "voodoo death." Walter B. Cannon's seminal essay, "'Voodoo' Death," did more than any other work to bring hoodoo into the realm of science. First published in *American Anthropologist* in 1942, it presented a novel argument that those who believed themselves cursed were indeed harmed by extreme stress. In the years since the publication of Cannon's article, others have taken up the problem. One of the more influential essays of the last quarter-century has been Harry Eastwell's "Voodoo Death and the Mechanism for Dispatch of the Dying in East Arnhem, Australia." According to Eastwell, fear of curses was usually present in individuals who had committed such acts as murder or other crimes that would likely anger members of their communities. What followed was an escalating cycle of psychological and social pressures. First, fear exacerbated any preexisting medical conditions, potentially damaging the victim's health. In time, friends and family members often also came to believe that the supposed victim was cursed. Their convictions reinforced those of the sufferer, making it difficult for him or her to lead a normal life. After a period of hope, the loved ones and the victim would surrender to despair, and the afflicted would prepare to die. On the sufferer's part, abandonment of everyday activities, including eating and drinking, followed. In cases examined by Eastwell, families facilitated the victims' deterioration by taking away water with the intent of helping the spirit part from the body. The result was death. Despite their essays' titles, however, neither Cannon nor Eastwell addressed Voodoo proper. On the contrary, both used cases from Australia to generalize about the potentially harmful effects of magic.[14]

Mental-health professionals were the first to apply the anthropologists' theories of Voodoo death to African American hoodoo cases. In addition, while anthropologists highlighted the negative power of magic, psychologists and psychiatrists came to see its beneficial properties. For instance, in a 1966 article in *Psychosomatic Medicine* psychiatrist David C. Tinling reported on seven incidences of "hexed" African Americans at the University of Rochester Medical Center in New York. Each patient complained of symptoms that initially defied diagnosis. In some cases doctors eventually discovered physical or mental roots for the ailments. Others remained unidentified. Tinling concluded that as part of treatment physicians should ask patients whether they had been victims of hoodoo. Doing so would help them to differentiate between physical or mental disorders and disorders prompted largely by conjure. While the former could often be treated with orthodox medicine and psychology, the latter required the services of rootworkers.[15]

A few years after Tinling's article appeared, Ronald M. Wintrob went even further, stating that doctors and psychiatrists should always incorporate hoodoo into their treatments of those who had faith in its power. To do so, healthcare professionals should ask patients about their beliefs, allowing them to build trust and a rapport with their caregivers. Moreover, he stated that "medical personnel should expect their patients who believe in malign magic to consult a native healer or a rootworker before, during, or after treatment." Throughout the 1970s, similar articles appeared with increasing frequency in periodicals aimed at doctors, nurses, psychiatrists and psychologists, and the general public. Their popularity continues to the present.[16]

Conjure has drawn on sources outside psychology, however. Chief among these is parapsychology, a fringe science with the sole aim of finding scientific explanations for various aspects of the supernatural. Parapsychology originated as a branch of psychology during the late nineteenth century. In the 1920s it emerged as a distinct field. William McDougall, an Oxford psychologist, coined the term *parapsychology* after he moved to Duke University and began to study what was more commonly known as psychic phenomena. By 1937 the field had a laboratory at Duke University and its own scholarly journal. The Parapsychological Association became the first professional organization for paranormal researchers in 1957.[17]

Most parapsychologists devote themselves to the search for proof of extrasensory perception, psychokinesis, and life after death. Recently, however, some have begun to examine magic. For instance, according to Michael Winkelman's "Magic: A Theoretical Reassessment," it can be explained as the workings of psi phenomenon. In this interpretation, differences between cultures are only superficial and derive from local religious beliefs and values. Although research specifically addressing hoodoo is rare, parapsychology indirectly promotes it by providing an ostensibly scientific explanation for its power. For instance, whereas blacks have traditionally attributed conjurers' powers to God or spirits, parapsychologists would more likely identify extrasensory perception (ESP) or psychokinesis as their source.[18]

Parapsychology rivals psychology in its influence on hoodoo. James McTeer, who offered psychological explanations for hoodoo's supposed effectiveness, also claimed to have inherited ESP from his mother and grandmother. The most telling example of hoodoo's assimilation of parapsychology is the proliferation of "psychics" catering to black customers. A perusal of African American newspapers is the easiest way to identify such professionals. For instance, one page in a recent issue of the *Miami Times* includes two advertisements for psychics. Close examination of their texts reveals that these "psychics" hoped that African Americans would recognize them as rootworkers. One advertisement states that "Niva" can "remove spells, voodoo, evil, curse jinx, [and] demons." The second, by "Sister Lisa," states that she sells roots, candles, and incense, all common hoodoo paraphernalia.[19]

A few scientists have sought the source of conjure's power in biology. In 1967 an article in the *Journal of the American Medical Association* argued that poisons were responsible for at least some hoodoo-induced sicknesses. The most important work supporting a biological basis for conjure, however, has been Faith Mitchell's *Hoodoo Medicine*. Mitchell, a medical anthropologist, collected dozens of herbal remedies among the Gullah of the South Carolina Sea Islands. In addition to describing their traditional uses among African Americans, she also listed their official pharmacological properties.[20]

Although many conjurers and believers have accepted psychological or parapsychological explanations for hoodoo's reputed powers, the number who admit to using herbal remedies and other biologically active agents is small. Certainly, the threat of prosecution for practicing medicine without a license is a powerful disincentive. At the same time, most conjurers now rely on manufactured spiritual supplies from large mail-order companies. Herbal remedies are no longer readily available. Most important, however, African Americans now have greater access to trained doctors. Despite these hurdles, a few practitioners have adopted elements of the biological explanation for hoodoo. For instance, Phoenix Savage, a small-scale hoodooist who works primarily for family and friends, reports that her most requested products are medicinal items for the treatment of specific ailments. Nevertheless, most of her clients use her products in conjunction with the services of a physician. Despite their rarity at present, the number of practitioners accepting a biological basis for conjure is likely to grow because herbalism is becoming increasingly popular among Americans of all races.[21]

Modern hoodooists have also drawn heavily from the occult and spiritual revival known as the New Age movement. The New Age movement is a complex topic and deserves some introduction. Its roots extend back to the first half of the nineteenth century. In the United States the 1830s and 1840s were decades of remarkable religious ferment that witnessed the rise of several new religions, including Mormonism, Transcendentalism, and Spiritualism. Transcendentalism and Spiritualism, both incorporating a strong mystic element, contributed strongly to the promotion of occult traditions in the United States. Later in the century another new religion, Theosophy, proclaimed the oneness of all life, consciousness, and power, an idea that would inspire much of New Age thought. In addition, it stressed the use of science to explain the workings of the supernatural, a position reinforced by parapsychology in the twentieth century. At the same time that Theosophy was taking hold, proponents of New Thought were proclaiming a philosophy of health that stressed "inner healing." According to its followers, each human had a spiritual nature. The key to health was recognizing one's spiritual being and allowing the divine to work cures in the flesh. Ultimately, wrong thoughts translated into physical illness, while right thoughts led to health. In sum, New Thought was a philosophy of positive thinking, another idea that would reappear in the New Age movement.[22]

The more recent New Age movement was sparked primarily by the interaction of increased East Asian immigration and the rise of the counterculture. Asian Buddhists, Hindus, and Sikhs were in the United States well before the twentieth century, but their numbers were limited by the tight regulations of the Oriental Exclusion Act of 1924. In 1965, however, President Lyndon Johnson and Congress rescinded the act. The result was a massive influx of new East Asian immigrants, including religious teachers. For the New Age movement the timing was fortuitous. As the Vietnam War dragged on and racial strife divided the nation, the younger generation abjured the values of white middle-class Protestant America. In many cases part of their rejection was the abandonment of Christianity. Following the flood of Asian immigrants, Eastern religions were the obvious countercultural choice. Zen Buddhism, transcendental meditation, and yoga were but a few of the most popular faiths. Like older American occultism, they tended to stress mysticism, oneness with the universe, and realization of one's own divine potential.[23]

The movement peaked after the decline of the counterculture that gave it birth. By the 1970s and 1980s it had spread beyond its Eastern base to incorporate a wide range of other practices and faiths, including extraterrestrial cults, astrology, neopaganism, and magical herbalism. Today, however, the movement is in decline. According to a 1991 *New York Times* survey, only twenty-eight thousand Americans identified themselves as "New Agers." Many others share the ideology but eschew the term *New Age* because of the media's popularization of it during the 1980s. The future of the movement is likewise threatened by an aging membership composed largely of baby boomers who became interested in it during the years of the counterculture. Ironically, while many began their involvement as part of a rebellion against societal norms, most have now moved into the middle class. They tend to be white, educated, upwardly mobile, and socially respectable. Despite the movement's declining presence, it has dramatically affected American culture. Herbalism has become widely accepted as a healthful activity. Polls indicate that approximately one-third of Californians participate in yoga or meditation on a daily basis. Some scholars estimate that as many as 25 percent of all Americans have participated in some aspect of the movement.[24]

The key elements of the New Age movement are not easy to define, yet common features do recur throughout. For instance, most of its members embrace pacifism, political reform, feminism, and environmentalism, all of which they adopted from the counterculture of the 1960s and 1970s. More important, most scholars agree that the movement's diverse adherents share a faith in self-spirituality. According to scholar Paul Heelas, self-spirituality comprises three main elements. First, New Agers hold that personal experience should take precedence over belief. In their view, belief is an organizational system that inhibits spiritual development. Second, each person is a spiritual being whose own mind is the only valid source of truth. Finally, to realize one's spiritual potential, one must abandon socialized values and institutions, including organized religion and societal norms of conduct.[25]

Self-spirituality created several other features shared by all or most of the groups within the movement. Among the most important of these are strong individualism, subjective morality, belief in the power of magic, holistic approaches to health, religious pluralism understood as different paths to truth, and denial of centralized spiritual authority. Despite their rejection of organized religion, many of those influenced by the New Age movement see no contradiction in borrowing from a variety of traditional religions in their search for personal spiritual uplift. Indeed, adherents of virtually all aspects of the movement, from Eastern mysticism to Wicca, claim to follow ancient faiths. Moreover, while individuals typically adhere to particular paths, such as Wicca, their chosen identities frequently do little to keep them from borrowing practices from other religions, ranging from Hinduism to Sufi Islam to ancient Gnosticism. These shared features, however, are not merely a means of imposing order on a mass of unconnected faiths: they are responsible for the diversity of the New Age movement.[26]

The movement's history of eclecticism and its philosophy of self-spirituality made it attractive to a few hoodooists. Priestess Miriam Chamani is an excellent example of an African American Voodoo and hoodoo practitioner who draws heavily from New Age philosophy. Born into a family of Mississippi Baptists, Chamani's first step on the path toward Voodoo came out of her experience in a Spiritual church, which commonly utilizes herbal medicine and recognizes the existence of many spirits. She began practicing Voodoo in 1975. Though her introduction to Voodoo came from traditional sources, she has nevertheless incorporated New Age self-spirituality into her own beliefs and practices. For instance, when asked whether she had been initiated into the religion, she replied that life initiates people, who are driven by "thoughts far beyond their birthing." Further elaborating, she stated that withdrawal from the church allows greater freedom and self-expression. According to Chamani, submitting to religious ministers, Christian or otherwise, limits higher expressions of God. She has also incorporated other elements of New Age philosophy into her practice. Chamani described a vision in which she looked ahead and saw many paths branching before her. When she looked behind, she discovered that the many paths were actually only one. Chamani interpreted her experience as a representation of the oneness of all religious faiths.[27]

Hoodoo gained more than just new concepts from the movement. New Age religions proved to be a fertile field for the recruitment of new believers. Initially, hoodoo did not attract members of a movement designed to be countercultural. After all, it had long been a part of American culture and had become deeply infused with Christianity. More important, like most whites, New Agers were not familiar with African American culture. Since the 1980s and early 1990s, however, increasing numbers of New Agers have turned to African American belief systems for spiritual growth. Within a world-view that advocated self-spirituality and religious relativism, condemnation of African American magic proved impossible. On the contrary, many now see it as a worthy source for personal spiritual development. The result has been an influx of white hoodoo practitioners, a revival of Voodoo and other African religious elements in the work of some practitioners, and a tendency to merge conjure with a variety of other magical and religious traditions.

One of the best examples of New Age–influenced Voodooists is the Reverend Claudia Williams. Like most New Age conjurers, she is white. Furthermore, she began her involvement in alternative religions as a Wiccan, which she found boring after a time. She says that unlike Wicca, Voodoo is complex and grows with the practitioner. Her magical practice consists primarily in private "spellwork" for clients whose needs generally involve love, protection, or money. Like Voodooists of the nineteenth century, she claims to work most closely with gods originating in Africa. Her closest relationships are reportedly with Oya and Shango, a goddess and a god present in both Haitian Vodou and Santería. At the same time, as a minister of ancient ways, she also incorporates elements of Native American religions, Hinduism, and other faiths into her personal system of belief and practice.[28]

Williams is not alone in the way she practices Voodoo. Sallie Ann Glassman, of New Orleans, also a white, began her involvement in New Age and occult practices as a child growing up in the Northeast. To her, these practices were too strongly tied to secrecy and individual will and seemed to ignore the needs of the community. Eventually she turned to Haitian Vodou as an alternative, undergoing initiation as a mambo, or priestess, in Haiti. Despite her abandonment of New Age philosophy, Glassman still shows the influence of her background. For instance, she gives her religious affiliation as "Vodou and Jewish," in keeping with the New Age concept of religious unity and relativism. She has also abandoned the Haitian practice of animal sacrifice. Instead, she offers some of her own life force to the spirits through yoga.[29]

S. Jason Black and Christopher S. Hyatt, the authors of *Urban Voodoo*, likewise show the influence of a New Age background in their practice. Though they openly disdain many aspects of the movement, particularly Wicca, they readily incorporate crystal balls, Tibetan Buddhist chants, and European ceremonial magic into their rituals. Just as important, they suggest that practitioners avoid adopting Haitian Vodou with all of its morals and mythology intact. Instead, Black and Hyatt argue that the "great virtue of Voodoo in contrast to other paths is direct experience and the pursuit of results [through magic]." Further keeping within New Age self-spirituality, they advocate self-initiation over traditional methods. Like Williams and Glassman, Black and Hyatt are both white. Whether they like it or not, they are as strongly influenced by the movement as any Wiccan.[30]

Conjure has further developed by interacting with the massive influx of immigrants whose faith in the supernaturalism is similar to that of African Americans. During the second half of the twentieth century large numbers of Latin Americans immigrated to the United States, driven by a variety of economic and political forces. With them they brought African European syncretic religions and magical traditions, including Puerto Rican Espiritismo, Cuban Palo Mayombe, Mexican *curanderismo* (healing) and *brujería* (magic), Haitian Vodou, Trinidadian Shango, and Brazilian Candomble. In recent years, however, the most influential syncretic faith has been Cuban Santería.[31]

Santería, like Louisiana Voodoo, includes a variety of gods, primarily derived from the Yoruba pantheon. As in Africa, these are arranged in a hierarchical order. At the top presides Olodumare, the remote creator of the universe, roughly equivalent to the Christian God. Below Olodumare are the *orishas,* each of which has an equivalent Catholic saint. Next in rank are ancestral spirits, collectively known as *eguns.* Further down the spiritual hierarchy are humans, plants and animals, and nonliving things. All life, including Olodumare, is filled with Ashe, an absolute spiritual force.[32]

Magic is an important part of Santería. For instance, Santerían priests, *babalawos,* practice divination for paying clients. One method involves casting kola nuts or their substitutes and interpreting the resulting pattern. In the United States most *babalawos* divine using the *opele,* a long chain to which tortoiseshell discs are attached at regular intervals. The *opeles* are typically lowered onto a flat surface by practitioners, who hold onto the chains at their center. As with kola nuts, the resulting patterns tell clients' fortunes.[33]

Divination is but a part of the *babalawos'* craft. After diagnosing a magically induced illness or other problem through the use of kola nuts or *opeles,* they prescribe cures. Treatments usually involve rituals and sacrifices. For instance, in one case encountered by Joseph M. Murphy, a young woman consulted a *babalawo* who divined that she had an ovarian cyst. He recommended that the woman visit a doctor, take a special herbal bath, and make a sacrifice to Oshun, the god of rivers, fresh water, and erotic love. The woman most likely obtained her magical bath materials from a botanica, Santería's equivalent of a conjure shop. In addition to herbal baths, botanicas sell statues of saints, candles, oils, and other goods.[34]

Believers in Santería have lived in the United States since well before the twentieth century, but the Cuban revolution of 1959 boosted their numbers into the hundreds of thousands, if not millions. The first Cubans to arrive were generally from the upper and middle classes. As time passed, the socioeconomic status of the immigrants declined. Most of those arriving after 1962 were from lower-middle- and working-class families. By 1979 Dade County, Florida, alone had 430,000 inhabitants of Cuban origin. Today sizeable communities exist throughout the nation, with particularly high concentrations in major cities, including New York City, Washington, DC, and Union City, New Jersey. Cubans, especially those of the working class, brought Santería with them. Moreover, in the United States many immigrants adopted the religion as an important cultural symbol. The result has been an increase in its practice among Cuban Americans. In addition, some Americans and immigrants from other Latin American nations have entered the Santería fold. According to George Brandon, "Santeria now almost certainly has more devotees in the United States than it had in Cuba at the time of the revolution."[35]

Santería's similarity to hoodoo has made it a support of older African American beliefs. For instance, when several venerable conjure shops closed in recent years, blacks turned to Santerían botanicas.³⁶ F and F Botanica and Candle Shop in New Orleans is one of the best examples. The store was initially founded in 1976 by a Cuban follower of Santería, Enrique Cortez. The store is now owned by a Baptist Puerto Rican who says that it is open to all beliefs. To many patrons, however, it is a "hoodoo store."³⁷ Santería's appeal to hoodoo practitioners is sometimes recognized by African American conjurers. According to "Deborah," a "spiritual worker" of Bessemer, Alabama, modern African American magic is primarily Latin American in origin.³⁸

Santería has also done much to draw new believers to hoodoo. While science and the New Age movement made Voodoo acceptable to many whites, the growth of Santería made African American magic and syncretic religions acceptable parts of black identity. In some cases experience with successful Santerían rituals persuaded blacks to adopt it as a religious faith. For example, a woman named Lorita Mitchell turned to Santería in a desperate effort to find a cure for her son's cancer. Apparently as a result of following a ritual prescribed by the owner of a local botanica, her son's cancer disappeared. Today both Lorita Mitchell and her son are members of the Santerían priesthood.³⁹

Others turned to Santería and other syncretic faiths as an expression of black nationalism. The most extreme example is Oba Oseijeman Adefumni I of Oyotunji. Adefumni began life as Walter King of Detroit. As a young man he traveled to New York to become an artist and dancer. While there, he encountered Cuban adherents of Santería.⁴⁰ Inspired by the religion's African features, he became deeply involved, traveling to Cuba for initiation as a priest of Obatala. Over time he became involved in the civil rights movement, advocating a form of separatism based on Yoruba religion. In time he came to believe that the movement had been a failure. As a result, he left New York and his old life behind, but he did not abandon his ideology of black nationalism. Settling in South Carolina, he realized his dream as the village of Oyotunji, literally meaning "return of the horseman" or "return to Oyo," a famous Yoruban city. The village was to be a recreation of Africa in America. To this end, he declared it an independent nation, adopting the name Adefumni I and the title *king*. King Adefumni also abandoned the Catholic elements of Santería in favor of "pure" Yoruba religion. Though the villagers now number in the thirties, there were about two hundred during the 1970s.⁴¹

Few are as radical in their response to Santería as Adefumni. More typical is Ava Kay Jones, a New Orleans Voodoo priestess. Growing up in rural Louisiana, she knew about hoodoo. Enrique Cortez, owner of the F and F

Botanica and Candle Shop, however, introduced her to the religion of Santería. Combined with her previous knowledge of hoodoo, it became what author Rod Davis calls "Orisha Voudou."[42] Jones saw no reason to abandon Catholicism. As she explains it, "I don't agree with all the Church dogma, but if we're dealing with what Christ taught, then I'm a Christian in that sense."[43] At the same time, Jones demonstrates an attachment to cultural nationalism. One of the best examples of her leanings was her initiation as a priestess of the goddess Oya. It took place in Atlanta, Georgia, and involved important leaders of African, Afro-Latin, and African American religions, including King Adefumni. It was the first initiation into Orisha Voudou carried out by American blacks. During the ceremony, Adefumni made the ceremony's ideological value clear, stating, "All across America now in every major city you are going to find that the gods of Africa have descended." Using the language of the civil rights movement, he continued, "Gradually, we shall overcome—through these initiations, which so many of the people, of the voudou inside of the people, are seeking."[44] The initiation was a far cry from the condemnatory articles that once appeared in the *New Republic* and *Ebony*. Santería has helped some African Americans embrace their spiritual history instead of rejecting it as superstition.

None of the three forces that have shaped conjure in the second half of the twentieth century has operated in isolation from the others. Instead, a form of neo-Voodoo has developed, characterized by interaction between them. Many modern practitioners fuse elements of science, New Age philosophy, and syncretic religions in lesser or greater degrees depending upon their personal ideologies. For example, Claudia Williams, who entered Voodoo by way of the New Age, encountered Latin American syncretic religions much earlier. As a child, she lived above a Santerían botanica. Though she was interested in the faith and learned much about it, her parents did not encourage her. Similarly, although James McTeer generally explained the success of rootwork in terms of parapsychology and psychology, he was also strongly attached to several New Age concepts. In *Fifty Years as a Low Country Witch Doctor* he expressed belief in the unity of all religions through a universal "Supreme Force," in reincarnation, and in a variety of other features common in Eastern-influenced New Age philosophy.[45]

Just as the three forces that compose neo-Voodoo have interacted among themselves, they have also contributed to traditional forms of hoodoo. For instance, Catherine Yronwode, owner of the Lucky Mojo Curio Company, sells conjure products "made the way they were made in your grandma's day—the way they SHOULD be made today."[46] At the same time, she has pragmatically adapted to changing circumstances, stocking items aimed at believers in Latin American syncretic faiths. As part of her personal life, Yronwode also practices tantric yoga, an Indian form of sacred sex linked to New Age philosophy in the United States.[47] Today, even tourist hoodoo draws on neo-Voodoo. According to the Web site of the New Orleans Historic Voodoo Museum, the source of Voodoo's power is Kundalini, a supposed river of energy that flows through each individual. The concept of Kundalini originated in India and is strongly tied to various forms of yoga. The Web site goes on to proclaim that "everything you do is to lift yourself to higher consciousness." In addition, New Orleans draws many neo-Voodooists, who benefit from the city's position as the most important center of tourist Voodoo. The influence of neo-Voodoo is virtually inescapable.[48]

Despite neo-Voodoo's pervasive influence, its eclectic character ensures that its adherents will differ on a variety of issues. For instance, practitioners disagree over the terms they apply to themselves, the sources of their powers, and the number of believers. In some cases such disagreements have developed into schools of thought. One of the most obvious divisions is between those who seek to practice historical hoodoo and those who are willing to incorporate outside ideas. For some, like Jason Black, hoodoo is just a part of a much broader occult world-view. As a result, they see no reason to draw sharp distinctions between conjure and other nonblack occult practices. Others maintain that hoodoo is best approached in a "purer" form. For instance, while Jason Black carried out his own initiation, Ava Kay Jones and Sallie Ann Glassman underwent traditional inductions into Voodoo. Glassman, a white, even traveled to Haiti to study Vodou. When she was ready, priests initiated her into the religion. According to her, "priests" and "priestesses" who have not undergone traditional initiations are frauds. The most extreme version of purist Voodoo is that practiced by Oyotunji's Oba Oseijeman Adefumni I, who aims to eliminate all non-African influences on Yoruba religion as part of his separatist ideology. Still others, like Catherine Yronwode, take a middle road, practicing traditional hoodoo without seeking to "purify" it of non-African practices.[49]

Racial issues have further divided practitioners. White Voodooists and conjurers see hoodoo as a multicultural practice open to all races. According to some, but by no mean all, African Americans, however, hoodoo is part of their cultural heritage and therefore forbidden to outsiders.[50] Phoenix Savage, a black Pennsylvania-born hoodooist, stated, "I would suspect that I better represent hoodoo than the New Age white folks running a hoodoo business. I rather resent those types, from a cultural sense of things."[51] Not all are as moderate as Savage. At times, race-based disagreements have deteriorated into near violence. Sallie Ann Glassman reports that some African Americans oppose her performance of public Voodoo ceremonies, occasionally turning to insults and intimidation to dissuade her. Followers of Louis Farrakhan, leader of the Nation of Islam, have sent her threatening e-mails. A common theme of these verbal and written assaults is that whites should not practice a black religion. Both sides of the dispute cling to their beliefs with a deep conviction that they are right. Still, virtually all hoodooists of both races have a multicultural clientele. More important, those willing to threaten the other side are a minority. Thus far, no one has been physically harmed in the dispute.[52]

The future role of conjure in American society remains undetermined. In addition to internal differences in ideology, both neo-Voodoo and traditional hoodoo remain objects of attack. For example, in 1990 *Mother Jones* published a brief article, entitled "The War on Voodoo," that addressed Voodoo, Santería, and related beliefs as types of black magic tied to the drug trade. In 2001 the film director Spike Lee attacked Hollywood's depictions of what he called "the super-duper, magical Negro" in movies like *The Green Mile* and *The Legend of Bagger Vance*. He argued that such characters, who generally helped whites with their supernatural powers, detracted from real social issues and were thus a form of racism. Meanwhile, laws against practicing medicine without a license, mail fraud, and the like continue to work against conjure, though they are enforced less rigorously than they once were.[53]

Despite continuing threats to hoodoo, its expansion beyond the bounds of African American society is helping to preserve it for future generations. Some practitioners even argue that the United States is in the midst of an African American magical renaissance. One of the more striking examples of the rising interest is an e-mail-based correspondence course on hoodoo first offered by Catherine Yronwode in 2003. As of late 2003 there were 126 students enrolled in the class, and others continued to sign up at the rate of more than 2 per week. According to Yronwode, in addition to growing Latin American and white participation, many blacks are returning to conjure as a link to their history. "Deborah" confirms Yronwode's statements. According to her, hoodoo is stronger now than it was ten years ago. In fact, she entered the craft in order to combat evil witchcraft, which she believed had become a major problem by the mid-1980s. Although conjure continues to face attacks from without and dissension from within, the forces of modern science, New Age philosophy, and Latin American syncretic religions have helped it adapt to the twenty-first century.[54]

Conclusion
The Importance of Conjure
in African American Society

FOR TOO LONG, conjure has remained an obscure topic in American history. Nevertheless, it has been a significant part of the black experience. Like other features of African American society, hoodoo grew out of slavery. Together, the experiences of slave raids, the Middle Passage, and the rigors of involuntary labor guaranteed that the African way of life could not survive intact in the New World. Like the African American culture of which it was a part, conjure emerged as a composite of European, Native American, and African elements. At the same time, whites have persistently sought to suppress the practice. Still, hoodooists have continued to command great respect within their communities, even as old-fashioned conjure evolved into modern consumer hoodoo. Today many blacks and whites still turn to African American magic as a source of both spiritual enlightenment and practical supernaturalism.

In a time when magic is largely discredited as a valid practice and many scholars eschew religious faith, the study of conjure can seem unprofitable. Some might consider it a perpetuation of old stereotypes that depict blacks as slaves to superstition. The truth is far more complex. Conjure has served a variety of functions within African American society and played a pivotal role in shaping other aspects of black culture. Hoodoo's power was not just a figment of African Americans' imagination. On the contrary, widespread belief made it an effective force, even among many whites. Conjurers could use pharmacologically active herbs to treat illness, psychology to ease mental ailments, fear to bring about the deaths of enemies and acquittals at trials, or good advice to encourage patrons to succeed on their own. Whatever their tactics, they had genuine power to help people achieve a variety of ends, ranging from the mundane to the seemingly impossible. At the very least, they gave their clients hope for success, spurring them to continue their efforts.

Because of the authority and reputation it gave to individuals, hoodoo became an important force for social regulation. For instance, reliance on magic for vengeance limited the use of violence in settling disputes. During the antebellum period conjurers helped slaves cope with lives of servitude by providing roots that allegedly prevented whippings, powders designed to give them control over their masters, and a variety of similar charms. Slaves could even buy "poisons" that promised to sicken or kill their owners. With such magical powers at their disposal, physical violence was often unnecessary. A more recent example of conjure's function was that of John and Leroy Ivy, who attempted to kill Judge Thomas Gardner III, of Tupelo, Mississippi, in 1989. Their motivation was revenge for the judge's sentencing of John Ivy to forty years in prison on robbery charges. Rather than taking the direct route of murder, the Ivys turned to hoodoo. Doubtless, they believed it would be easier to carry out a murder by magic than by physical force. The plot collapsed after they asked the judge's black housekeeper to supply them with a lock of his hair and a photograph. Soon thereafter the Ivys were arrested on charges of conspiracy to commit murder.[1]

Conversely, fear of conjure has probably dissuaded some from taking actions that might result in a magical counterstroke. In parts of South Carolina, for example, people would threaten to "go to Beaufort" on those who made them angry. The significance of the statement was that Beaufort was the home of Dr. Buzzard.[2] Similarly, the common nineteenth-century practice of isolating suspected hoodooists from the rest of the population was an example of avoiding offense by limiting conjurers' social contact with the rest of the community.[3]

Stories about conjure also served as a means of communicating societal values. One striking example was a tale collected by Elon Ali Kulii. According to an informant living in Indianapolis, Indiana, her grandmother had once had an acquaintance who romantically pursued a man who had no interest in her. Although her friends advised her to give up, she turned for help to an "herb doctor," who gave her a powder to sprinkle along the path that the man usually followed to and from work. The spell seemed to work just as the woman intended. Soon, the man was madly in love with her, and the relationship quickly led to marriage. After about six months, however, the woman realized that she did not love her husband as much as she thought. She soon began to "fool around" with another man. Her dalliance did not last long. One day her husband walked in on her and her lover and in a jealous rage killed them both. Clearly, the morals of the tale, passed down to the young and inexperienced, are to let love follow its own course and to remain faithful to one's spouse.[4]

Historically, hoodoo has been distinguished from other forms of magic by its role as a tool of an oppressed race. Among the black populace, conjure was thought to be a source of protection against abuse by slave masters and unfair employers, economic success in a white-dominated business world, and hope to those charged with crimes under the Jim Crow justice system. From the standpoint of conjurers, the profession allowed them to assume a variety of roles otherwise closed to them by economics and white prejudice. For example, as herbal healers hoodooists filled the role of medical doctors. African Americans were pitifully poor between the Civil War and the civil rights movement. They could seldom afford the fees of university-trained physicians. The only viable alternatives were rootworkers. Hoodooists have also filled the roles of psychiatrists for those who could not call upon the services of mental-health professionals. Likewise, while during the Jim Crow era African Americans required all the legal help they could get, the study of the law was all but denied blacks. Once again, hoodooists filled the void, providing those who believed in magic with spells to sway judges, juries, and law-enforcement officials. In short, conjurers were the poor man's doctors, psychiatrists, and lawyers.[5]

Because of hoodoo's many uses, conjurers often attained positions of great influence. For instance, during the days of slavery conjurers frequently became community leaders, respected for their knowledge and feared for their occult power. Moreover, many whites also held hoodooists in high regard. After all, crossing a conjurer might result in poisoning.[6] After emancipation, wealth also followed hoodooists. In the 1930s black tenant farmers could expect to make as little as $1.50 a week for backbreaking labor. Even those who labored in relatively high-paying northern factories rarely made more than $20.00 a week. Moreover, black workers were more vulnerable to retrenchment than their white counterparts. At the very least, hoodooists entered the middle class as self-employed professionals. In many cases they did much better. Conjurers like Jean Bayou, Julius P. Caesar, Dr. Buzzard, and James Jordan generally made more each day than the highest-paid black factory workers did in a week. In some cases successful conjurers could make more in a day than a black tenant farmer could in a year. Not only did their wealth surpass that of almost all other African Americans, it also gave them an economic status well above that of the vast majority of whites. Elon Kulii affirms that many root doctors practicing today have become millionaires. He estimates that the hoodoo industry generated $3 billion annually during the late 1970s. Furthermore, as during the nineteenth and early twentieth centuries, economic prosperity continues to bring social prominence. Modern hoodooists, such as Bishop Master Robinson, remain widely respected members of their communities.[7]

In reference to African Americans, discussions of equality are usually conducted along the lines of race. Nevertheless, equality between the sexes has long been an issue for both blacks and whites. In the antebellum South "respectable" white women seldom worked outside the home. Property restrictions, strict control of female sexuality, and a lack of political opportunity were even more prevalent. Although the period since the Civil War has been one of enormous change in white females' political, sexual, and economic positions in American society, the separation between the private female and the public male has remained strong. While women have historically failed to achieve full equality with men, African American women proved unable to reach a parity with their white counterparts. Despite emancipation and the passage of the Nineteenth Amendment, black females were unable to vote in substantial numbers until the overthrow of Jim Crow during the 1960s and 1970s. In addition, they were even less likely than white women to hold high-status jobs. In the South, black women could most commonly be found working as tenant farmers, domestic servants, and laundresses, professions shunned by the vast majority of whites. Like black men, black women had little opportunity to improve their economic standing. For instance, Mississippi's female domestics earned an average of $2.00 each week for labor from sunup to sundown during the 1930s. Even when black women held the same jobs as whites, they usually received much lower wages.[8]

Conjuring was one of the few professions that allowed women to escape the domestic ideal and to avoid the necessity of menial labor. While women by no means constituted the majority of hoodoo practitioners, they were highly visible members of blacks' magical world. For instance, when Zora Neale Hurston interviewed New Orleans conjurers for "Hoodoo in America," she spoke primarily to men. Nevertheless, Ruth Mason, a female hoodooist, performed the most powerful and involved ritual in which Hurston participated.[9] In addition, all five of the male conjurers with whom Hurston spoke willingly instructed her in their craft. Also, she reported that "practically all of the hoodoo doctors of Louisiana" relied on spells traditionally attributed to the female Voodoo queen Marie Laveau.[10]

A 1987 incident graphically illustrated the sexual parity within conjure. Tommy Lee Berry and his wife, "Mama Betty" Berry, had once operated a successful rootworking business in the town of Blakely, Georgia. After their marriage ended in divorce, both spouses continued to practice hoodoo. Unfortunately for Mama Betty, she competed too successfully against her former husband. Tommy Lee gunned her down after she opened the door to two women seeking the aid of a spiritual adviser. Despite the unfortunate consequences for Mama Betty, conjure has been an equal-opportunity employment.[11]

In addition to conjure's social functions, it has also contributed strongly to other aspects of African American culture, most notably the arts, language, and religion. The art most strongly affected by hoodoo has been music. Songs referring to conjure were already in circulation by the nineteenth century. Some of these were designed to ward off evil magic. A worker from the Federal Writers' Project recorded one such song during the 1930s:

> Keep 'way from me, hoodoo and witch, Lead my path from de porehouse gate; I pines for golden harps and sich, Lawd, I'll jes' set down and wait. Old Satan am a liar and a conjurer, too—If you don't watch out, he'll conjure you.[12]

Others told stories of conjure. Henry F. Pyles remembered an example. The words recount the process by which a nineteenth-century hoodooist named Old Bab made his charms:

> Little pinch o' pepper,
> Little bunch o' wool.
>
> Mumbledy-mumbledy.
>
> Two, three Pammy Christy beans,
> Little piece o' rusty iron.
>
> Mumbledy-mumbledy.
>
> Wrop it in a rag and tie it with hair,
> Two from a hoss and one from a mare.

Mumbledy, mumbledy, mumbledy.

Wet it in whiskey
Boughten with silver;
That make you wash so hard your sweat pop out,
And he come to pass, sure![13]

Such songs foreshadowed blues music about hoodoo.[14]

African American visual art has also been influenced by conjure. For example, rootwork featured prominently in the works of Sam Doyle, a recently deceased folk artist from Beaufort, South Carolina. One of Doyle's best-known paintings was a portrait of Dr. Buzzard. For those more inclined toward popular culture, there are the comic book illustrations of Kenjji, of Detroit, Michigan. In early 2002 he debuted a black superhero known as the WitchDoctor in a book published by Griot Enterprises. To thwart evil, the WitchDoctor relies on his supernatural vision and the power of Voodoo. At the same time, he combats stereotypes of both African Americans and the religion, causes dear to his creator's heart.[15]

Conjurers have been common in African American literature as well. In the 1899 book *The Conjure Woman* Charles W. Chesnutt told of Uncle Julius, a prolific teller of conjure tales, and his relationships with whites. Chesnutt's stories, which often depict the hardships of slavery, were also an implicit critique of America's racist society. Today nationalist authors such as poet Ishmael Reed depict hoodooists as tricksters who undermine white power with magic. One need not be a nationalist, however, to use conjurers in one's writing. For many female African American authors conjure women are examples of powerful, independent black women. Alice Walker's *Third Life of Grange Copeland* provides an example. One character, Sister Madelaine, is a two-headed doctor who uses her income from conjure and fortunetelling to send her son to college. Though the son initially disdains his mother's "superstition," he comes to admire her profession and its attendant power after joining the civil rights movement. A similar character appears in Toni Morrison's *Sula*. Like Sister Madelaine, Morrison's conjurer is a strong black woman. Even the book's narrator, who ostensibly condemns her as evil, nevertheless expresses her admiration for the hoodooist's knowledge, child-rearing skills, magical acumen, and even her physical appearance.[16]

Language is another aspect of black culture that has been influenced by conjure. Words like *hoodoo, Voodoo,* and *mojo* have become household words even among whites. Similarly, the pejorative terms *hoochie-choochie man* and *hoochie-choochie woman* originally referred to hoodoo practitioners. Today, however, they are more commonly used as insults applied to the sexually immoral. More distinctive, however, are phrases derived from hoodoo that have lost their original significance. An informant interviewed by Elon Kulii in 1977, stated that she commended hosts who prepared especially good meals by stating, "This is so good you must have peed in this."[17] As the informant recognized, the phrase derived from black women's practice of urinating into the food that they were preparing for husbands or lovers. They believed that this would make their men unable to leave them for other women. The much more common phrase "I'll fix you," probably originated in conjure. Although it now used widely to mean that the speaker will take revenge on the listener, it initially referred to *fixing*, a conjuring term for laying curses.[18]

Conjure has had its greatest influence on religion. According to the theologian Theophus Smith, it has affected virtually all African Americans' worldviews. In *Conjuring Culture* he maintains that conjure must be understood as more than sorcery. Smith argues that blacks used hoodoo as a means of magically healing or transforming society. The Bible was the primary means of carrying out the reshaping. An example of biblical conjuring was blacks' emulation of Jesus. According to Smith, they did not act simply in imitation. Instead, African Americans hoped to learn how Christ used his victimization to change his oppressors. This potentially world-changing power of conjure made it a vital force during the civil rights movement and is one reason that it remains important today.[19]

While Smith's theological work applies to all black Christians, some denominations have had much stronger and more visible links to conjure. The nominally Christian Spiritual churches, which seem to have originated in Chicago and spread to New Orleans by 1920, have been the most strongly influenced by hoodoo. Many of the largely independent congregations accept much of mainstream Christian doctrine, including a slightly modified version of the Apostle's Creed, renamed the Divine Spiritual Creed. At the same time, they all incorporate a variety of distinctly non-Christian beliefs, including reincarnation. One reason for the Spirituals' unorthodox views is that their denomination is a mixture of many influences, including Catholicism, Pentecostalism, and white Spiritualism. The impact of hoodoo and Voodoo, however, is evident throughout the faith. For instance, the chief feature that sets Spirituals apart from orthodox Christians is their belief in a host of spirits, who often possess members of the congregation during services. In addition, as in Voodoo, these spirits frequently carry the names of saints. While they have lost any African names they once had, their numbers include a variety of spirits who have little to do with Catholicism. The most important of these is Black Hawk, an Indian spirit also associated with hoodoo. Others include White Hawk, Father Jones, and a variety of deceased Spiritual Church leaders. Some even recognize "Mother" Marie Laveau as an early church founder.[20]

Spirituals also engage in much hoodoo-like magic.[21] For example, the church's spiritual advisers use the supernatural to heal paying clients of various ailments. In many cases the ministers discover that their clients have "unnatural" illnesses brought on by possession by evil spirits or diabolic witchcraft. Some also aid those facing legal trouble by performing rituals or making charms. Such magic is also present during regular church services. During a Spiritual "cleansing service" witnessed by this author, those being purged of evil spirits stood upon a folded white cloth. Then a church leader struck each person with white flowers that had been dipped in a basin containing salt water. (Salt had long been a protective agent in African American conjure.) Church leaders also recommended that members use floor washes to protect themselves at home and that they secretly add various spiritual products to their children's bath water to help them grow to be good people.[22]

Despite the similarities among hoodoo, Voodoo, and the Spiritual Church, many church members deny that their beliefs have anything to do with the older practices. On the contrary, Bishop Barbara Gore, the current leader of the St. Benedict Spiritual Church, argues that Voodoo was and is an evil practice. According to her, although Spiritual ministers and Voodooists use some of the same magical materials, the former use them only for good. While Voodoo calls on evil spirits, Spirituals rely only on benevolent ones. Like many modern African American magical practitioners, members of Spiritual churches have distanced themselves from terms that white society has traditionally defined as evil, including *hoodoo, Voodoo,* and *conjure.* The change in terminology, however, has not drastically altered their magical practices.[23]

The Spiritual Church was not alone in its incorporation of conjure into its religious rituals. Black Pentecostalism has also been influenced by African American magic. Pentecostalism grew out of the nineteenth-century Holiness movement. Like mainstream Protestantism, the Holiness movement stressed personal salvation through belief in Jesus Christ. Unlike other Protestants, however, followers of the Holiness movement also advocated the doctrine of sanctification, a process by which believers progressively became more holy through the development of their faith. Though initially operating within established denominations, including the Baptists and Methodists, the Holiness movement took an independent course during the 1890s in order to protest the increasing liberalism and modernism of the mainstream churches. As part of its rejection of modernism, the movement turned to older forms of rural folk Christianity, including an emphasis on emotion. One consequence was that the movement began to appeal to African Americans. In fact, the first legally chartered Holiness church in the South was a black congregation of the Church of God in Christ.[24]

From this milieu arose Pentecostalism. Among its chief early proponents was William J. Seymour, a black former Texan Baptist who first gained national attention when he presided over a series of interracial revivals at the Azusa Street Mission of Los Angeles, California. These revivals were the first stirrings of what would emerge as the Pentecostal movement. Its stress on the "baptism of the Holy Spirit," which gave believers the ability to produce signs of their sanctification, such as the gifts of tongues, healing, and prophecy, set it apart from the Holiness movement.[25]

Today, approximately 20 percent of all American Pentecostals are African American. Pentecostalism's large black membership, along with its stress on spiritual gifts, opened it to contributions from conjure. Like members of Spiritual churches and believers in hoodoo, Pentecostals often understood illness in terms of demonic influence. Similarly, ministers and other church leaders were frequently the tools by which such maladies could be cured. Sometimes they used materials associated with hoodoo, including oils. In addition, many believed that major early leaders of the Pentecostal movement possessed objects imbued with supernatural power. William J. Seymour, for instance, reputedly owned a glass eye that he used to perform magic. Another prominent leader, Charles Harrison Mason, supposedly used roots to discern God's will, a practice already familiar to those who had experience with hoodoo.[26]

Conjurelike practices continue in some churches even today. According to Jonell Smith, the pastor of one of New Orleans's Full Gospel churches uses magic in his services. Smith, a member of a Spiritual church, was upset by what she saw as hypocrisy on the part the leadership of the rival church. While Spirituals openly deal with spirits, the leaders of the Full Gospel Church condemn the practice while surreptitiously doing the same. The only major difference, according to Smith, is that while Spirituals use saint candles and herbs, the

Full Gospel Church uses birthday candles and olive oil. As Smith's experience demonstrates, hoodoo survives in the seemingly most unlikely of places.[27]

The failure of historians to recognize the significance of hoodoo has been a mistake. First, it has been a constant presence from colonial times to the present. Throughout American history conjure has been a source of healing, luck, financial success, love, and revenge for clients. Today it can also be a form of New Age spirituality or an expression of black nationalism. For practitioners, it has historically been a path to wealth and power. At present the spiritual products industry generates millions, if not billions, of dollars in revenue. In addition, hoodoo is both one of black Americans' strongest links to their African past and a powerful case study in the impact of European and Native American ideas on black culture. Finally, its social functions and pervasive impact on other aspects of African American culture cannot be ignored.

The influence of conjure on African American society and culture is difficult to underestimate, but the most compelling reason for its study is that it is an ongoing practice. A 1995 article in Florida's *St. Petersburg Times* reported that court-case spells were common in Miami, home to both hoodoo and recent imports like Santería and Haitian Vodou. Kenneth Ausly, an investigator for the district attorney of Alabama's Monroe and Conecuh counties, confirmed that many African Americans relied on court-case magic in his state as well. Similarly, many spiritual supply shops and botanicas continue to prosper.[28]

On a darker note, conjure's evil side is also alive and well. Recently, the "King of Pop," Michael Jackson, reportedly paid a Voodoo doctor $150,000 to kill twenty-five of his enemies. Among those on Jackson's magical hit list were Steven Spielberg and David Geffen. Josephine V. Gray, of Germantown, Pennsylvania, has been under investigation twice in the last eleven years for crimes connected with the death of two former husbands and a lover. Though she allegedly committed her first murder in 1974, she eluded prison for more than twenty-five years. As one of the prosecutors explained, "There is a very unusual type of witness intimidation that had occurred in this case, which was the idea that Josephine Gray had the ability to practice black magic or witchcraft or voodoo." An assistant agreed, stating, "Fear permeated this entire case." As incidents like those involving Michael Jackson and Josephine Gray demonstrate, conjure is unlikely to disappear anytime soon.[29]

Notes

PREFACE

1. Yates, "Conjures and Cures"; Clar, "Folk Belief and Custom."
2. The following contrasts between conjure and syncretic religions also hold true for other Afro-European faiths present in the United States, such as Brazilian Candomble, Trinidadian Shango, Jamaican Obeah, and the homegrown Spiritual churches.
3. For a similar argument, see Puckett, *Folk Beliefs of the Southern Negro*, 174–77.
4. Hurston, *Mules and Men*, 275.
5. See Hurston, *Mules and Men*; and Carmer, *Stars Fell on Alabama*, 215–22. For accounts of syncretic religions, see Rigaud, *Secrets of Voodoo*, 43–78; and Brandon, *Santeria from Africa to the New World*, 79–120.
6. Steiner, "Superstitions," 263; Mary Alicia Owen, *Voodoo Tales*, 174.
7. Steiner, "Superstitions," 263. An example of a mail-order curio company is the Lucky Mojo Curio Company, which can be found online at www.luckymojo.com.
8. Mary Alicia Owen, *Voodoo Tales*, 209–22; Yronwode, interview by author; Yronwode, "Hoodoo." Many African Americans view *hoodoo* and *Voodoo* as synonyms, using both to refer to magic. The distinction between the two terms is a modern one, promulgated by Voodoo believers who wish to identify their faith as a legitimate religion and by hoodoo practitioners attempting to disassociate themselves from the religious connotations and negative stereotypes attached to Voodoo.
9. Mary Alicia Owen, *Voodoo Tales*, 209–22; Peete Cross, "Witchcraft in North Carolina"; Dorson, *Negro Folktales in Michigan*, 101; Yronwode, interview by author.
10. See Herskovits, *Myth of the Negro Past*, 224–51, for the most famous author to draw this distinction.

11. Hurston, *Mules and Men,* 281.

12. Yronwode, interview by author. Since the mid-twentieth century, "psychic" fortunetellers have also entered the scene. While these practitioners fulfill the same function as traditional readers, they claim to use a special mental gift to foretell the future rather than such traditional tools as playing cards or bones.

13. Ibid.

14. Hurston, "Hoodoo in America," 320; Steiner, "Braziel Robinson."

INTRODUCTION

1. Page, *Red Rock,* 292.

2. Bruce, *Plantation Negro as a Freedman,* 115.

3. Steiner, "Observations," 177; Mary Alicia Owen, *Voodoo Tales,* 219.

4. For the most important passages addressing Dr. Moses, see Page, *Red Rock,* 60, 103, 287, 291–93, 356–58. For a similar description of conjurers, see Herron, "Conjuring and Conjure Doctors."

5. For works on the mechanics of identity construction and cultural nationalism, see Andersen, *Imagined Communities;* Hobsbawm and Ranger, *Invention of Tradition;* and Conzen et al., "Invention of Ethnicity."

6. Norris, "Negro Superstitions," 95; Izard, "Diary of a Journey," 160.

7. Douglass, *Narrative of the Life,* 41–42, 47.

8. Norris, "Negro Superstitions," 90–91. See also "Religious Life of the Negro Slave," 816–25, which mentions conjuring as an important part of blacks' religion.

9. R., L., G., and A., "Conjure Doctors in the South"; W. and C., "About the Conjuring Doctors."

10. On the development of segregation and resistance to it, see Norrell, *Reaping the Whirlwind;* and Woodward, *Strange Career of Jim Crow.*

11. For an excellent discussion of the extent to which the academic world was science-centered during the late nineteenth century, see Novick, *That Noble Dream,* 31–44.

12. For excellent examples of the strength of racial uplift ideology, see the *Southern Workman.* Founded in 1872, its early issues ceaselessly promote self-improvement of blacks and Native Americans. See also Lears, *No Place of Grace.* Lears argues that individuals turned to antimodern pursuits, such as the arts and crafts movement, Orientalism, medievalism, and religious mysticism as ways of coping with the social and cultural onslaughts of modernity. In *The Populist Response to Industrial America* Norman Pollack applied a similar argument to midwestern Populism, which he believed was a revolt against industrial capitalism.

13. For the works of two of Harris's better-known imitators, see Charles Colcock Jones Jr., *Gullah Folktales;* and Mary Alicia Owen, *Voodoo Tales.*

14. For an account of scholarly efforts to erase sectionalism, see Novick, *That Noble Dream,* 72–80.

15. See Grimm and Grimm, *Complete Fairy Tales.*

16. These international expositions were held in Paris, London, and Chicago, respectively. For the text of Owen's talk, see Mary Alicia Owen, "Among the Voodoos."

17. Bronner, *American Folklore Studies,* 1–38. See also Bronner, *Folklife Studies in the Gilded Age;*

Cocchiara, *History of Folklore in Europe;* Newell, "Myths of Voodoo Worship"; and Newell, "Reports of Voodoo Worship." Haitian Vodou, as will be explained later, was the ancestor of the Voodoo of Louisiana. I use the term *Vodou* for the religion of Haiti primarily because the more familiar spelling, *Voodoo,* has fallen from favor among practitioners. On the other hand, I retain *Voodoo* when referring to American practices because of its long-established usage and because of the ease with which readers will be able to distinguish the Haitian and American incarnations of the syncretic faiths.

18. Steiner, "Observations."

19. Folk-Lore and Ethnology, *Southern Workman* 22 (1893): 180.

20. Technically not an academic journal, the *Southern Workman* approached conjure with the same level of sophistication as the *Journal of American Folklore.* For this reason, and because the newspaper was published by an academic institution, I refer to it as a scholarly publication so far as it relates to hoodoo.

21. Bacon, "Conjuring and Conjure-Doctors." Four years before Bacon published her piece, Mary Alicia Owen's paper at the 1891 International Folk-lore Congress, "Among the Voodoos," classified Missouri Voodoo charms into "good tricks," "bad tricks," "all that pertains to the body," and "commanded things." Owen's presentation, however, was less influential than Bacon's essay.

22. Herron, "Conjuring and Conjure-Doctors," 117. See also Daniel Webster Davis, "Conjuration."

23. Not all contributors to the *Southern Workman* were necessarily black. As was common at similar institutions, many instructors at the Hampton Normal School were white. Nevertheless, authors of both races generally approached their topics with the interests of their black readers in mind.

24. Bruce, *Plantation Negro as a Freedman,* 111–25; Stoyer, *My Life in the South,* 52–59; William Wells Brown, *My Southern Home,* 68–82, quotations from 69 and 74. See also Louis Hughes, *Thirty Years a Slave,* 108.

25. Charles Colcock Jones Jr., *Gullah Folktales,* 111–13, 177–84; Mary Alicia Owen, *Voodoo Tales;* Boyle, *Devil Tales,* quotation from xi.

26. Pitkin, *Angel by Brevet,* 5–7, quotation from 7 (Pitkin's novel, though fictional, relies on factual accounts of upper-class white involvement with African American magic); Page, *Red Rock,* 60, 103, 287, 291–93, 356–58. See also Cable, *Grandissimes.*

27. Hearn, "Last of the Voudoos," 726; "Believed in North Carolina Also."

28. Cable, "Dance in Place Congo"; Cable, "Creole Slave Songs."

29. Park, "Voodooism in Tennessee"; Shepard, "Superstitions of the Negro"; Sara M. Handy, "Negro Superstitions"; Elam, "Case of Hoodoo."

30. See the unsigned editorial preface to Dana, "Voodoo," 529.

31. For an account of changing scholarly views of the southern past, see Novick, *That Noble Dream,* 72–80. The two most prominent sympathetic treatments of southern experiences during the Civil War and Reconstruction are Beard and Beard, *Rise of American Civilization;* and Dunning, *Reconstruction, Political and Economic.*

32. Puckett, *Folk Beliefs of the Southern Negro,* 1–78, 167–310, quotation from 2.

33. Ibid., 1–78.

34. Ibid., 167–310. See also C.H.W., review of *Folk Beliefs of the Southern Negro.*

35. Penkower, *Federal Writers' Project*, esp. 1–29, 238–48.

36. Kennedy, *Palmetto Country*, esp. 127–32, 163–82; Saxon, Tallant, and Dreyer, *Gumbo Ya-Ya*.

37. Grossman, *Land of Hope*.

38. Weinstein, "Radicalism in the Midst of Normalcy"; Naison, *Communists in Harlem*; Nelson, *Workers on the Waterfront*; Korstad and Lichtenstein, "Opportunities Found and Lost"; Cronon, *Black Moses*.

39. For many, whites were also important as the primary consumers of their artistic productions. In fact, many of the creations of the Harlem Renaissance represent an acceptance of the prevailing white stereotypes of blacks as primitive and exotic. For a brief synopsis of this idea, see Bone, "Negro Renaissance," 122–24.

40. Huggins, *Harlem Renaissance*, 3–12; Hutchinson, *Harlem Renaissance in Black and White*; Mishkin, *Harlem and Irish Renaissances*; Kramer and Russ, *Harlem Renaissance Re-examined*.

41. Renda, *Taking Haiti*, 10–39. For the most influential account of Haitian Vodou during this period, see Seabrook, *Magic Island*.

42. Hurston, "Hoodoo in America"; Hurston, *Mules and Men*, esp. 181–285; Hurston, *Tell My Horse*; Renda, *Taking Haiti*, 288–300.

43. Hurston, *Mules and Men*, 183.

44. Hurston, "Hoodoo in America"; Hurston, *Mules and Men*, 181–285.

45. Brown, "Hoodoo Blues." For the full text of this song and many others, see Yronwode, "Blues Lyrics and Hoodoo."

46 Yronwode, "Blues Lyrics and Hoodoo"; Clar, "Folk Belief and Custom."

47. Not surprisingly, during the twentieth century those who remembered the original Dr. Buzzard considered Robinson an imitator. Nevertheless, this second Dr. Buzzard was to outstrip his forebear in fame, which persists to this day. Thus, unless otherwise specified, I am speaking of Robinson when I refer to Dr. Buzzard hereafter (see Hyatt, *Hoodoo—Conjuration—Witchcraft—Rootwork*, iii–iv; Johnson, *Fabled Doctor Jim Jordan*; and McTeer, *Fifty Years*).

48. See also Hurston, *Moses, Man of the Mountain*; and Hurston, *Tell My Horse*, which also deal with aspects of African and African American magical beliefs.

49. Herskovits, *Myth of the Negro Past*, 235–51. Herskovits's most important opponent was Edward Franklin Frazier, who argued in *Black Bourgeoisie* that blacks had lost their culture through the process of enslavement. Herskovits, an anthropologist, so influenced succeeding generations of historians and social scientists that it is difficult to find one who would argue that African culture died during the Middle Passage. For another study of African survivals, see Georgia Writers' Project, Savannah Unit, *Drums and Shadows*.

50. Bass, "Mojo"; Lea, "Two-head Doctors." For a similar treatment, see Carmer, *Stars Fell on Alabama*, 215–22.

51. Lea, "Two-head Doctors," 236.

52. The most important exception to this general trend was the medical field's discovery of conjure as an important psychosomatic force (see, e.g., "Voodoo Kills by Despair"). Unfortunately, medicine's isolation from social science limited such articles' influence on the broader society.

53. Penkower, *Federal Writers' Project*, 181–214.

54. Dalfiume, *Desegregation of the U.S. Armed Forces;* Blum, *V Was for Victory;* Korstad and Lichtenstein, "Opportunities Found and Lost."

55. Chappell, *Inside Agitators;* Chafe, *Civilities and Civil Rights.* For overviews of the political goals of the movement, see Lawson, *Black Ballots;* and Lawson, *In Pursuit of Power.* For King's role, see Branch, *Parting the Waters.*

56. Propp, *Morphology of the Folktale;* Langston Hughes and Bontemps, *Book of Negro Folklore,* especially 103–5, 183–207. The most important exception to this rule was Norman E. Whitten's "Contemporary Patterns of Malign Occultism." Whitten's essay set the trend for later folkloric investigations of conjure by seeking to identify a peculiar logic behind African American magic.

57. Clayton, "Truth about Voodoo," 54.

58. In addition to Tivnan's "Voodoo That New Yorkers Do," another typical article on Santería is see Fred Grimm, "Ritual Sacrifices Turn Miami River Red." For a scholarly work on Santería, see Brandon, *Santeria from Africa to the New World.*

59. See Meyer Kallen, *Culture and Democracy;* Boas, *Anthropology and Modern Life;* and Mead, *Coming of Age in Samoa.*

60. See Harvey, *Condition of Postmodernity,* esp. 43. See also Schlesinger, *Disuniting of America.*

61. Melody Baker, *New Consciousness,* 15–16.

62. Faber, *New Age Thinking,* esp. 1–16; Basil, *Not Necessarily the New Age.* For the effects of cultural pluralism and postmodernism on the field of history, see Novick, *That Noble Dream,* 415–629. It should be noted that most Wiccans now recognize that their religion was founded in the twentieth century, though it drew on older practices.

63. McTeer, *Fifty Years,* 12–20, quotation from 27.

64. For works by some of the most popular proponents of Black Power, see Carmichael and Hamilton, *Black Power;* and Malcolm X with Haley, *Autobiography of Malcolm X.* See also Lawson, *In Pursuit of Power;* and Schlesinger, *Disuniting of America,* 63–71, 73–99. Black Power's drive for autonomy formed the basis of what would be known as "Afrocentrism" by the late 1980s. Afrocentrism is an intellectual movement that locates the origins of Western culture in ancient Egypt, which its proponents imagine to have been peopled by blacks. Intended as a form of mental compensation for past injustices, this expression of "multiculturalism" is simply a form of cultural chauvinism, which is often linked closely to racist ideologies, such as those propounded by the Nation of Islam.

65. Lindroth, "Images of Subversion," quotation from 185. Two of Reed's more pertinent works are *Mumbo Jumbo* and *Conjure.* See also Zamir, "Interview with Ishmael Reed."

66. See also Faith Mitchell, *Hoodoo Medicine;* and Malbrough, *Charms, Spells, and Formulas.*

67. Rhodes, "Marie Laveau, Voodoo Queen," quotation from 31.

68. Snake, *Doktor Snake's Voodoo Spellbook.* Ironically, interest in conjure has been less centered on New Orleans than in the past, with a growing number of books examining magic among the Gullah people of the South Carolina Sea Islands. McTeer's *Fifty Years as a Low Country Witch Doctor* was the most important influence on this trend. For an entertaining collection based heavily on McTeer's work, see Pinckney, *Blue Roots.*

69. See Blassingame, *Slave Community,* 40–41, 109–13; Rawick, *American Slavery,* 1:48–51; Joyner,

Down by the Riverside, 144–52; Genovese, *Roll, Jordan, Roll*, 215–24, 231, 255; Levine, *Black Culture and Black Consciousness*, 55–80; and Raboteau, *Slave Religion*, 75–87, 275–88.

70. Lest the readers dismiss my brief discussion of the racial politics as mere speculation, I must state that I have personally encountered it. For example, I once attempted to publish an essay on hoodoo. An anonymous reviewer rejected it on the grounds that it was "racially insensitive" and "insulting." On another occasion an African American author who had published works on hoodoo strongly discouraged me from writing on the subject. One of his stated reasons was that I was not black.

71. Some article-length works on hoodoo have also appeared. A few of the more notable examples are Chireau, "Conjure and Christianity"; Leone and Fry, "Conjuring in the Big House Kitchen"; Snow, "Mail Order Magic"; and David H. Brown, "Conjure/Doctors.".

72. Hyatt became interested in conjure while conducting research for his pioneering book *Folk-Lore from Adams County Illinois*, a work that he intended as a record of all aspects of folklore within a single rural county. He amassed much information dealing with magic, including hoodoo, which he later included in his book (see Hyatt, *Folk-Lore from Adams County Illinois*, esp. 455–545).

73. It should be noted that in the field of folklore Hyatt's work is well respected.

74. Smith uses the spelling *conjuror* to emphasize his interpretation.

75. See Klingelhofer, "Aspects of Early Afro-American Material Culture"; Ferguson, "Looking for the 'Afro' in Colono-Indian Pottery"; and Ferguson, "The Cross Is a Magic Sign." For other examples, see Patten, "Mankala and Minkisi"; Orser, "Archaeology of African-American Slave Religion"; and Fennell, "Conjuring Boundaries."

76. Shortly before this book went to press, another major work on conjure appeared: Yvonne Chirean's *Black Magic*. It will doubtless prove an important source for future scholars.

1. *Vodu* AND *Minkisi*

1. See Herskovits, *Myth of the Negro Past*.

2. A rare exception to this rule has been Robert Farris Thompson, whose excellent book *Flash of the Spirit* examines the links between African American art and philosophy and their counterparts among diverse African peoples. Just as important, Michael Gomez has furthered historians' understanding of the impacts of distinct African religions on different parts of the South through his book *Exchanging Our Country Marks*.

3. The word *tribe* has fallen from favor among many American historians, who prefer to use *ethnic groups* or similar terms to refer to different peoples of Africa. Ultimately, however, this practice reflects African American and American ideals of political correctness, which those who advocate them have attempted to foist on Africans, who typically prefer to continue to use the traditional *tribe*.

4. A. Gomez, *Exchanging Our Country Marks*, 38–58, 114–53, 150.

5. Ibid.

6. The term *hoodoo* had spread throughout the South by the late nineteenth or early twentieth century. For this reason, it is employed throughout this work as a synonym for conjure, though it likely originated in Louisiana. Some later authors draw a sharp distinction between the religion

of Voodoo and the magic of hoodoo. Today, this distinction does exist, but during the nineteenth century and earlier neither African Americans nor whites attempted to separate them. For an example of this error, see Turlington, *Complete Idiot's Guide® to Voodoo*, 283.

7. Pitkin, *Angel by Brevet*, 167; Porteous, "Gri-gri Case"; Puckett, *Folk Beliefs of the Southern Negro*, 19; Mary Alicia Owen, "Among the Voodoos," 241; Cappick, *Key West Story*; Lopez, "Nanigo Dance"; Cannella with Crowe, "Nañigo"; Kennedy, "Ñañigo in Florida"; Hauptmann, "Spanish Folklore from Tampa Florida"; Pinckney, *Blue Roots*, 1–18; Hyatt, *Hoodoo—Conjuration—Witchcraft—Rootwork*, 11, 17, 275, 278, 280–81, 284, 308, 310, 314, 336, 337.

8. Likewise, Missouri's *noodoo* almost certainly also derived from *Voodoo*.

9. *Zinzin*, never a common term, is virtually unknown today.

10. Ellis, "On Vōdu Worship"; Pitkin, *Angel by Brevet*, 167; Porteous, "Gri-gri Case"; Nicholas Owen, *Journal of a Slave Dealer*, 49–50; Thompson, *Flash of the Spirit*, 105, 117, 166–67; Puckett, *Folk Beliefs of the Southern Negro*, 19; Mary Alicia Owen, "Among the Voodoos," 241; Hyatt, *Hoodoo—Conjuration—Witchcraft—Rootwork*, 11, 17, 275, 278, 280–81, 284, 308, 310, 314, 336, 337; Gomez, *Exchanging Our Country Marks*, 50–56. According to Ward, *Voodoo Queen*, 11, *wanga* derives from *nganga*, a Kongolese term for a diviner.

11. Thompson, *Flash of the Spirit*, 105, 117, 166–67; Puckett, *Folk Beliefs of the Southern Negro*, 19; Hyatt, *Hoodoo—Conjuration—Witchcraft—Rootwork*, 11, 17, 275, 278, 280–81, 284, 308, 310, 314, 336, 337; Gomez, *Exchanging Our Country Marks*, 50–56. For the use of the variant *Joe Moe*, see John Daniels, interview by B.N. (NC), in Rawick, *American Slave*, 14:231. In the above case, the Joe Moe was used for a malevolent purpose.

12. Courlander, *Treasury of African Folklore*, 159–60, 187–88; Opoku, *West African Traditional Religion*, 9–10, 14–18.

13. Opoku, *West African Traditional Religion*, 9–10, 14–18; Ellis, *Tshi-Speaking Peoples*, 34–38.

14. MacGaffey, *Religion and Society in Central Africa*, 63–89.

15. Long, *Spiritual Merchants*, 3–96; Cable, *Grandissimes*, 99, 101, 135, 182, 184, 257, 272, 311, 447, 453–56, 468; Pitkin, *Angel by Brevet*, 185–213, 260–92. Voodoo queens were female priestesses, who generally presided over communal ceremonies.

16. Pitkin, *Angel by Brevet*, 195.

17. Long, *Spiritual Merchants*, 3–96; Cable, *Grandissimes*, 99, 101, 135, 182, 184, 257, 272, 311, 447, 453–56, 468; Pitkin, *Angel by Brevet*, 185–213, 260–92; Courlander, *Treasury of African Folklore*, 159–60, 187–88; Jacobs and Kaslow, *Spiritual Churches of New Orleans*, 82–92.

18. Ellis, *Yoruba-Speaking Peoples*, 34–124; Murphy, *Santería*, 7–36; Opoku, *West African Traditional Religion*, 54–90; MacGaffey, *Religion and Society in Central Africa*, 53, 59, 79; Kennedy, "Ñañigo in Florida"; Hauptmann, "Spanish Folklore from Tampa Florida"; Georgia Writers' Project, Savannah Unit, *Drums and Shadows*, 113, 125, 145, 160, 167.

19. Louisiana, for instance, had an almost equal number of blacks and whites in the decades preceding the Civil War. Whites outnumbered blacks by about 7,000 in 1860, though in preceding decades, the slight imbalance had leaned in favor of African Americans. Florida, in contrast, was sparsely populated, with the more than 77,000 white Floridians outnumbering African Americans by around 15,000. In Missouri, the imbalance was much greater, with whites outnumbering

blacks by about five to one in 1820, increasing to almost nine to one in 1860 (for more details, see Roller and Twyman, *Encyclopedia of Southern History,* s.v. "South Carolina," "Louisiana," "Florida," and "Missouri").

20. Frey and Wood, *Come Shouting to Zion,* 63–148; Asbury, *French Quarter,* 254–83; Hurston, "Hoodoo in America," 317–19; Pitkin, *Angel by Brevet,* 194–96; Cable, *Grandissimes,* 182, 184; Métraux, *Voodoo in Haiti,* 323–58; Gomez, *Exchanging Our Country Marks,* 23; Boggs, "Spanish Folklore from Tampa Florida," 1–4.

21. Frey and Wood, *Come Shouting to Zion,* 63–148; Gomez, *Exchanging Our Country Marks,* 23.

22. Ellis, *Yoruba-Speaking Peoples,* 34–124; Opoku, *West African Traditional Religion,* 54–90; MacGaffey, *Religion and Society in Central Africa,* 53, 59, 79; Kennedy, "Ñañigo in Florida"; Hauptmann, "Spanish Folklore from Tampa Florida."

23. Oliver and Fage, *Short History of Africa,* 106–9; Joseph E. Harris, *Africans and Their History,* 135–38.

24. Mary Alicia Owen, "Among the Voodoos," 232–33; Hurston, "Hoodoo in America," 357–60.

25. William Adams, interview by Sheldon F. Gauthier (Tarrant County, AL), in Rawick, *American Slave,* suppl. 2, 2:16–22; Carmer, *Stars Fell on Alabama,* 218.

26. Georgia Writers' Project, Savannah Unit, *Drums and Shadows,* 36, 42, 44, 75, 84, 93–94, 102, 125.

27. Bones were another, less common conjure material associated with the dead. For example, during the excavation of an Indian mound on Georgia's Savannah River black laborers collected the metacarpal bones from the skeletons they unearthed, believing that they would protect them from conjure (see Steiner, "Observations," 178).

28. Bendenbaugh, "Contribution from South Carolina," 46; Georgia Writers' Project, Savannah Unit, *Drums and Shadows,* 36, 42, 44, 75, 84, 93–94, 102, 125; Steiner, "Observations"; Long, *Spiritual Merchants,* 91.

29. Nicholas Owen, *Journal of a Slave Dealer,* 50–51.

30. Mary Alicia Owen, "Among the Voodoos," 232.

31. Ibid., 232–33; Mary Alicia Owen, *Voodoo Tales,* 169–89.

32. Long, *Spiritual Merchants,* 6–8; Blier, "Vodun."

33. Bibb, *Narrative of the Life,* 25–32; Ellis, *Ewe-Speaking Peoples,* 94; Ellis, *Yoruba-Speaking Peoples,* 119; Mary Alicia Owen, "Among the Voodoos," 232–33.

34. Thompson, *Flash of the Spirit,* 117–31; Thompson, *Face of the Gods,* 47–107; Steiner, "Observations"; Long, *Spiritual Merchants,* 6–8, 102; Bibb, *Narrative of the Life,* 25–32. Voodoo dolls, common in folklore but rare in practice, likewise had precedents in west-central Africa.

35. MacGaffey, *Religion and Society in Central Africa,* 162; Bacon, "Conjuring and Conjure-Doctors," 210; Hyatt, *Hoodoo—Conjuration—Witchcraft—Rootwork,* 5–6, 2618; Steiner, "Observations," 179.

36. Folk-Lore and Ethnology, *Southern Workman* 28 (1899): 314–15; Hyatt, *Hoodoo—Conjuration—Witchcraft—Rootwork,* 5–6; Ellis, *Ewe-Speaking Peoples,* 94.

37. Kingsley, *Travels in West Africa,* 470–71. For African American examples of animal infestations, see Puckett, *Folk Beliefs of the Southern Negro,* 249–55.

38. Stine, Cabak, and Groover, "Blue Beads as African-American Cultural Symbols."

39. Ferguson, "The Cross Is a Magic Sign"; Thompson, *Flash of the Spirit,* 108–16; Thompson, *Face of the Gods,* 49–50; Tallant, *Voodoo in New Orleans,* 129; Steiner, "Superstitions," 262; Gomez,

Exchanging Our Country Marks, 204–6; MacGaffey, *Religion and Society in Central Africa,* 52; Puckett, *Folk Beliefs of the Southern Negro,* 220–21, 290–91.

40. Thompson, *Flash of the Spirit,* 108–16; Thompson, *Face of the Gods,* 49–50; Gomez, *Exchanging Our Country Marks,* 204–6; MacGaffey, *Religion and Society in Central Africa,* 52; Puckett, *Folk Beliefs of the Southern Negro,* 220–21, 290–91.

41. Opoku, *West African Traditional Religion,* 148; Puckett, *Folk Beliefs of the Southern Negro,* 220.

42. Kingsley, *Travels in West Africa,* 446, 469; Opoku, *West African Traditional Religion,* 148; Georgia Writers' Project, Savannah Unit, *Drums and Shadows,* 43, 61, 200, 206; Puckett, *Folk Beliefs of the Southern Negro,* 220; Long, *Spiritual Merchants,* 15.

43. MacGaffey, *Religion and Society in Central Africa,* 160–65.

44. Opoku, *West African Traditional Religion,* 11–13, 74–91, 140–51; Parrinder, *West African Religion,* 137–71.

45. "Hags and Their Ways."

46. McTeer, *Fifty Years,* 21–30.

47. Buel, *Sunlight and Shadow,* 516–42; Pitkin, *Angel by Brevet,* 185–213, 260–92.

48. Opoku, *West African Traditional Religion,* 91–100.

49. MacGaffey, *Religion and Society in Central Africa,* 135–36.

50. Bass, "Mojo," 88–89.

51. Steiner, "Braziel Robinson."

52. These two societies eventually spread beyond the Mande, gaining a presence among many West African groups.

53. Gomez, *Exchanging Our Country Marks,* 94–102.

54. Ibid., 99–102; Murphy, *Santería,* 32–35; Kennedy, "Ñañigo in Florida"; Hauptmann, "Spanish Folklore from Tampa Florida"; Cappick, *Key West Story,* 9, 16 May 1958.

55. Gomez, *Exchanging Our Country Marks,* 99–102; Mary Alicia Owen, "Among the Voodoos," 231; Hurston, "Hoodoo in America."

56. Hurston's accounts of hoodoo initiations are the most detailed of any recorded. Unfortunately, we have only her word that they took place at all. She is known to have occasionally plagiarized other works for her publications. Recently, Carolyn Morrow Long discovered that many of the Voodoo formulas that Hurston claimed to have learned from New Orleans practitioners had probably been copied from a do-it-yourself book of spells. Nevertheless, although she may have fabricated or exaggerated the rituals that she underwent, that secret societies and their initiations did survive should not be doubted (see Carolyn Morrow Long, e-mail message to author, 5 February 2003; and Hurston, *Folklore, Memoirs, and Other Writings,* 966).

57. Hurston, "Hoodoo in America," 357–60.

58. Ibid.

59. Ibid.

60. Ibid.; Opoku, *West African Traditional Religion,* 112–23.

61. Hurston, "Hoodoo in America," 357–60; Opoku, *West African Traditional Religion,* 112–23. Other aspects of the initiation, such as the wearing of new clothes, appeared in both priestly initiations and those of men's and women's societies (see Opoku, *West African Traditional Religion,* 75–90).

62. Hurston, "Hoodoo in America," 357–60; Opoku, *West African Traditional Religion,* 112–23; Mary Alicia Owen, "Among the Voodoos," 231–38.

63. Hurston, "Hoodoo in America," 357–60; Opoku, *West African Traditional Religion,* 112–23.

64. For more on these methods of becoming a conjurer, see chapter 4.

65. Opoku, *West African Traditional Religion,* 75–90, 140–51; Parrinder, *West African Religion,* 156–17; McTeer, *Fifty Years,* 21–30; Pinckney, *Blue Roots,* 119–20; Hurston, "Hoodoo in America," 357–60, 390–91.

66. Joyner, *Down by the Riverside,* 83, 146, 284; Raboteau, *Slave Religion,* 146; Herron, "Conjuring and Conjure Doctors," 117; Puckett, *Folk Beliefs of the Southern Negro,* 214–15; Opoku, *West African Traditional Religion,* 75–90, 140–51; Parrinder, *West African Religion,* 156–71; Hurston, "Hoodoo in America," 357–60, 390–91.

67. Opoku, *West African Traditional Religion,* 144.

68. Ibid., 75–90, 140–51; Bass, "Mojo"; Parrinder, *West African Religion,* 156–71; Hyatt, *Hoodoo—Conjuration—Witchcraft—Rootwork,* 97–111; Hurston, "Hoodoo in America," 390–91.

69. Carmer, *Stars Fell on Alabama,* 218.

70. Opoku, *West African Traditional Religion,* 75–90, 140–51; Parrinder, *West African Religion,* 156–71; Blier, "Vodun," 65; Hurston, "Hoodoo in America."

2. WITCHES AND MEDICINE MEN

1. R., L., G., and A., "Conjure Doctors in the South," 30. Asbury, *French Quarter,* 254–59; Porteous, "Gri-gri Case," 61–63; Tallant, "Chronology of Voodoo"; Joyner, *Down by the Riverside,* 144.

2. On the reality of witchcraft, see Russell, *Witchcraft in the Middle Ages,* 20–23. Russell argues that while many victims of witchcraft accusations were innocent, witchcraft itself was a genuine practice, using satanic pacts and magic as a way of rejecting the dominant social order.

3. Ibid., 1–43, 232–33; Levack, *Witch-Hunt in Early Modern Europe,* 19–22. The classic witch hunters' manual is Institoris, *Malleus Maleficarum.*

4. Fischer, *Albion's Seed,* 127–30, 340–44, 526–30, 704–10.

5. Ibid., 704–10; Combs, "Sympathetic Magic in the Kentucky Mountains"; Cross, "Witchcraft in North Carolina," 236–41.

6. Cross, "Witchcraft in North Carolina," 236–41; Fischer, *Albion's Seed,* 704–10. In the Bells' case the witch hunters failed.

7. Fischer, *Albion's Seed,* 704–10; Combs, "Sympathetic Magic in the Kentucky Mountains," 328–30; Cross, "Witchcraft in North Carolina," 236–41; Hand, *Popular Beliefs and Superstitions,* 121–36.

8. Parrinder, *West African Religion,* 135–36, 165–68; Hurston, "Hoodoo in America," 390–91; Hyatt, *Hoodoo—Conjuration—Witchcraft—Rootwork,* 97–111; Gomez, *Exchanging Our Country Marks,* 94–102; Kennedy, "Ñañigo in Florida"; Mary Alicia Owen, "Among the Voodoos," 231.

9. Parrinder, *West African Religion,* 135–36, 165–69; Steiner, "Braziel Robinson," 226–27; Hand, *Popular Beliefs and Superstitions,* 121; Tallant, *Voodoo in New Orleans,* 88–97; Cross, "Witchcraft in North Carolina," 236–41; Carmer, *Stars Fell on Alabama,* 122–25.

10. Thomas, *Religion and the Decline of Magic,* 212–22, 231–52; Combs, "Sympathetic Magic in

the Kentucky Mountains," 330; Hand, *Popular Beliefs and Superstitions*, 155–82; Long, *Spiritual Merchants*, 74, 230; Gainer, *Witches, Ghosts, and Signs*, 112–20, 139–42.

11. Dobbs, *Foundations of Newton's Alchemy;* Thomas, *Religion and the Decline of Magic*, 222–31.

12. Thomas, *Religion and the Decline of Magic*, 222–31. See also *The Complete Book of Fortune* for some examples of European fortunetelling practices.

13. Thomas, *Religion and the Decline of Magic*, 177–222; Tallant, "Chronology of Voodoo," 245–54; Reiss, *Medicine in Colonial America*, 183–232; Keeney, "Unless Powerful Sick"; Moss, *Southern Folk Medicine;* Hohman, *Pow-Wows, or Long Lost Friend*, 26; Conway, *Magic of Herbs*, 27–30. For a book of magical cures extant during the early colonial period, see Best and Brightman, *Book of Secrets*.

14. Though authors have traditionally portrayed Tituba as black, she was more likely a South American Indian or mixed Native American and black (see Breslaw, "Tituba's Confession"; and McMillan, "Black Magic").

15. Warner, *Studies in the South and West,* 64–74, quotation from 68–69.

16. McMillan, "Black Magic"; Hyatt, *Hoodoo—Conjuration—Witchcraft—Rootwork,* 5–6.

17. Chireau, "Conjure and Christianity," 235; Perdue, Barden, and Phillips, *Weevils in the Wheat,* 11; Fry, *Night Riders in Black Folk History,* 59–81; Hyatt, *Hoodoo—Conjuration—Witchcraft—Rootwork,* iii–iv; Cable, *Grandissimes,* 147–56; Long, *Spiritual Merchants,* 16.

18. Cable, *Grandissimes,* 182; Pitkin, *Angel by Brevet,* 185–213, 260–92; Jacobs and Kaslow, *Spiritual Churches of New Orleans,* 82–92; Hauptmann, "Spanish Folklore from Tampa Florida"; Long, *Spiritual Merchants,* 50–51; Hurston, *Tell My Horse,* 116. In Haitian Vodou, Damballah Ouedo, identical to Louisiana's Monsieur Danny, was the equivalent of St. Patrick owing to the saint's association with serpents in Catholic iconography. St. Michael, frequently shown defeating a serpentine devil in religious art, came to be identified with Monsieur Danny in a similar manner. Satan, to whom whites often attributed all conjure, ranked alongside the saints in the Latin zone. For example, Nañigo's Elegba, the trickster god, was identical to the devil, according to at least one observer. The same may have occasionally been true for Papa Lébat, who was also sometimes regarded as an evil god.

19. Adams, interview, in Rawick, *American Slave,* suppl. 2, 2:16–22. See also Theophus H. Smith, *Conjuring Culture.*

20. Pennethorne Hughes, *Witchcraft,* 154, 165; Levack, *Witch-Hunt in Early Modern Europe,* 33; Waite, *Book of Ceremonial Magic,* 236–96; Long, *Spiritual Merchants,* 74, 121, 230; Moss, *Southern Folk Medicine,* 153–54; Hyatt, *Hoodoo—Conjuration—Witchcraft—Rootwork,* 11, 17, 275, 278, 280–81, 284, 308, 310, 314, 336, 337; Whitney and Bullock, *Folk-Lore from Maryland,* 81–83; S., in "Letter from Hampton Graduates," 28.

21. Warner, *Studies in the South and West,* 64–74. See also Thompson, *Face of the Gods,* for a discussion of African-style altars.

22. Cable, *Grandissimes,* 100–101; Pitkin, *Angel by Brevet,* 193; Hyatt, *Hoodoo—Conjuration—Witchcraft—Rootwork,* 797–862; Dues, *Catholic Customs and Traditions,* 186–88.

23. Warner, *Studies in the South and West,* 64–74; Pitkin, *Angel by Brevet,* 185–210.

24. Hyatt, *Hoodoo—Conjuration—Witchcraft—Rootwork,* 880–88, quotation from 880.

25. Hyatt, *Hoodoo—Conjuration—Witchcraft—Rootwork,* 872, 877–88; Farmer, *Oxford Dictionary*

of Saints, s.v. "Rita of Cascia." Nine was a popular number in hoodoo, especially in the Louisiana area (see, e.g., Hurston's initiation at the hands of Samuel Thompson, in which the number recurs frequently: "Hoodoo in America," 357–60).

26. Hurston, *Mules and Men,* 280.

27. Adams, interview, in Rawick, *American Slave,* suppl. 2, 2:16–19. For some of the following examples, I rely on Hyatt's *Hoodoo—Conjuration—Witchcraft—Rootwork* because of the lack of nineteenth-century sources detailing the passages tied to particular results.

28. Hyatt, *Hoodoo—Conjuration—Witchcraft—Rootwork,* 523, 673. See also Theophus H. Smith, *Conjuring Culture,* esp. 3–15. Smith argues that African Americans chose their verses based on the genre of the particular book. For instance, Exodus was used for "conjuring-God-for-freedom," while the Gospels were more useful for "curing violence."

29. Scot, *Discoverie of Witchcraft,* 227, 230.

30. "Religious Life of the Negro Slave," 822; Lucy Kimball, interview by Francois Ludgere Diard (Mobile, AL), 7 May 1937, in Rawick, *American Slave,* suppl. 1, 1:230; Opie and Tatem, *Dictionary of Superstitions,* 193–94.

31. Fennell, "Conjuring Boundaries," 297–98, 300–301.

32. Hurston, *Mules and Men,* 279; Hyatt, *Hoodoo—Conjuration—Witchcraft—Rootwork,* 440–41, 553–54; Weyer, *Witches, Devils, and Doctors,* 424; Mary Alicia Owen, *Voodoo Tales,* 113; Grieve, *Modern Herbal,* 749–50.

33. Carrie Pollard, interview by Ruby Pickens Tartt (Livingston, AL), 23 May 1937, in Rawick, *American Slave,* 6, pt. 1:319; *Complete Book of Fortune,* 13–57, 250–68; *Aunt Sally's Policy Players' Dream Book,* 52–61; M. P. Handy, "Witchcraft among the Negroes," 666; Hyatt, *Folk-Lore from Adams County Illinois,* 488–98; Waring, *Dictionary of Omens and Superstitions,* s.v. "Evil Eye"; Sara M. Handy, "Negro Superstitions," 739.

34. Nash, *Red, White, and Black,* 174–75, 303–8; Saxon, Tallant, and Dreyer, *Gumbo Ya-Ya,* 159–60.

35. Puckett, *Folk Beliefs of the Southern Negro,* 206.

36. Ibid.; Moss, *Southern Folk Medicine,* 152–62; Hand, *Popular Beliefs and Superstitions,* 113, 151, 155–57; Hyatt, *Hoodoo—Conjuration—Witchcraft—Rootwork,* iii–iv; Chireau, "Conjure and Christianity"; Long, *Spiritual Merchants,* 16; Cable, *Grandissimes,* 147–56.

37. Nash, *Red, White, and Black,* 170–71, 308–14; Hudson, *Southeastern Indians,* 465–67.

38. McReynolds, *Seminoles,* 23, 48, 179, 185, 263, 302–12; Hudson, *Southeastern Indians,* 465–67; Kennedy, *Palmetto Country,* 131–33.

39. Benson, *Life among the Choctaw Indians,* 34.

40. Ibid.; Hudson, *Southeastern Indians,* 457, 461, 465–66, 469.

41. Bibb, *Narrative of the Life,* 150–53, quotation from 153; Hudson, *Southeastern Indians,* 457, 461, 465–66, 469.

42. Mooney, "Cherokee Theory and Practice," 44. So great was Native Americans' reputation for medicinal lore that *Indian doctor* was a term used by many whites to designate all practitioners of herbalism. Dr. Jean Bayou, a nineteenth-century Voodoo conjurer, was sometimes known as one. The title was likely inspired, at least in part, by Peter Smith's herbal manual, *The Indian Doctor's Dispensatory* (see Long, *Spiritual Merchants,* 44–45).

43. Joseph William Carter, interview by Launa Creel (Vanderburgh County, IN), in Rawick, *American Slave*, 6, pt. 2:47.

44. Mary Alicia Owen, *Voodoo Tales,* 3, 6, 8; Mary Alicia Owen, "Among the Voodoos," 241; Berry, *Spirit of Black Hawk,* 97–101.

45. Hudson, *Southeastern Indians,* 127–32, 169–73; Carmody and Carmody, *Native American Religions,* 15–40; Hultkrantz, *Belief and Worship,* 91–114. Although the Cherokee were but one of the many peoples who encountered African Americans, their cosmology was typical of the southeastern religious beliefs. Moreover, during the nineteenth century significant numbers of Cherokees had lived in a majority of the southern states, including Tennessee, Alabama, Georgia, Kentucky, Virginia, North Carolina, South Carolina, West Virginia, Arkansas, Texas, and Oklahoma. A few escaped removal to the Indian Territory by fleeing to Mexico, where their descendants still dwell. Others managed to remain in the Southeast (Mooney, *Myths of the Cherokee,* 14–181).

46. Mooney, *Myths of the Cherokee,* 14–181; Hudson, *Southeastern Indians,* 127–32, 169–73; Carmody and Carmody, *Native American Religions,* 15–40; Hultkrantz, *Belief and Worship,* 91–114.

47. Ibid.

48. Hudson, *Southeastern Indians,* 131–32, 136–39, 165–68; Mooney, *Myths of the Cherokee,* 295–96; Lankford, *Native American Legends,* 102–5.

49. Hudson, *Southeastern Indians,* 131–32, 136–39, 165–68; Mooney, *Myths of the Cherokee,* 295–96; Mary Alicia Owen, "Among the Voodoos," 236–37; Lankford, *Native American Legends,* 102–5.

50. Hudson, *Southeastern Indians,* 174–83, 336–65; Mooney, *Myths of the Cherokee,* 303–7; Carmody and Carmody, *Native American Religions,* 58–31; Hultkrantz, *Religions of the American Indians,* 116–28. There were also other magical specialists, the most notable being weather specialists, who purported to bring rain as needed (see Hudson, *Southeastern Indians,* 337–38).

51. Hudson, *Southeastern Indians,* 337–40, 362–63.

52. Ibid., 344; Hultkrantz, *Religions of the American Indians,* 131–32; Opoku, *West African Traditional Religion,* 91–100; MacGaffey, *Religion and Society in Central Africa,* 135–36; Bass, "Mojo," 88–89; Steiner, "Braziel Robinson."

53. Mooney, "Cherokee Theory and Practice," 46; Vogel, *American Indian Medicine,* 15–17; Hudson, *Southeastern Indians,* 172, 360. Sometimes animal ghosts would take up residence in those who angered them, creating similar ailments.

54. Hudson, *Southeastern Indians,* 244, 247, 252, 370, 489; Hultkrantz, *Religions of the American Indians,* 66–83.

55. Steiner, "Observations," 177.

56. Steiner, "Superstitions," 269; Steiner, "Observations," 179; Vogel, *American Indian Medicine,* 224–25, 236; Bergen, *Animal and Plant Lore,* 78; Hamel and Chiltoskey, *Cherokee Plants and Their Uses,* 23; Foster and Duke, *Field Guide to Medicinal Plants and Herbs,* 54–56, 155, 244.

57. Hurston, "Uncle Monday," 863–65; Mary Alicia Owen, "Among the Voodoos," 246–48; Parrinder, *West African Religion,* 11.

58. Hudson, *Southeastern Indians,* 166–69, quotation from 167.

59. Mary Alicia Owen, "Among the Voodoos," 246–48; Hudson, *Southeastern Indians,* 166–69; Hultkrantz, *Religions of the American Indians,* 60–62; Howard with Lena, *Oklahoma Seminoles,*

88–90. Despite the similarities between African American conjure stones and Native American magical crystals, we cannot wholly reject the possibility that the stones originated in Africa. Stones sacred to specific gods did exist in parts of West Africa, including the kingdom of Dahomey. Nevertheless, because these stones did not appear outside of the Latin zone, they probably were not African imports. If they had been, one would expect to find them throughout the South or at least throughout the Latin-settled areas. Likewise, Africans and African Americans in many parts of the South sometimes incorporated stones and crystals into charms, but their powers were a far cry from the might attributed to the conjure stones of Missouri or Uncle Monday's singing stone. Moreover, there is little evidence of conjure stones' existence in New Orleans, the area most strongly linked to the Caribbean, where such African beliefs might have been expected to survive (see Galke, "Did the Gods of Africa Die?").

60. For a discussion of this process, see Gomez, *Exchanging Our Country Marks*, 1–16.

61. Pinckney, *Blue Roots,* 6; Wilkie, "Magic and Empowerment on the Plantation"; Puckett, *Folk Beliefs of the Southern Negro,* 315.

62. Hyatt, *Hoodoo—Conjuration—Witchcraft—Rootwork,* 862–88, quotation from 863; Métraux, *Voodoo in Haiti,* 274, 277, 327; Hurston, *Mules and Men,* 279–80; Tallant, *Voodoo in New Orleans,* 204; Berry, *Spirit of Black Hawk,* 25–52; Jacobs and Kaslow, *Spiritual Churches of New Orleans,* 136–47; Long, *Spiritual Merchants,* 54.

63. Berry, *Spirit of Black Hawk,* 25–52.

3. THE CONJURERS' WORLD

1. Taylor, "Hoodoo Doctor," 77–80, quotation from 80.
2. Ibid., 77–80.
3. Ibid.
4. Leone and Fry, "Conjuring in the Big House Kitchen," 383; Breslaw, "Tituba's Confession"; "Negro Cesar's Cure for Poison," quotation from 103.
5. For a later instance in which *poison* specifically denotes magical influence, see R., L., G., and A., "Conjure Doctors in the South," 30.
6. Sam Jordan, interview by J. S. Thomas (Oklahoma City, OK), 7 June 1937, in Baker and Baker, *WPA Oklahoma Slave Narratives,* 234–35.
7. Domenech, *Missionary Adventures in Texas and Mexico,* 303–8.
8. R., L., G., and A., "Conjure Doctors in the South," 30.
9. Bruce, *Plantation Negro as a Freedman,* 120–21; Sparkman, "The Negro," quoted in Joyner, *Down by the Riverside,* 144.
10. Hyatt, *Hoodoo—Conjuration—Witchcraft—Rootwork,* ii–iii.
11. Ibid.; Catterall, *Judicial Cases,* 2:413–14. Posey eventually persuaded another slave, named Appling, to murder his wife. After Appling succeeded in drowning the hapless woman, Posey murdered him to hide the crime. Eventually Posey was convicted of both killings.
12. Wyatt-Brown, *Southern Honor,* 313, 315–16, 424–25; Pitkin, and *Angel by Brevet.* For further examples, see Tallant, *Voodoo in New Orleans;* and Marie B. Williams, "Night with the Voudous," 404.

13. Gainer, *Witches, Ghosts, and Signs*, 135–77; Peterson, "Witch of Franklin"; Hyatt, *Hoodoo—Conjuration—Witchcraft—Rootwork*, iii–iv.

14. Deuteronomy 18:10–11.

15. William Wells Brown, *My Southern Home*, 68; Livermore, *Story of My Life*, 254–58.

16. Raboteau, *Slave Religion*, 231–39.

17. Bruce, *Plantation Negro as a Freedman*, 115; S., in "Letters from Hampton Graduates."

18. Bacon, "Conjuring and Conjure-Doctors," 210; R., L., G., and A., "Conjure Doctors in the South," 30.

19. Steiner, "Observations," 179.

20. Hyatt, *Hoodoo—Conjuration—Witchcraft—Rootwork*, 5–6, 2618. See also Hand, "Plugging, Nailing, Wedging."

21. Irene Poole, "Hush Water for Talkative Women," interview by Susie R. O'Brien (Uniontown, AL), 10 June 1937, in Rawick, *American Slave*, 6, pt. 1:320–22; "Some Conjure Doctors We Have Heard Of."

22. A variety of methods existed to prevent being conjured. Keeping frizzly chickens in one's yard, wearing silver dimes around one's ankles, and carrying a bone from a black cat were but a few. Despite purportedly adverting conjure, these practices help illustrate its negative power. Only more magic could thwart evil conjure (see Puckett, *Folk Beliefs of the Southern Negro*, 287–91).

23. When operating to remove spells, these sorcerers were often called "healers," "conjure doctors," "hoodoo doctors," or similar appellations, referring to their benevolent actions.

24. R., L., G., and A., "Conjure Doctors in the South," 30; Hyatt, *Hoodoo—Conjuration—Witchcraft—Rootwork*, 332; Bacon, "Conjuring and Conjure-Doctors," 210–11.

25. Anthropologists have historically used the term *Voodoo death* to refer to curses in general. Therefore, they have viewed African American conjure as but one manifestation of a widespread phenomenon (Cannon, "Voodoo Death").

26. Eastwell, "Voodoo Death"; Colligan, "Extreme Psychic Trauma"; Marvin Harris, "Death by Voodoo."

27. Bruce, *Plantation Negro as a Freedman*, 118.

28. Snow, "Sorcerers, Saints, and Charlatans," 93; Jordan, "Voodoo Medicine." See also Moerman, "Anthropology of Symbolic Healing."

29. Adams, interview, in Rawick, *American Slave*, suppl. 2, 2:20.

30. Faith Mitchell, *Hoodoo Medicine*, 41–100; Savitt, *Medicine and Slavery*, 149–84; Harriet Barrett, interview by B. E. Davis (Palestine County, TX), in Rawick, *American Slave*, suppl. 2, 2:201; Albert L. Robinson (Conecuh County, AL), June 1937, in ibid., suppl. 1, 1:330–31. It should be noted that much of the medicine practiced by white doctors was likewise based on the use of herbs and other naturally occurring substances.

31. Hyatt, *Hoodoo—Conjuration—Witchcraft—Rootwork*, 332; Bacon, "Conjuring and Conjure-Doctors," 210. For European parallels, see Thomas, *Religion and the Decline of Magic*, 216–22.

32. Hyatt, *Hoodoo—Conjuration—Witchcraft—Rootwork*, 4–6, 332; Bacon, "Conjuring and Conjure-Doctors," 210.

33. Bibb, *Narrative of the Life*, 26–27, quotation from 26.

34. Douglass, *Narrative of the Life*, 41–42.

35. John Barker, interview by Florence Angermiller (Kinney County, TX), 12 September 1937, in Rawick, *American Slave*, suppl. 2, 2:166. Barker failed to describe these apparently supernatural beasts.

36. Poole, interview, in Rawick, *American Slave*, 6:320–22.

37. Hoodoo doctors, like lawyers, rarely concerned themselves with the guilt or innocence of clients.

38. Hyatt, *Hoodoo—Conjuration—Witchcraft—Rootwork*, 1423–49, 3633–34; Pinckney, *Blue Roots*, 101–20. For a historian who recognized the power of conjure in black lives, see Robin D. G. Kelley, "We Are Not What We Seem," 88–89.

39. Wilkie, "Magic and Empowerment on the Plantation," 136–46.

40. Puckett, *Folk Beliefs of the Southern Negro*, 207, 282–87; Sara M. Handy, "Negro Superstitions," 737–38; William Wells Brown, *Narrative of the Life*, 91–92; William Wells Brown, *My Southern Home*, 68–82; Hyatt, *Hoodoo—Conjuration—Witchcraft—Rootwork*, 667.

41. Puckett, *Folk Beliefs of the Southern Negro*, 207, 282–87; Sara M. Handy, "Negro Superstitions," 737–38; William Wells Brown, *Narrative of the Life*, 91–92; Henry F. Pyles, interview by Robert Vinson Lackey (Tulsa, OK), Spring 1937, in Baker and Baker, *WPA Oklahoma Slave Narratives*, 328–29; Hyatt, *Hoodoo—Conjuration—Witchcraft—Rootwork*, 667.

42. William Wells Brown, *My Southern Home*, 68–82, quotation from 70.

43. Bruce, *Plantation Negro as a Freedman*, 111–25.

44. Bibb, *Narrative of the Life*, 25–32; Douglass, *Narrative of the Life*, 41–47, quotation from 43.

45. William Wells Brown, *Narrative of the Life*, 90–92; William Wells Brown, *My Southern Home*.

46. William Wells Brown, *Narrative of the Life*, 91; Smalley, "Sugar-Making in Louisiana," 112; R., L., G., and A, "Conjure Doctors in the South," 30; W. and C., "About the Conjuring Doctors," 38; Hearn, "Last of the Voudoos."

47. Roller and Twyman, *Encyclopedia of Southern History*, s.v. "Tenant Farming"; Hearn, "Last of the Voudoos"; Wolf, "Aunt Caroline Dye."

48. Taylor, "Hoodoo Doctor." Unfortunately for historians, Taylor did not mention whether the hoodooist held an elected office or an informal position of political leadership, analogous to that of a party boss.

49. Mulira, "Case of Voodoo in New Orleans," 37; Suttles, "African Religious Survivals"; Nat Turner, *The Confessions of Nat Turner, the Leader of the Late Insurrections in Southampton, Va.*, in Andrews and Gates, *Slave Narratives*, 251.

50. Long, *Spiritual Merchants*, 45–52; Tallant, *Voodoo in New Orleans*, 51–151; Saxon, *Fabulous New Orleans*, 237–46.

51. "Death of Marie Laveau."

52. Long, *Spiritual Merchants*, 45–52; Tallant, *Voodoo in New Orleans*, 51–151; Saxon, *Fabulous New Orleans*, 237–46.

53. Long, *Spiritual Merchants*, 45–52; Tallant, *Voodoo in New Orleans*, 51–151; Saxon, *Fabulous New Orleans*, 237–46; Gandolfo, *Marie Laveau of New Orleans*, 16; Gandolfo, *Voodoo Vé-Vé's and Talismans*, 16.

54. Carmer, *Stars Fell on Alabama*, 122–25; Dorson, *American Negro Folklore*, 141–42.

55. Charles Colcock Jones Jr., *Gullah Folktales*, 111–13; Mary Alicia Owen, *Voodoo Tales*, 102–19.

56. According to Hyatt, *Hoodoo—Conjuration—Witchcraft—Rootwork,* 923, *zippy* means "lively" and "smart." *Uncle* and *Aunt* have long been terms of respect in African American culture.

4. THE CONJURERS THEMSELVES

1. For purposes of analysis, *religion* refers to an aspect of spirituality that includes worship of divine beings. Thus, religion is god focused. In contrast, *magic, conjure,* and related terms are human focused, designating those elements of spirituality aimed at changing human circumstances by influencing divine or supernatural forces.
2. Long, *Spiritual Merchants,* 40–51; Tallant, *Voodoo in New Orleans,* 3–51.
3. See Moreau de Saint-Méry, *Description topographique.*
4. Long, *Spiritual Merchants,* 40–51; Cable, "Creole Slave Songs," 815–21; Tallant, *Voodoo in New Orleans,* 3–51. More recent scholars have questioned the sexual focus of the St. John's Eve dances.
5. Long, *Spiritual Merchants,* 40–51; Buel, *Sunlight and Shadow,* 516–42. See also Touchstone, "Voodoo in New Orleans," which argues that the dances had become a form of pseudo-Voodoo aimed at making money off whites by the late 1800s.
6. Warner, *Studies in the South and West,* 64–69, quotation from 69.
7. Ibid., 64–74.
8. Mary Alicia Owen, "Among the Voodoos," 236–41. Unfortunately, Owen is one of only a handful of sources on Missouri Voodoo, and her accounts cannot be fully verified.
9. In Cuba, *ñañigo* was a term for a secret society. In the popular mind, and sometimes in reality, such societies were deeply involved in the Cuban underworld, making them widely feared as a criminal force. In *Palmetto Country* Stetson Kennedy defined Nañigo as only the most elite cult of the broader *brujería* faith. Kennedy's formulation more closely replicated the Cuban relationship of a ñañigo to Santería and related Cuban syncretic religions than those of other authors. Nevertheless, I have followed the practice of most early-twentieth-century authors (including Kennedy in another work) in using *Nañigo* to represent the entire faith (see Kennedy, *Palmetto Country,* 175–79; and Murphy, *Santería,* 32–34).
10. Boggs, "Spanish Folklore from Tampa Florida," 1–12; Kennedy, "Ñañigo in Florida"; Hauptmann, "Spanish Folklore from Tampa Florida."
11. Lopez, "Nanigo Dance," 2–3; Boggs, "Spanish Folklore from Tampa Florida," 1–12; Kennedy, "Ñañigo in Florida."
12. Cannella with Crowe, "Nañigo," 1–3; Boggs, "Spanish Folklore from Tampa Florida," 1–12; Kennedy, "Ñañigo in Florida." These identifications of the attributes of Yemaya and Elegba are suspect and do not match those for the same gods in Santería.
13. Cappick, *Key West Story,* 9, 16 May 1958. Obeah is a Bahamian syncretic religion similar to Vodou and Santería.
14. Ibid.
15. Georgia Writers' Project, Savannah Unit, *Drums and Shadows,* 113, 125, 131; Joyner, *Down by the Riverside,* 144–50; Botkin, *Lay My Burden Down,* quotation from 39.

16. Pitkin, *Angel by Brevet,* 185–213, 260–92; Cable, *Grandissimes,* 99–101, 135, 182–84, 257, 272, 311, 447; Mary Alicia Owen, "Among the Voodoos," 241–42.

17. Adams, interview, in Rawick, *American Slave,* suppl. 2, 2:16–22.

18. "Some Conjure Doctors We Have Heard Of," 37.

19. This concept of God is the same in Haitian Vodou (see Métraux, *Voodoo in Haiti,* 83–84).

20. "Some Conjure Doctors We Have Heard Of"; W. and C., "About the Conjuring Doctors"; Cable, *Grandissimes,* 453–56, 468; Mary Alicia Owen, "Among the Voodoos," 232–33.

21. Mary Alicia Owen, "Among the Voodoos," 232–33.

22. Joyner, *Down by the Riverside,* 144–50; Adams, interview, in Rawick, *American Slave,* suppl. 2, 2:16–22; "Some Conjure Doctors We Have Heard Of," 38; Herron, "Conjuring and Conjure Doctors," 117; Hurston, "Hoodoo in America," 390–91; Mary Alicia Owen, "Among the Voodoos," 231–35. See also Livermore, *Story of My Life,* 254–55, which describes an exhorter/conjurer who prayed to both God and the devil during a church service.

23. For more on the methods of gaining supernatural powers, see chapter 1.

24. Adams, interview, in Rawick, *American Slave,* suppl. 2, 2:17.

25. Ibid.

26. Joyner, *Down by the Riverside,* 83, 146, 284; Raboteau, *Slave Religion,* 146; Herron, "Conjuring and Conjure Doctors," 117; Theophus H. Smith, *Conjuring Culture,* 162–74; Sojourner Truth, *Narrative of Sojourner Truth, a Northern Slave, Emancipated from Bodily Servitude by the State of New York, in 1828,* in Andrews and Gates, *Slave Narratives,* 567–676; Puckett, *Folk Beliefs of the Southern Negro,* 214–15.

27. Bass, "Mojo," 83; Steiner, "Observations," 178–79.

28. Bass, "Mojo," 83.

29. Hearn, "Last of the Voudoos"; Georgia Writer's Project, Savannah Unit, *Drums and Shadows,* 7, 24, 28, 67–69, 121, 168–69, 177.

30. Tallant, *Voodoo in New Orleans,* 33–39; Hurston, "Hoodoo in America," 326–62; McTeer, *Fifty Years,* 21–30; Pinckney, *Blue Roots,* 119–20.

31. Hurston, "Hoodoo in America," 390–91, quotation from 390.

32. Hyatt, *Hoodoo—Conjuration—Witchcraft—Rootwork,* 97–111.

33. Hurston, "Hoodoo in America." For an example of one of the more elaborate initiation ceremonies undergone by Hurston, see chapter 1.

34. Mary Alicia Owen, "Among the Voodoos," 231–32.

35. McNeil, *Ghost Stories from the American South,* 115–19; Carmer, *Stars Fell on Alabama,* 193, 215–18. Since the woman Carmer met was evidently mature and possibly past middle age, this initiation likely happened during the nineteenth century. In addition, Carter's initiation, which took place in southeastern Alabama, may have been influenced by the Voodoo or Nañigo practiced in the nearby Latin-settled states of Louisiana and Florida or even in the territory around Mobile, Alabama, a former French settlement.

36. Carmer, *Stars Fell on Alabama,* 193, 215–18.

37. Mary Alicia Owen, "Among the Voodoos," 230–38.

38. Hurston, "Hoodoo in America," 380–82; Hurston, *Mules and Men,* 213–21.

39. Carmer, *Stars Fell on Alabama,* 218.

40. Ibid., 217–18; Adams, interview, in Rawick, *American Slave*, suppl. 2, 2:17.

41. For an exhaustive treatment of patterns in conjure, see Bell, "Pattern, Structure, and Logic." See also Whitten, "Contemporary Patterns of Malign Occultism."

42. Bass, "Mojo," 87–88, quotation from 88. For more on Divinity, see Bass, "Little Man."

43. Pyles, interview, in Baker and Baker, *WPA Oklahoma Slave Narratives*, 328–29; Mary Alicia Owen, "Among the Voodoos," 233.

44. Mary Alicia Owen, "Among the Voodoos," 233; Pinckney, *Blue Roots*, 54–55, 95, 102, 107, 155; Samuel Simeon Andrews, interview by Rachel A. Austin (Jacksonville, FL), 27 October 1936, in Rawick, *American Slave*, 17:10–20; Hyatt, *Hoodoo—Conjuration—Witchcraft—Rootwork*, 284–86.

45. Ann Parker, interview by Mary A. Hicks (Raleigh, NC), 27 October 1936, in Rawick, *American Slave*, 15:157; William Wells Brown, *My Southern Home*, 70; Breslaw, "Tituba's Confession"; Bibb, *Narrative of the Life*, 26–27; Douglass, *Narrative of the Life*, 41–42.

46. For the primary influence behind my understanding of the process of curing conjure, see Bacon, "Conjuring and Conjure-Doctors," 210–11.

47. Bacon, "Conjuring and Conjure-Doctors," 210–11.

48. Daniel Webster Davis, "Conjuration." In this account Davis altered the order of the steps, stating that the doctor offered to turn back the spell immediately after finding the buried charm, before completing the cure.

49. Hyatt, *Hoodoo—Conjuration—Witchcraft—Rootwork*, 923–24; Herron, "Conjuring and Conjure Doctors," 251–52.

50. For examples of contagious magic, see Hurston, *Mules and Men*, 274–75. Hurston also provides an example, supposedly utilized by Marie Laveau herself, in "Hoodoo in America," 332–33. The famed Voodoo dolls of popular conceptions of African American sorcery were yet another form of contagious magic. I do not give them further attention for the simple fact that they were rare in the American South.

51. Steiner, "Observations," 177–80; M. P. Handy, "Witchcraft among the Negroes," 666.

52. Steiner, "Observations," 177–80. For a more complete explanation of the principles of sympathy and contagion, see Frazer, *Golden Bough*, 12–52.

53. Hyatt, *Hoodoo—Conjuration—Witchcraft—Rootwork*, 926–28.

54. Ibid.

55. Ibid.

56. For thorough investigations of John the Conqueror and its origins, see Long, "John the Conqueror"; Tyler, "Elusive History"; and Long, *Spiritual Merchants*, 221–46. According to Long, the plant originally gained its importance as a love charm owing to its phallic appearance. Whatever its original functions, its uses had grown more diverse by the late nineteenth century.

57. Folk-Lore and Ethnology, *Southern Workman* 28 (1899): 112.

58. Haskell, "Sacrificial Offerings," 267; Hyatt, *Hoodoo—Conjuration—Witchcraft—Rootwork*, 923–29; Folk-Lore and Ethnology, *Southern Workman* 28 (1899): 112; Andrews, interview, in Rawick, *American Slave*, 17:10–20; Mary Alicia Owen, *Voodoo Tales*, 113, 174.

59. Haskell, "Sacrificial Offerings," 267; Mary Alicia Owen, "Among the Voodoos," 231; Folk-Lore and Ethnology, *Southern Workman* 28 (1899): 315.

60. Folk-Lore and Ethnology, *Southern Workman* 28 (1899): 112 and 24 (1893): 155; Hurston, *Mules and Men*, 220–21; Tallant, *Voodoo in New Orleans*, 24–32; Hearn, "New Orleans Superstitions"; M. P. Handy, "Witchcraft among the Negroes," 666–67.

61. Cornelia Robinson, interview by Preston Klein (Opelika, AL), 1937, in Rawick, *American Slave*, 6, pt. 1:331.

62. Silvia Witherspoon, "Foots Gets Tired from Choppin' Cotton," interview by Susie R. O'Brien and John Morgan Smith (AL), 25 June 1937, in ibid., 431.

63. Puckett, *Folk Beliefs of the Southern Negro*, 207–10.

64. Smiley, "Folk-lore," 365.

65. Ibid.

66. Daniel Webster Davis, "Conjuration," 252.

67. Long, *Spiritual Merchants*, 38–58; Hearn, "Last of the Voudoos."

68. Livermore, *Story of My Life*, 254–58; Mary Alicia Owen, "Among the Voodoos," 240, 242.

69. Long, *Spiritual Merchants*, 38–58; Livermore, *Story of My Life*, 254–58; Mary Alicia Owen, "Among the Voodoos"; Gomez, *Exchanging Our Country Marks*, 284–85; R., L., G., and A., "Conjure Doctors in the South," 30; Hearn, "Last of the Voudoos"; Carmer, *Stars Fell on Alabama*, 215–22; Tallant, *Voodoo in New Orleans*, 9–47; Daniel Webster Davis, "Conjuration," 251.

70. McTeer, *Fifty Years*, 21–30; Tallant, *Voodoo in New Orleans*; Hyatt, *Hoodoo—Conjuration—Witchcraft—Rootwork*, 5–6, 891–905.

71. Taylor, "Hoodoo Doctor"; Hyatt, *Hoodoo—Conjuration—Witchcraft—Rootwork*, 891–905.

72. R., L., G., and A., "Conjure Doctors in the South," 30.

73. Long, *Spiritual Merchants*, 38–52; Mary Alicia Owen, "Among the Voodoos," 242–44.

74. Taylor, "Hoodoo Doctor"; R., L., G., and A., "Conjure Doctors in the South," 30; Herron, "Conjuring and Conjure Doctors," 251–52; Bruce, *Plantation Negro as a Freedman*, 111–25; Bacon, "Conjuring and Conjure-Doctors"; W. and C., "About the Conjuring Doctors," 38; Mary Alicia Owen, "Among the Voodoos," 242–44, quotation from 244; Hyatt, *Hoodoo—Conjuration—Witchcraft—Rootwork*, 891–905.

75. Hyatt, *Hoodoo—Conjuration—Witchcraft—Rootwork*, 923–29.

76. Daniel Webster Davis, "Conjuration," 251.

77. Ibid., 251–52.

78. R., L., G., and A., "Conjure Doctors in the South," 30. The sex of the author whose aunt was cured is unclear, so I have arbitrarily treated the person as male based on the probability that he was.

79. Adams, interview, in Rawick, *American Slave*, suppl. 2, 2:19.

5. CONJURE SHOPS AND MANUFACTURING

1. Long, *Spiritual Merchants*, 99–126.

2. Hyatt, *Hoodoo—Conjuration—Witchcraft—Rootwork*, 620, 691–94, 744–888, 3293–3419. I have been unable to find mention of nation sacks in nineteenth-century sources.

3. Ibid.

4. Castellanos, *New Orleans as It Was*, 90.

5. Touchstone, "Voodoo in New Orleans," 375–86.

6. Ibid.; Castellanos, *New Orleans as It Was*, 90.

7. Touchstone, "Voodoo in New Orleans," 375–86; "Voudou-'Fetish.'"

8. Lopez, "Nanigo Dance," 2–3; Boggs, "Spanish Folklore from Tampa Florida"; Kennedy, "Ñañigo in Florida," 155.

9. Hyatt, *Hoodoo—Conjuration—Witchcraft—Rootwork*, 288–89, 667–68, 896, quotation from 667, emphases in the original.

10. Hurston, "Hoodoo in America," 317; Hyatt, *Hoodoo—Conjuration—Witchcraft—Rootwork*, 288–89, 896.

11. Hurston, "Hoodoo in America," 317.

12. Kulii, "Root Doctors and Psychics"; Maduro, "Hoodoo Possession in San Francisco"; Wintrob, "Influence of Others." See also Grossman, *Land of Hope*.

13. Long, *Spiritual Merchants*, xv–xviii; Tallant, *Voodoo in New Orleans*, 65–66; Tallant, *Voodoo Queen*, 131–33, 147; Cable, *Grandissimes*, 123, 147–56, 291–93, 325, 412. According to Ward, *Voodoo Queen*, 42–43, at least one white-owned pharmacy in New Orleans, founded in 1823, stocked hoodoo supplies.

14. Brown and Cooper, "Structural Continuity," 16–18; Mary Alicia Owen, *Voodoo Tales*, 171.

15. Daniel Webster Davis, "Conjuration," 251.

16. Zora Neale Hurston, "Negro in Florida, 1528–1940," 117–18, quotation from 117.

17. Ibid., 117–18. The store visited by Hurston was likely the Eureka Store (see Kennedy, *Palmetto Country*, 166–69).

18. Long, *Spiritual Merchants*, 143–57; Hyatt, *Hoodoo—Conjuration—Witchcraft—Rootwork*, 1625–26, 3224.

19. F. L. Robinson, interview by author; Long, *Spiritual Merchants*, 143–57, 253–61; Thomas Williams, interview by author.

20. Richard Miller, interview by author; Long, *Spiritual Merchants*, 153–54; Figueroa, interview by author. During my time in Figueroa's shop, I met an adherent of Santería and some members of a Spiritual church, as well as people simply looking for magical aids.

21. Long, *Spiritual Merchants*, 100–102; Hurston, *Mules and Men*, 277–80.

22. Long, *Spiritual Merchants*, 130–43; Hyatt, *Hoodoo—Conjuration—Witchcraft—Rootwork*, 1640–50; "Husbands and Lovers Are Voodoo Sage's Specialty"; Snow, "Mail Order Magic"; McGowan, *Gullah Mailman*, 92; McTeer, *Fifty Years*, 23; McTeer, *High Sheriff*, 18–41, quotation from 34.

23. Long, *Spiritual Merchants*, 253–64. For an example of an online mail-order hoodoo shop, see the Lucky Mojo Curio Company Web site, www.luckymojo.com.

24. Long, *Spiritual Merchants*, 187–219, 261–63.

25. Ibid., 161–63; Yronwode, interview by author.

26. Mary Alicia Owen, *Voodoo Tales*, 113; Tyler, "Elusive History," 164–66; Long, "John the Conqueror"; Clayton, "Truth about Voodoo," 61.

27. Long, *Spiritual Merchants*, 120–26; Richardson, "Bolita."

28. See Hurston, "Hoodoo in America," 328–57. A revised edition of the *Life and Works of Marie Laveau* is now in print under the title *Original Black and White Magic*. Another work has appropri-

ated the former title (see Laveau, *Original Black and White Magic;* and Canizares, *Life and Works of Marie Laveau*).

29. Yronwode, "Sonny Boy Products at the Egypt Candle Store"; F. L. Robinson, interview by author.

30. See Long, *Spiritual Merchants,* 125.

31. Yronwode, "Hoodoo"; Long, *Spiritual Merchants,* 122; Yronwode, "Secrets of the Psalms."

32. For more on the idea of the Oriental, see Said, *Orientalism.*

33. See Long, *Spiritual Merchants,* 118–19; and Claremont, *Legends of Incense,* 59–69, 82–89. According to Long, Eastern beliefs became so strongly associated with hoodoo during the first half of the twentieth century that some conjure shops came to be known as "Hindu stores."

34. McTeer, *High Sheriff,* 35.

35. Clayton, "Truth about Voodoo," 56; Winslow, "Bishop E. E. Everett," 61.

36. Winslow, "Bishop E. E. Everett," 59–80. No conjure shop that I have visited differs in any notable respect from that operated by Bishop Everett, with the exception that many proprietors are not themselves practitioners of magic.

37. Miller and Miller, *Miller's* catalog (ca. 2001), 12.

38. *Sonny Boy Blue Book Guide,* 9. See also Rondo and Rondo, *Rondo's Temple Sales Co.* catalog.

39. Long, *Spiritual Merchants,* 194, 199–201, 203–4. See also Hyatt, *Hoodoo—Conjuration—Witchcraft—Rootwork,* 1075–88.

40. James Harvey Young, *Toadstool Millionaires,* 144–244; James Harvey Young, *American Self-Dosage Medicines,* 1–31.

41. James Harvey Young, *Toadstool Millionaires,* 190–202; Flannery, "Good for Man or Beast," 10–11; Hyatt, *Hoodoo—Conjuration—Witchcraft—Rootwork,* 1097–1114, 1158–71, 4514; Long, *Spiritual Merchants,* 124–25; Rucker, *Black Herman's Secrets.* According to Hyatt, the Dr. Buzzard mentioned by Henry was neither the original white conjurer nor the later Stephaney Robinson (see Hyatt, *Hoodoo—Conjuration—Witchcraft—Rootwork,* 4514).

42. "Warner's Safe Kidney and Liver Cure."

43. James Harvey Young, *American Self-Dosage Medicines,* 1; "Why Be Sick!" *Lost manhood* was a polite euphemism for impotence.

44. "Why Be Sick!"

45. According to Carolyn Morrow Long, the *Chicago Defender* published its first advertisement for supernatural products in 1910. Nine years later the first advertisement for products traditionally associated with hoodoo appeared (Long, *Spiritual Merchants,* 130).

46. "Interesting Facts."

47. "Roots and Herbs of All Kinds Bought and Sold."

48. "Madam Ida B. Jefferson."

49. "Dr. Buzzard's Son."

50. James Harvey Young, *Toadstool Millionaires,* 205–44; Flannery, "Good for Man or Beast," 16–17; James Harvey Young, *American Self-Dosage Medicines,* 25–31.

51. Long, *Spiritual Merchants,* 127–37; McTeer, *Fifty Years,* 23; Hyatt, *Hoodoo—Conjuration—Witchcraft—Rootwork,* 1075.

52. Snow, "Mail Order Magic," 47.

53. Rondo and Rondo, *Rondo's Temple Sales Co.* catalog, 2.

54. Ibid., 25–29.

55. Ritzer, *The McDonaldization of Society*, 11–16. For other relevant works on consumerism and commodification, see Mullins, *Race and Affluence;* and McCracken, *Culture and Consumption,* 104–17.

56. Bibb, *Narrative of the Life,* 26–27; Rondo and Rondo, *Rondo's Temple Sales Co.* catalog, 15; Pyles, interview, in Baker and Baker, *WPA Oklahoma Slave Narratives,* 328–29; Miller and Miller, *Miller's* catalog (ca. 2001), 20. See also Mathers, *Key of Solomon the King.*

57. *Sonny Boy Blue Book Guide,* 10, 12, 14, 16.

58. Ibid., 8–21; Laveau, *Original Black and White Magic,* 11.

59. F. L. Robinson, interview by author.

60. Mooney, "Cherokee Theory and Practice," 44; James Harvey Young, *Toadstool Millionaires,* 173–79. For further elaboration and examples, see Long, *Spiritual Merchants,* 106–19.

61. *Sonny Boy Blue Book Guide,* 2–3, quotation from 2.

62. Ibid.; Snow, "Mail Order Magic," 47, 51–52; Miller and Miller, *Miller's* catalog (c. 2001), 39, 42.

63. Eugenia Brown, interview by author; Carmer, *Stars Fell on Alabama,* 215–22; Pinckney, *Blue Roots,* 102, 119–20, 149–50; Johnson, *Fabled Doctor Jim Jordan,* 46.

64. Hearn, "Last of the Voudoos"; Hyatt, *Hoodoo—Conjuration—Witchcraft—Rootwork,* 1642; Breaux and McKinney, "Hoodoo Price List"; Rhett, interview by author. Rhett could not remember whether the conjurer was Dr. Buzzard or Dr. Eagle. Dr. Eagle is the more likely candidate since he lived until at least the 1970s.

65. Johnson, *Fabled Doctor Jim Jordan,* 60.

66. McTeer, *Fifty Years,* 23–24, quotation from 24.

67. Ibid., 23–24.

68. Wolf, "Aunt Caroline Dye," 340.

69. Johnson, *Fabled Doctor Jim Jordan,* 67–78, quotation from 68; Pinckney, *Blue Roots,* 154.

70. Johnson, *Fabled Doctor Jim Jordan,* 57–67, 132–33; Fields with Fields, *Lemon Swamp and Other Places,* 121; Georgia Writers' Project, Savannah Unit, *Drums and Shadows,* 31, 60; Hyatt, *Hoodoo—Conjuration—Witchcraft—Rootwork,* 891–905, 1414–23, 1515–17, 1646, 4513–27, 4749–51.

71. Eugenia Brown, interview by author; Steiner, "Superstitions," 262.

72. Tallant, *Voodoo in New Orleans,* 94–95. For some recent examples of hoodoo advertisements, see *Miami Times,* 26 March 1998, 5D.

73. Johnson, *Fabled Doctor Jim Jordan,* 56–59; F. L. Robinson, interview by author; Thomas Williams, interview by author.

74. Hyatt, *Hoodoo—Conjuration—Witchcraft—Rootwork,* 1645–46, 2784, 4612.

75. F. L. Robinson, interview by author; Thomas Williams, interview by author. For examples of the changing terminology, see "Spiritual Medium"; and "Opportunity Awaits You." Some nonpractitioners have also adopted such terminology. For instance, while looking for Robinson in Micanopy, Florida, I asked a woman if she knew of any "hoodoo doctors in the area." She replied that there had once been one but that he had died. Then she took me to meet Robinson, whom she described as a "healer."

76. Kulii, "Look at Hoodoo."

77. Johnson, *Fabled Doctor Jim Jordan*, 132–33; Long, *Spiritual Merchants*, 149–50.
78. Thomas Williams, interview by author; Long, *Spiritual Merchants*, 262.

6. THE MAGIC CONTINUES

1. Claudia Williams, interview by author.
2. Deborah [pseud.], interview by author.
3. Long, *Spiritual Merchants*, 261–63; Daniel Webster Davis, "Conjuration," 251; Cable, *Grandissimes*, 123, 147–56, 291–93, 325, 412.
4. Touchstone, "Voodoo in New Orleans," 375–86; Coleman, *Historical Sketch Book*, 229–31; Kennedy, "Ñañigo in Florida," 155.
5. Historically, dolls were rare but not unknown in hoodoo.
6. "Welcome to Voodoo Authentica (TM)."
7. "Welcome to the New Orleans Historic Voodoo Museum." For an example of a Voodoo tour, see "Voodoo and Cemetery Tour."
8. Charles deV. Williams, "Gullah Tours"; "Welcome to Voodoo Authentica (TM)"; "Welcome to the New Orleans Historic Voodoo Museum." Voodoo Rain is a product of Everfresh/LaCROIX Beverages.
9. *New Orleans Historic Voodoo Museum; Marie Laveau's Magic Herb Packets*. My own experience confirms the tourist orientation of Marie Laveau's House of Voodoo. When I visited the shop in November 2001, I asked an employee if he would be able to give me his views on hoodoo. To my surprise, he said that he did not know enough to help me.
10. Saxon, "Voodoo," 135; Clayton, "Truth about Voodoo," 54, 60–61; Bims, "Would You *Believe* It."
11. Kulii, "Look at Hoodoo," 411–12, 417, 385.
12. McTeer, *Fifty Years*, 12–14, 27.
13. Thomas Williams, interview by author.
14. Cannon, "Voodoo Death," 186–90; Marvin Harris, "Death by Voodoo," 16; Eastwell, "Voodoo Death," 8–17.
15. Tinling, "Voodoo, Root Work, and Medicine."
16. Wintrob, "Influence of Others," 324–26, quotation from 326. For examples of some recent articles, see Straight, "Throw Downs, Fixin, Rooting, and Hexing"; and Jeremy Brown, "Vital Signs." See also Watson, *Black Folk Medicine;* and Fontenot, *Secret Doctors*.
17. Auerbach, *ESP, Hauntings, and Poltergeists*, 65–77. Duke University has since severed its ties with the parapsychology laboratory.
18. Winkelman, "Magic"; Auerbach, *ESP, Hauntings, and Poltergeists*, 15–55. Auerbach defines *psi* as "exchanges of information between living things (mainly people, of course), or between living things and the environment, or . . . influences of living things on the environment, which occur without the use of what we call the 'normal' senses, and do not seem to be explicable by the 'known' physical laws of nature" (ibid., 15–16). See also Wolman, *Handbook of Parapsychology*.
19. McTeer, *Fifty Years*, 12–14, 27; "Psychic Readings by Niva"; "Sister Lisa." See also Kulii, "Look at Hoodoo," 93–116, which offers a different perspective on the transformation of hoodooists into psychics.

20. Saphir et al., "Voodoo Poisoning in Buffalo, NY"; Faith Mitchell, *Hoodoo Medicine,* 41–100.
21. Savage, interview by author.
22. Kyle, *New Age Movement,* 27–39; Alexander, "Roots of the New Age."
23. Kyle, *New Age Movement,* 10–11, 49–53, 57–74.
24. Ibid., 4–5, 10–11, 53–74; Heelas, *New Age Movement,* 106–32; Lewis, "Approaches to the Study of the New Age Movement," 11–12.
25. Heelas, *New Age Movement,* 18–28; Kyle, *New Age Movement,* 52; Faber, *New Age Thinking,* 1–16; Melody Baker, *New Consciousness,* 15–16.
26. Heelas, *New Age Movement,* 18–28, 225–26; Kyle, *New Age Movement,* 18–20, 41–55; Melton et al., *New Age Encyclopedia,* xv–xviii.
27. Chamani, interview by author. The Spiritual churches are not to be confused with predominantly white spiritualism. For more on the Spiritual churches, see the conclusion.
28. Claudia Williams, interview by author; Brandon, *Santeria from Africa to the New World,* 77.
29. Glassman, interview by author.
30. Black and Hyatt, *Urban Voodoo,* 122, 142, 179–88, quotation from 122; Glassman, interview by author.
31. Brandon, *Santeria from Africa to the New World,* 1–2.
32. Ibid., 13–17, 74–78.
33. Ibid., 140–42; Murphy, *Santería,* 39–48, 62–69, 181.
34. Ibid.
35. Brandon, *Santeria from Africa to the New World,* 104–20, quotation from 104.
36. In the Southwest, the same is true of *yerberías,* shops that serve the needs of Mexican practitioners of traditional *curanderismo* and *brujería* (Long, *Spiritual Merchants,* 159, 179–80, 255).
37. Brandon, *Santeria from Africa to the New World,* 104; Long, *Spiritual Merchants,* 255; Figueroa, interview by author; Smith and Smith, conversations with and overheard by author; Rod Davis, *American Voudou,* 56–59. During my approximately thirty minutes in the store, seven patrons visited. All but one were African American.
38. Deborah [pseud.], interview by author.
39. Cuthrell-Curry, "African-Derived Religion"; Rod Davis, *American Voudou,* 17–59.
40. Rod Davis, *American Voudou,* 183–84. King, unlike most African Americans who encounter Santería, did so before the Cuban revolution.
41. Ibid., 177–90; Pinckney, *Blue Roots,* 135–45. See also Brown and Chappelle, "African Religions." These authors discuss black Americans' interest in African faiths.
42. Rod Davis, *American Voudou,* 28–38, 299–312. Davis writes the term *orisha voudou.* I have chosen to capitalize it in keeping with the principle of capitalizing the names of religions.
43. Ibid., 36.
44. Ibid., 299–312, quotation from 310.
45. Claudia Williams, interview by author; McTeer, *Fifty Years,* 12–14, 27, 79–85, 95–105.
46. Yronwode, "Anointing Oils."
47. Yronwode, "Lucky Mojo Curio Co."; Yronwode, "Catherine Yronwode." Yronwode is not alone in her willingness to sell products associated with Santería. Virtually all hoodoo shops stock items tied to Santería and other syncretic faiths, particularly saint candles.

48. Griffen and Reugger, "What Is Voodoo?" Melton et al., *New Age Encyclopedia*, s.v. "Kundalini Yoga."

49. Black and Hyatt, *Urban Voodoo*, 117–25; Rod Davis, *American Voudou*, 299–312; Glassman, interview by author; Yronwode, interview by author.

50. This disagreement is not universal. For example, Miriam Chamani asserts that Voodoo knows no race (see Chamani, interview by author).

51. Phoenix Savage, e-mail message to author, 10 July 2002. I have corrected a few spelling errors in this quotation.

52. Savage, interview by author; Glassman, interview by author.

53. Gorov, "War on Voodoo"; "Lee Rails against Hollywood."

54. Catherine Yronwode, e-mail message to author, 10 March 2003; Yronwode, interview by author; Deborah [pseud.], interview by author; Yronwode, "Hoodoo Magic Spells Correspondence Course 2003."

CONCLUSION

1. Wyatt-Brown, *Southern Honor*, 313, 315–16, 424–25; "Special Judge Hears Case." Unfortunately, I have been unable to discover the result of the second Ivy trial. One of the first authors to investigate the social function of conjure was Leonora Herron, whose "Conjuring and Conjure Doctors" appeared in 1891. According to Herron, blacks saw magic as a way of procuring justice in an unjust system.

2. Fields with Fields, *Lemon Swamp and Other Places*, 121.

3. Bass, "Mojo," 83.

4. Kulii, "Look at Hoodoo," 357–58.

5. Puckett, *Folk Beliefs of the Southern Negro*, 167–69, 207–9, 259–62. For another early discussion of the conjurers' multiple roles, see Du Bois, "Religion of the American Negro."

6. Wyatt-Brown, *Southern Honor*, 424–25; Izard, "Diary of a Journey," 160.

7. Pinckney, *Blue Roots*, 102, 119–20, 149–50; Johnson, *Fabled Doctor Jim Jordan*, 46, 60; Hearn, "Last of the Voudoos"; Hyatt, *Hoodoo—Conjuration—Witchcraft—Rootwork*, 1642; Jacqueline Jones, *Labor of Love, Labor of Sorrow*, 128, 166–67, 206–7; Carmer, *Stars Fell on Alabama*, 215–18; Puckett, *Folk Beliefs of the Southern Negro*, 207–9; Kulii, "Look at Hoodoo," 151–52; F. L. Robinson, interview by author.

8. Jacqueline Jones, *Labor of Love, Labor of Sorrow*, 44–151, 196–231. For full discussions of women's roles in American and southern society, see Evans, *Born for Liberty*; Scott, *Southern Lady*; and Epstein, *Woman's Place*.

9. Hurston, "Hoodoo in America," 368–71. This spell was a dance before an image of death. The intended result was the death of a client's former lover.

10. Ibid., 326–27, 357–60, 362–63, 368–71, 380–82, 387–88, 390–91, quotation from 327.

11. "'Root Doctor' Held." Works aimed at a popular audience, such as Carl Carmer's *Stars Fell on Alabama* and Charles W. Chesnutt's *Conjure Woman*, gave women an even more important role in conjuring. The popular image of conjurers as female reflects European beliefs about witchcraft, which was strongly associated with women (see Levack, *Witch-Hunt in Early Modern Europe*, 124–31).

12. Willis Easter, interview by Federal Writers' Project employee (Texas), in Rawick, *American Slave*, 4, pt. 2:3, quoted in Raboteau, *Slave Religion*, 286.

13. Botkin, *Lay My Burden Down*, 29.

14. Yronwode, "Blues Lyrics and Hoodoo"; Clar, "Folk Belief and Custom."

15. Tsuzuki, *Sam Doyle;* Blair, "X-ray Vision Is Needed."

16. Chesnutt, *Conjure Woman,* v–xix, 36–63, 103–31; Lindroth, "Images of Subversion"; Reed, *Mumbo Jumbo;* Reed, *Conjure;* Houston A. Baker Jr., *Workings of the Spirit,* 97–99; Walker, *Third Life of Grange Copeland;* Morrison, *Sula.* See also Pryse and Spillers, *Conjuring.* For information about a well-known white author who found inspiration in hoodoo, see Yates, "Conjures and Cures," 137–49.

17. Major, *Juba to Jive,* 109, 208, 239–40, 306–7, 496–97; Kulii, "Look at Hoodoo," 264. The informant's earlier statements indicate that she referred to a compliment used by other African Americans.

18. Kulii, "Look at Hoodoo," 261–64.

19. Theophus H. Smith, *Conjuring Culture,* 3–15, 183–205. To stress his broader definition of conjuring, Smith uses *conjuror* rather than the standard *conjurer* to designate hoodoo practitioners. He adopts this title for its implications of exhortation rather than simply casting of spells.

Smith's book is divided into three parts, and each part is subdivided into chapters examining particular books and sets of books from the Bible and their conjuring use. In the first part, which deals with ethnographic issues, Smith contends that Genesis, Exodus, and the Law of Moses define African Americans' magical cosmogony, their belief in conjuring God for freedom, and their belief in curing social wrongs by means of the supernatural. In part 2 Smith suggests that the Bible's Spirituals (Psalms), Prophecy, and Wisdom books define blacks' theories of aesthetics and vocations and their world-view. In part 3 he argues that the Gospels, Praxis (Book of Acts), and Apocalypse shape African American theology on curing violence, acts and activism, and judgement and revelation.

20. Jacobs and Kaslow, *Spiritual Churches of New Orleans,* 30–48, 74, 125–48, 209.

21. It should be noted that Spirituals do not refer to such practices as magic. To them, it is simply part of the dealings with spirits common in their faith. I use *magic* because of the term's simplicity and the consequent ease with which magic can be compared with hoodoo.

22. Jacobs and Kaslow, *Spiritual Churches of New Orleans,* 149–69; Gore, interview by author.

23. Gore, interview by author.

24. Chireau, "Conjuring," 248–57; Synan, *Holiness-Pentecostal Tradition,* 70–71.

25. MacRobert, "Black Roots of Pentecostalism"; Chireau, "Conjuring," 248–57.

26. Chireau, "Conjuring," 257–67; Wacker, *Heaven Below,* 65, 91–92, 104–5, 153, 206–7, 226–35; Synan, *Holiness-Pentecostal Tradition,* 167–86.

27. Smith and Smith, conversations with and overheard by author.

28. "Where the Best Defense Is a Good Hex"; Ausly, interview by Eugenia Brown.

29. "Magazine: Jackson Resorts to Voodoo"; "Md. Woman Facing Murder Charges Again."

Note on Sources

ANYONE DOING RESEARCH on African American magic faces serious historical challenges. Sources on the subject are scarce, especially in comparison with sources on the more traditional topics of historical examination, such as slave life or blacks' struggle to overturn segregation. There are several reasons for this scarcity in the written record. First, the primary believers in hoodoo have belonged to the working class, and they have produced very few records. The substandard education that southern states provided blacks created this problem. For some, however, conjure has been so maligned that they would hesitate to reveal their participation. By the standards of the dominant white culture, hoodoo has appeared to be just another superstition of a second-class race. Few whites found reason to record its practices. Educated middle-class blacks possessed similar biases, viewing hoodoo as a backward aspect of African American society that helped keep them shackled to a legacy of inequality. In short, believers rarely wrote of it. Nonbelievers did not care to do so and frowned upon those who did. As a result, the limited number of primary works on hoodoo requires researchers to draw from a wider variety of sources than would be typical for a historical study.

Documentary records on hoodoo are limited, but other means of recovering the past do exist. Yet the investigator must be wary. For instance, most of the primary sources, especially those covering the period before the late twentieth century, were wholly or partially produced by whites. The few that have black origins were chiefly the work of members of the educated middle class, who usually disparaged conjure's efficacy. Also, beliefs shaped what was recorded, as commonly occurs regarding spiritual matters. For example, when explaining how a pre–World War II hoodoo doctor cured a woman of swelling in her leg, a believing observer might have described seeing the practitioner pull a live snake from the afflicted limb. Modern readers would likely discount the tale or attribute it to trickery on the part of the conjurer, much as many an educated white or black observer of the event would have done. Folklore and deception have always been part of the sources addressing conjure.

The sources for this volume range from archival documents and published memoirs to novels and blues music. Of course, the use of such diverse and sometimes unorthodox sources required rigorous standards to determine reliability. The methodology used in this study was based on the intimacy of individual authors with their subject and the consistency of the recorded observations with other accounts. Sources by practitioners, participants, firsthand observers, and scholarly investigators were privileged over sources produced by those who came by knowledge secondhand or who wrote for entertainment purposes, to argue for or against the practice of conjure, or to sell hoodoo supplies. For instance, an interview of a practicing African American conjurer took precedence over a white author's recounting of his or her childhood memory of hoodoo stories. Similarly, a published memoir of an escaped slave was preferred to the writings of a novelist. The chronological closeness to the period under study was likewise a factor in judging the reliability of particular works.

The principle of consistency helped differentiate between fact and fiction, regardless of whether a source was based on firsthand experience. As a general rule, unless there was more than one source for particular information, it was either disregarded or treated as highly suspect. For instance, Edwin Granberry's fictionalized account of hoodoo in Florida, "Black Jupiter" (1932), speaks of a particular conjurer whom believers thought was a god, but no other sources speak of hoodooists with a similarly exalted status. Such deification was rarely, if ever, the case in reality. On the other hand, George Washington Cable's *Grandissimes* (1891), a fictional work critiquing race relations in nineteenth-century New Orleans, mentions the names of several Voodoo deities. Their existence could be largely verified by consulting independent sources on Louisianian Voodoo and scholarly works on Haitian Vodou. Most other sources have undergone similar tests of validity.

The presence of folkloric elements in purportedly factual sources was not so great a problem as might first appear. Indeed, the presence of mythic elements in descriptions of practitioners and their powers was troublesome when I was trying to determine the income of the average hoodoo doctor, the use of herbal medicines in rootwork, or the pervasiveness of belief in conjure. On the other hand, the folkloric aspects of such sources proved unimportant when I was examining some questions on hoodoo and even helped to answer others. For instance, the fact that believers frequently attributed illnesses to the effects of evil magic in no way interfered with my investigation of the effectiveness or ineffectiveness of rootworkers' treatments. At the same time, though modern scholars would almost universally dismiss the idea that hoodooists could actually kill their enemies by locking their bowels or magically inserting reptiles into their bodies, believers have continued to fear such powers. Beliefs about the reputed abilities of conjurers better explain practitioners' social standing, believers' fear of malevolent hoodoo, and the survival of hoodoo shops than do objective facts.

The primary materials researched for this book can be roughly divided into four categories: documents, artistic productions, interviews conducted by me, and works originally designed to serve as secondary sources. Each possessed its own uniquely useful features, as well as notable drawbacks.

As in most historical studies, the most important primary sources were documents—works designed to describe conjure and conjurers, sources intended for believers, and specialized studies by scholars working outside of the social sciences. Those works describing practitioners and their profession consisted of archival manuscripts, published materials containing references to conjure, and collected interviews of African Americans. Among the archival sources utilized were papers on conjure composed by the Federal Writers' Project and a smattering of writings by individuals who had encountered hoodooists or studied their supernatural arts. The published materials describing conjure were much more numerous and wide ranging, comprising articles from news periodicals, diaries, memoirs and autobiographies, letters, court proceedings, and the like. By far the most important documentary sources, though, were collections of published interviews, the most important of which were Harry Middleton Hyatt's *Hoodoo—Conjuration—Witchcraft—Rootwork* (1970–78) and *The American Slave: A Composite Autobiography* (1972–78), edited by George P. Rawick. These two works were massive undertakings, dwarfing all other sources on conjure in breadth, depth, variety, and sheer volume. Hyatt's collection is composed solely of transcribed interviews with conjurers and knowledgeable believers assembled during the first half of the twentieth century. Rawick's collection presents a similarly vast amount of supernatural material on the antebellum and immediate postwar period, though much of it is scattered throughout the hundreds of interviews with ex-slaves found within its volumes.

Of course, documentary works describing conjure and conjurers firsthand best illustrate their subject. Descriptions as detailed and as accurate could only rarely be found elsewhere. The main problem with almost all of the documentary sources is that they fit squarely into a category of works produced by atypical individuals. The vast majority were written by whites who were often unsympathetic to their subject. Some authors even used conjure to argue for the inferiority of blacks. A prime example is Philip A. Bruce, author of *The Plantation Negro as a Freedman: Observations on His Character, Condition, and Prospects in Virginia* (1889). Whether hostile, critical, or simply condescending, such works frequently present distorted visions of hoodoo by stressing its negative or supposedly backward qualities. Works by African American authors, who were typically educated members of the middle class, frequently suffer from similar prejudices. Even Hyatt's *Hoodoo—Conjuration—Witchcraft—Rootwork* and Rawick's *American Slave* have elements of atypicality. While the interviewees were black, the interviewers were almost exclusively white. Thus, the information conveyed by the African Americans would be influenced by how much the speakers wanted to reveal or keep hidden from the eyes of historically oppressive outsiders. Hyatt created a further problem by paying his informants. Although money might draw out secrets that would otherwise have remained hidden, it was also a tempting motive for creativity.

Many of the documentary sources describing hoodooists and their profession were produced well after the events and practices they delineate took place, increasing the possibility of inaccuracy or exaggeration. The interviews recorded in *The American Slave*, for example, took place in the late 1930s, some seven decades after the years they describe. Inaccuracy or exaggeration resulting from such a time lag can be overcome by comparing questionable statements to those found in sources produced during the antebellum period and the late nineteenth century. Some excellent examples of such sources are news articles, such as "The Voudou-'Fetish,'" in the *Daily Picayune* (1873); autobiographies, such as *Narrative of the Life and Adventures of Henry Bibb, an American Slave* (1850); Samuel Taylor's "Hoodoo Doctor, 30 April 1890"; and numerous late-nineteenth-century letters to the editor of the *Southern Workman* describing the practice of conjure.

Documentary sources intended for believers and specialized non-social-science studies fill in the gaps in descriptive accounts and help to counterbalance their unrepresentative features. Works intended for those accepting hoodoo as a valid system include advertisements for spiritual supplies in periodicals such as the *Chicago Defender;* spiritual supply store catalogs; do-it-yourself hoodoo books, such as *Aunt Sally's Policy Players' Dream Book* (1889) and Herman Rucker's *Black Herman's Secrets of Magic, Mystery, and Legerdemain* (1938); and actual items used in conjure, ranging from roots to the latest aerosol sprays. (The last, though not strictly documents, serve in much the same capacity. In a sense, they are descriptions of a practice given tangible form. Moreover, many hoodoo items carry their instructions on their packaging, making them bona fide sources in even the strictest terms.) These sources help substantiate the methods, pervasiveness, and materials used in African American magic during any period from the late nineteenth century to the present. Nevertheless, because they were usually the work of entrepreneurs aiming to sell their wares, their authors or manufacturers had a vested interest in exaggerating their products' effectiveness and positive features. Many business-minded producers have also introduced magical items from other cultures with a reputation for magic or spirituality in order to broaden their goods' appeal. On the other hand, as business endeavors, these works have had to fit into the preexisting hoodoo belief system, limiting the distance they could drift from actual practice. In addition, by presenting conjure in a predominantly positive light, they help offset the many negatively biased descriptive sources. Do-it-yourself books have the added advantage of giving detailed instructions for performing spells, going into greater depth than most works by outside observers.

Sources by scholars specializing in areas outside of the social sciences help to further balance the prejudices of the other documentary sources and bridge the chronological gap. Works by physicians, psychiatrists, and psychologists are the most important of this type; notable examples include Ronald M. Wintrob's "Influence of Others: Witchcraft and Rootwork as Explanations of Behavior Disturbances" (1973) and Marvin Harris's "Death by Voodoo" (1984). Such sources typically provide firsthand accounts of recent instances of hoodoo, along with analyses of conjure's effects on patients. Their accounts supply a scientific approach to the power of African American magic absent from other sources. Of course, healthcare workers are as subject to bias as anyone else, and many do not accept the spiritual implications of hoodoo. Nevertheless, their efforts to understand conjure as a practical means of healing or harming patients have given scholars uniquely objective descriptions of the measurable physical and psychological aspects of hoodoo.

Archaeological works too, by laying bare the remains of past lives, including the physical remnants of hoodoo charms and rituals, help put hoodoo into its proper place in African Americans' daily lives. At the same time, they do not rely on informants' potentially faulty memories. On the other hand, archaeology is extremely limited in what it can tell scholars. Archaeologists must rely heavily on interpretation to understand what they have uncovered. Without outside evidence to indicate what an item was used for, its identification as a vestige of conjure remains questionable. Even when an item's identity is firmly established, archaeologists must use documentary sources to discover the fine points of its functions and the rituals surrounding its use. One of the best examples of a source that uses documentary sources is Mark P. Leone and Gladys-Marie Fry's "Conjuring in the Big House Kitchen: An Interpretation of African American Belief Systems Based on the Uses of Archaeology and Folklore Sources" (1999).

A second type of primary sources, artistic works, can also be very valuable to students of African American magic. Their chief value is that they place hoodoo within the specific contexts of artists and their subjects. Literary works and visual arts are especially valuable in the former sense. Novels, most notably Helen Pitkin's *Angel by Brevet* (1904) and George Washington Cable's *Grandissimes*, indicate the degree of conjure's penetration into the nineteenth-century white society of their authors. Other works, like Charles Chesnutt's *Conjure Woman* (1899), do the same with respect to the society of that century's educated middle-class blacks. Chesnutt went a step further, using conjure as a means of articulating blacks' struggle for equality, an important indicator of the magical system's societal value. More recently, the novelist Alice Walker and the poet Ishmael Reed have followed similar courses. Paintings and drawings involving conjure, such as the folk art of Sam Doyle, can occasionally show us the face of a hoodoo doctor, but they always indicate the importance of blacks' supernaturalism by depicting it for the world to see.

In addition to placing conjure within the milieu of the artistic world, some artworks also shed light on the practice of hoodoo. Once again, Pitkin's *Angel by Brevet* is a key example. Pitkin described New Orleans Voodoo rituals in greater detail than any other author has done. Although her story is fictional, the rituals she writes about were purportedly based on actual observations. Indeed, many of the ceremonies she describes can be at least partially verified by consulting reliable documentary sources. Novelists, though motivated by a combination of artistic and economic concerns, can sometimes weave convincing portraits of the experiences of believers.

Music is at least as valuable for scholarly objectivity as literature and the visual arts. Hoodoo has rarely made a showing in white tunes; however, conjure has been a frequent feature of African American songs since well before the Civil War, being especially evident in the blues of the early twentieth century. Blues songs are rife with references to hoodoo men, nation sacks, graveyard dirt, and the like. Unlike most literary works, the blues was a solidly black genre for both composers and listeners, neutralizing the question of bias. The great drawback of the blues is that its references to particular conjure items and prominent hoodooists rely on listeners' knowledge of them for interpretation. Much like archaeological works, their value is limited outside the broader context supplied by other primary sources.

Another category of primary sources employed in this study were personal interviews with conjurers, operators of spiritual supply shops, and knowledgeable observers. These interviews, conducted by me in person in various cities throughout the South and by phone with persons as far away as California, do not constitute a scientific sampling of the population that practices or believes in conjure. Nevertheless, they provided important insights into modern hoodoo that would have been unobtainable otherwise. Most important, face-to-face conversations with practitioners and their clients or customers allowed for the testing of hypotheses. For instance, when speaking with owners of hoodoo shops, I frequently asked about their ethnic and religious background. By doing so, I was able to test other writers' assertion that white practitioners were frequently of recent European Jewish descent. In addition, personal interaction with conjurers and shop owners allowed me to ask specific questions not addressed in most other sources, such as why hoodooists had adopted their profession, what their most popular goods and services were, and what the volume of their sales was, as well as questions about their personal belief in conjure or their lack thereof. Without direct contact with knowledgeable insiders, many features of modern hoodoo, including its links to the New Age movement, its growing appeal to younger whites and blacks, and its strong reliance on scientific theories as explanations for success, would have remained obscure, even undiscovered by me. Despite these many benefits, my interviews suffer from the same drawbacks as earlier collections of interviews. Like so many early investigators, I am a white outsider. My background both shaped my interpretations of facts and excluded me from any information that interviewees might feel uncomfortable about revealing.

The final category of primary sources used here, works designed to serve as secondary sources, is especially important for those examining conjure. In addition to their standard use as secondary sources, putting hoodoo in context and serving as interpretive models, some of the best primary sources were originally intended to be secondary sources. This group includes the numerous brief studies of hoodoo that appeared in the *Journal of American Folklore* and *Southern Workman* during the late nineteenth and early twentieth centuries, as well as the many other articles that appeared in newspapers, magazines, journals, and reports during the same period. These sources illustrate the importance of conjure during the period in which they appeared. Others preserve details of African American magic that appear nowhere else. For example, many articles in a series that appeared in the *Southern Workman* near the end of the nineteenth century drew from a collection of more than one hundred letters addressing hoodoo that have since been lost. The information they contained is preserved in the articles in an abridged form. Similarly, the works of nineteenth- and early-twentieth-century folklorists often simply listed the beliefs attached to particular omens and magical items, including a minimum of interpretation.

A few authors of intended secondary sources interject their own observation of conjure into their interpretations of it. Writers' observations commonly appear in articles; however, the three major book-length studies of hoodoo, Newbell Niles Puckett's *Folk Beliefs of the Southern Negro* (1926), Zora Neale Hurston's "Hoodoo in America" (1931), and Carolyn Morrow Long's *Spiritual Merchants: Religion, Magic, and Commerce* (2001), also include their authors' descriptions and impressions of conjure as practiced at the time they conducted their research. During the 1920s Puckett personally interviewed several African American believers, among them a few practitioners. For a time he also successfully posed as a hoodoo doctor in order to gain deeper insight into the practice. Thus, *Folk Beliefs* can be justly termed either a primary or a secondary source, depending on the kind of information one seeks. The same can be said for *Spiritual Merchants*. Long visited spiritual supply shops and manufacturers throughout the nation and spoke with their owners, gaining information about and observing the inner workings of the industry firsthand. Slightly less than one-fifth of *Spiritual Merchants* describes the history of these individual businesses and what Long encountered while visiting them and/or interviewing their proprietors.

Hurston's "Hoodoo in America" is a unique case. As the only book-length scholarly treatment of conjure by an African American, it offers insights into conjure obtainable nowhere else. Few sources rival this work by Hurston in the depth of its descriptions of individual spells, conjure materials, herbal medicines used by rootworkers, and practitioners' initiations into the profession. Like Puckett, Hurston posed as a conjurer to obtain her information and multiple initiations. Moreover, as an African American, Hurston is less vulnerable to accusations of outsider misinterpretation than are whites like Puckett and Long.

At the same time, the uniqueness of Hurston's writings opens them to questions about their accuracy. In particular, her accounts of initiations into New Orleans hoodoo are suspect. Very few other sources from the period describe such ceremonies. It is possible that Hurston fabricated some of her experiences. She might also have embellished her stories for the sake of attracting readers or making a name for herself in the scholarly world.

I have chosen to accept Hurston's accounts of initiations on several grounds. First, she had the advantage of being an African American; this fact alone would account for the confidence she received from hoodooists. In addition, the overall consistency of other features of her work, such as descriptions of spells and important herbs used in rootwork, with independently verified facts circumstantially attests to her truthfulness. Next, the existence of a few reliable late-nineteenth-century descriptions of hoodoo initiations also argues in favor of at least the possibility that such ceremonies survived in New Orleans. After all, the nineteenth century was only a generation in the past at the time that Hurston conducted her research, and over the course of the early twentieth century the law had grown more rigid in its prosecution of hoodooists for mail fraud and practicing medicine without a license. It is reasonable to assume that many practitioners may have become increasingly unwilling to share their knowledge of the more elaborate hoodoo ceremonies. Also, occasional twentieth-century sources, including Pitkin's *Angel by Brevet* and a few of the Federal Writers' Project interviews, record instances of rituals similar in complexity to those in Hurston's initiations, though they were sometimes performed for purposes other than initiation. Finally, and perhaps most tellingly, African American scholars, practitioners, and believers have yet to denounce Hurston's work as a fabrication. Although "Hoodoo in America" is suspiciously unique, it must not be dismissed out of hand.

In sum, while the historical record on conjure is limited in comparison with the material addressing other subjects, the sources vary widely in form, are diverse in content, and are frequently rich in detail. The documentary works, artistic works, authorial interviews, and intended secondary sources that served as the foundation for this book each have both positive features and notable drawbacks. When studied together, however, they offer a clear view of the changing face of conjure through the years.

Bibliography

Alexander, Kay. "Roots of the New Age." In *Perspectives on the New Age*, edited by James R. Lewis and J. Gordon Mellon, 30–47. Albany: State University of New York, 1992.
Andersen, Benedict. *Imagined Communities: Reflections on the Origin and Spread of Nationalism.* London: Verso, 1993.
Andrews, William L., and Henry Louis Gates Jr., eds. *Slave Narratives.* New York: Literary Classics of the United States, 2000.
Antippas, A. P. *A Brief History of Voodoo: Slavery and the Survival of the African Gods.* New Orleans: Marie Laveau's House of Voodoo, 1988.
Asbury, Herbert. *The French Quarter: An Informal History of the New Orleans Underworld.* New York: Knopf, 1936.
Auerbach, Loyd. *ESP, Hauntings, and Poltergeists: A Parapsychologist's Handbook.* New York: Warner Books, 1986.
Aunt Sally's Policy Players' Dream Book and Wheel of Fortune. New York: H. J. Wehman, 1889. Reprint, Los Angeles: Indio Products, n.d.
Ausly, Kenneth. Interview by Eugenia Brown. 26 June 2002. Owassa, AL. Notes. Author's personal collection, Birmingham, AL.
Bacon, A. M. "Conjuring and Conjure-Doctors." Folk-Lore and Ethnology. *Southern Workman* 24 (1895): 193–94, 209–11.
Baker, Houston A., Jr. *Workings of the Spirit: The Poetics of Afro-American Women's Writing.* Chicago: University of Chicago Press, 1991.

Baker, Melody. *A New Consciousness: The True Spirit of the New Age.* Duluth, MN: New Thought, 1991.

Baker, T. Lindsay, and Julie P. Baker, eds. *The WPA Oklahoma Slave Narratives.* Norman: University of Oklahoma Press, 1996.

Basil, Robert. *Not Necessarily the New Age: Critical Essays.* Buffalo, NY: Prometheus Books, 1988.

Bass, Ruth. "The Little Man." *Scribner's Magazine* 97 (February 1935): 120–23.

———. "Mojo: The Strange Magic That Works in the South Today." *Scribner's Magazine* 87 (January 1930): 83–90.

Beard, Charles A., and Mary R. Beard. *The Rise of American Civilization.* With decorations by Wilfred Jones. 2 vols. New York: Macmillan, 1927.

"Believed in North Carolina Also." *Daily Equator-Democrat,* 10 July 1889.

Bell, Michael E. "Pattern, Structure, and Logic in Afro-American Hoodoo Performance." Ph.D. diss., Indiana University, 1980.

Bendenbaugh, J. W. "A Contribution from South Carolina." Folk-Lore and Ethnology. *Southern Workman* 23 (1894): 46–47.

Benson, Henry Clark. *Life among the Choctaw Indians and Sketches of the South-west.* With an Introduction by T. A. Morris. Cincinnati: L. Swormstedt and A. Poe, 1860. Reprint, New York: Johnson Reprint, 1970.

Berendt, John. *Midnight in the Garden of Good and Evil: A Savannah Story.* New York: Random House, 1994.

Bergen, Fanny D., ed. *Animal and Plant Lore: Collected from the Oral Tradition of English Speaking Folk.* With an introduction by Joseph Y. Bergen. Vol. 7 of *Memoirs of the American Folk-Lore Society.* Boston: Houghton, Mifflin, 1899.

Berry, Jason. *The Spirit of Black Hawk: A Mystery of Africans and Indians.* Jackson: University Press of Mississippi, 1995.

Best, Michael R., and Frank H. Brightman, eds. *The Book of Secrets of Albertus Magnus of the Virtues of Herbs, Stones and Certain Beasts—Also a Book of the Marvels of the World.* Studies in Tudor and Stuart Literature, edited by F. H. Mares and A. T. Brissenden, vol. 2. Oxford: Oxford University Press, 1973.

Bibb, Henry. *Narrative of the Life and Adventures of Henry Bibb, an American Slave.* 3rd ed., with an introduction by Lucius C. Matlack. New York: privately printed, 1850.

Bims, Hamilton. "Would You *Believe* It . . . Superstition Lives!" *Ebony,* July 1976, 118–22.

Black, S. Jason, and Christopher S. Hyatt. *Urban Voodoo: A Beginner's Guide to Afro-Caribbean Magic.* Tempe, AZ: New Falcon, 1995.

Blair, Jayson. "X-ray Vision Is Needed to Find Black Superheroes." *New York Times,* sec. 4, 5 May 2002, p. 16.

Blassingame, John. *The Slave Community: Plantation Life in the Antebellum South.* 2nd ed. New York: Oxford University Press, 1979.

Blier, Suzanne Preston. "Vodun: West African Roots of Vodou." In *Sacred Arts of Haitian Vodou*, edited by Donald L. Cosentino, 73–76. Los Angeles: University of California Fowler Museum of Cultural History, 1995.

Blum, John Morton. *V Was for Victory: Politics and American Culture during World War II*. New York: Harcourt Brace Jovanovich, 1976.

Boas, Franz. *Anthropology and Modern Life*. Rev. ed. New York: W. W. Norton, 1932.

Boggs, Ralph Steele. "Spanish Folklore from Tampa Florida." *Southern Folklore Quarterly* 1 (1937): 1–12.

Bone, Robert A. "The Negro Renaissance." In *The Twenties: The Critical Issues*, edited by Joan Hoff Wilson, 118–28. Critical Issues in American History Series, edited by Barton J. Bernstein. Boston: Little, Brown, 1972.

Botkin, B. A., ed. *Lay My Burden Down: A Folk History of Slavery*. Athens: University of Georgia Press, 1945.

Boyle, Virginia Frazer. *Devil Tales*. With illustrations by A. B. Frost. 1900. Reprint, Freeport, NY: Books for Libraries, 1972.

Branch, Taylor. *Parting the Waters: America in the King Years, 1954–1963*. New York: Simon and Schuster, 1988.

Brandon, George. *Santeria from Africa to the New World: The Dead Sell Memories*. Bloomington: Indiana University Press, 1993.

Breaux, Hazel, and Robert McKinney. "Hoodoo Price List." Robert Tallant Papers, 320–21. City Archives, New Orleans Public Library, New Orleans.

Breslaw, Elaine G. "Tituba's Confession: The Multicultural Dimensions of the 1692 Salem Witch-Hunt." *Ethnohistory* 44 (1997): 535–56.

Bronner, Simon. *American Folklore Studies: An Intellectual History*. Lawrence: University Press of Kansas, 1986.

———, ed. *Folklife Studies in the Gilded Age: Object, Rite, and Custom in Victorian America*. Ann Arbor and London: University Microfilms, 1987.

Brown, Bessie. "Hoodoo Blues." Composed by Spenser Williams. Columbia 14029, 3 July 1924.

Brown, Charles S., and Yvonne R. Chappelle. "African Religions and the Quest for Afro-American Heritage." In *African Religions: A Symposium*, edited by Newell S. Booth Jr., 241–54. New York: NOK, 1977.

Brown, David H. "Conjure/Doctors: An Exploration of a Black Discourse in America, Antebellum to 1940." *Folklore Forum* 23 (1990): 3–45.

Brown, Eugenia. Interview by author. 9 May 2002. Evergreen, AL. Notes. Author's personal collection, Birmingham, AL.

Brown, Jeremy. "Vital Signs: A Deadly Specter." *Discover Magazine*, September 1995, 48–51.

Brown, Kenneth L., and Doreen C. Cooper. "Structural Continuity in an African-American Slave and Tenant Community." *Historical Archaeology* 24 (1990): 7–19.

Brown, William Wells. *My Southern Home: Or, the South and Its People.* Boston: A. G. Brown, 1880. Reprint, Upper Saddle River, NJ: Gregg, 1968.

———. *Narrative of the Life of William Wells Brown, an American Slave.* London: Charles Gilpin, 1850.

Bruce, Philip A. *The Plantation Negro as a Freedman: Observations on His Character, Condition, and Prospects in Virginia.* New York: G. P. Putnam's Sons, 1889.

Buel, James William. *Sunlight and Shadow of America's Great Cities.* Philadelphia: West Philadelphia, 1889.

Burns, Khephra. "The Queen of Voodoo." *Essence* 23 (May 1992): 80.

Cable, George Washington. "Creole Slave Songs." With illustrations by E. W. Kemble. *Century Magazine* 31 (1886): 807–28.

———. "The Dance in Place Congo." With illustrations by E. W. Kemble. *Century Magazine* 31 (1886): 517–32.

———. *The Grandissimes: A Story of Creole Life.* New York: Charles Scribner's Sons, 1891.

Canizares, Raul. *The Life and Works of Marie Laveau: Gris-gris, Cleansings, Charms, Hexes.* Plainview, NY: Original Publications, 2001.

Cannella, Felix, with F. Hilton Crowe. "Ñañigo," 26 May 1936. In "American Guide: Ybor City." Tampa: Federal Writers' Project, [1939]. P. K. Yonge Library of Florida History, Department of Special and Area Studies Collection, George A. Smathers Libraries, University of Florida, Gainesville.

Cannon, Walter B. "Voodoo Death." *American Anthropologist* 44 (1942). Reprinted in *Psychosomatic Medicine* 19 (1957): 182–90.

Cappick, Marie. "The Key West Story, 1818–1950." *Coral Tribune*, 2, 9, 16, 23 May, 6 June 1958.

Carmer, Carl. *Stars Fell on Alabama.* With an Introduction by J. Wayne Flynt. Tuscaloosa: University of Alabama Press, 1985.

Carmichael, Stokely, and Charles V. Hamilton. *Black Power: The Politics of Liberation America.* New York: Random House, 1967.

Carmody, Denise Lardner, and John Tully Carmody. *Native American Religions: An Introduction.* New York: Paulist Press, 1993.

Castellanos, Henry C. *New Orleans as It Was: Episodes of Louisiana Life.* New Orleans: L. Graham & Son, 1895.

Catterall, Helen Tunnicliff, ed. *Judicial Cases concerning American Slavery and the Negro.* 5 vols. 1926. Reprint, New York: Negro Universities Press, 1968.

Chafe, William Henry. *Civilities and Civil Rights: Greensboro, North Carolina, and the Black Struggle for Freedom.* New York: Oxford University Press, 1980.

Chamani, Miriam. Interview by author. 15 November 2001. New Orleans, LA. Notes and audio recording. Author's personal collection, Birmingham, AL.

Chappell, David L. *Inside Agitators: White Southerners in the Civil Rights Movement.* Baltimore: Johns Hopkins University Press, 1994.

Chesnutt, Charles W. *The Conjure Woman.* With an Introduction by Robert M. Farnsworth. Ann Arbor: University of Michigan Press, 1969.
Chireau, Yvonne. *Black Magic: Religion and the African American Conjuring Tradition.* Berkeley and Los Angeles: University of California Press, 2003.
———. "Conjure and Christianity in the Nineteenth Century: Religious Elements in African American Magic." *Religion and American Culture: A Journal of Interpretation* 7 (1997): 225–46.
———. "Conjuring: An Analysis of African American Folk Beliefs and Practices." Ph.D. diss., Princeton University, 1994.
C.H.W. Review of *Folk Beliefs of the Southern Negro,* by Newbell Niles Puckett. *Southern Workman* 55 (1926): 574–75.
Clar, Mimi. "Folk Belief and Custom in the Blues." *Western Folklore* 19 (1960): 173–89.
Claremont, Lewis de. *Legends of Incense, Herb and Oil Magic.* Rev. ed. Arlington, TX: Dorene, 1966.
Clayton, Edward T. "The Truth about Voodoo." *Ebony,* April 1951, 54–61.
Cocchiara, Giuseppe. *The History of Folklore in Europe.* Translated by John N. McDaniel. Translations in Folklore Studies, edited by Dan Ben-Amos. Philadelphia: Institute for the Study of Human Issues, 1981.
Coleman, William H., ed. *Historical Sketch Book and Guide to New Orleans and Environs.* New York, 1885.
Colligan, Douglas. "Extreme Psychic Trauma Is the Power behind Voodoo Death." *Science Digest,* August 1976, 44–48.
Combs, Josiah Henry. "Sympathetic Magic in the Kentucky Mountains: Some Curious Folk-survivals." *Journal of American Folk-Lore* 27 (1914): 328–30.
The Complete Book of Fortune: How to Reveal the Secrets of the Past, the Present and the Future. 1936. Reprint, New York: Crescent Books, 1990.
Conway, David. *The Magic of Herbs.* New York: E. P. Dutton, 1973.
Conzen, Kathleen Neils, David A. Gerber, Ewa Morawska, George E. Pozzetta, and Rudolph J. Vecoli. "The Invention of Ethnicity: A Perspective from the U.S.A." *Journal of American Ethnic History* 12 (1992): 3–41.
Courlander, Harold. *A Treasury of African Folklore: The Oral Literature, Traditions, Myths, Legends, Epics, Tales, Recollections, Wisdom, Sayings, and Humor of Africa.* New York: Crown, 1975.
Crellin, John K., and Jane Philpott. *A Reference Guide to Medicinal Plants: Herbal Medicine Past and Present.* Durham, NC: Duke University Press, 1990.
Cronon, E. David. *Black Moses: The Story of Marcus Garvey and the Negro Improvement Association.* With a foreword by John Hope Franklin. Madison: University of Wisconsin Press, 1955.
Cross, Tom Peete. "Witchcraft in North Carolina." *Studies in Philology* 16 (1919): 217–87.

Cuthrell-Curry, Mary. "African-Derived Religion in the African-American Community in the United States." In *World Spirituality: An Encyclopedic History of the Religious Quest*, vol. 2, *African Spirituality: Forms, Meanings, and Expressions*, edited by Jacob K. Olupona, with a foreword by Charles Long, 450–66. New York: Crossroad, 2000.

Dalfiume, Richard. *Desegregation of the U.S. Armed Forces.* Columbia: University of Missouri Press, 1969.

Dana, Marvin. "Voodoo: Its Effect on the Negro Race." *Metropolitan Magazine* 28 (1908): 529–38.

Davis, Daniel Webster. "Conjuration." Folk-Lore and Ethnology. *Southern Workman* 27 (1898): 251–52.

Davis, Rod. *American Voudou: Journey into a Hidden World.* Denton: University of North Texas Press, 1999.

"Death of Marie Laveau." *Daily Picayune*, 17 May 1881, 8.

Deborah. Interview by author. 15 July 2002. Bessemer, AL. Notes. Author's personal collection, Birmingham, AL.

DeLaurence, Lauren William. *The Great Book of Magical Art, Hindu Magic, and East Indian Occultism.* N.p., 1902.

Dobbs, B. J. T. *The Foundations of Newton's Alchemy: or, "The Hunting of the Greene Lyon."* Cambridge: Cambridge University Press, 1975.

Domenech, Emmanuel Henri Dieudonné. *Missionary Adventures in Texas and Mexico: A Personal Narrative of Six Years' Sojourn in Those Regions.* London: Longman, Brown, Green, Longmans, and Roberts, 1858.

Dorson, Richard M., ed. *American Negro Folklore.* Greenwich, CT: Fawcett, 1967.

———. *Negro Folktales in Michigan.* Cambridge, MA: Harvard University Press, 1956.

Douglass, Frederick. *Narrative of the Life of Frederick Douglass.* With an introduction by William Lloyd Garrison, a letter from Wendell Phillips, Esq., and a new introductory note. New York: Dover, 1995.

"Dr. Buzzard's Son." *Miami Times*, 28 November 1974, 33.

Du Bois, William Edward Burghardt. "The Religion of the American Negro." *New World* 9 (1900): 614–25.

Dues, Greg. *Catholic Customs and Traditions: A Popular Guide.* Rev. ed. Mystic, CT: Twenty-third Publications, 1992.

Dunning, William Archibald. *Reconstruction, Political and Economic, 1865–1877.* New York: Harper and Brothers, 1907.

Eastwell, Harry D. "Voodoo Death and the Mechanism for Dispatch of the Dying in East Arnhem, Australia." *American Anthropologist* 84 (1982): 5–18.

Elam, William Cecil. "A Case of Hoodoo." *Lippincott's Monthly Magazine* 54 (1894): 138–41.

Ellis, A. B. *The Ewe-Speaking Peoples of the Slave Coast of West Africa: Their Religion, Manners, Customs, Laws, Languages, &c.* London: Chapman and Hall, 1890.

———. "On Vōdu Worship." *Popular Science Monthly* 38 (March 1891): 651–63.

———. *The Tshi-Speaking Peoples of the Gold Coast of West Africa: Their Religion, Manners, Customs, Laws, Language, Etc.* London: Chapman and Hall, 1887.

———. *The Yoruba-Speaking Peoples of the Slave Coast of West Africa: Their Religion, Manners, Customs, Laws, Language, Etc.* Chicago: Benin, 1964.

The Encyclopedia of American Popular Beliefs and Superstitions. Berkeley and Los Angeles: University of California Press, forthcoming.

Epstein, Cynthia Fuchs. *Woman's Place: Options and Limits in Professional Careers.* Berkeley and Los Angeles: University of California Press, 1970.

Evans, Sara M. *Born for Liberty: A History of Women in America.* New York: Free Press, 1989.

"The Evil Eye." *History's Mysteries.* Executive producer Bram Rods. Los Angeles: Film Roos, 1999.

Faber, Mel D. *New Age Thinking: A Psychoanalytic Critique.* Religion and Beliefs Series, 5. Ottawa, ON: University of Ottawa Press, 1996.

Farmer, David Hugh. *The Oxford Dictionary of Saints.* 3rd ed. Oxford: Oxford University Press, 1992.

Fennell, Christopher C. "Conjuring Boundaries: Inferring Past Identities from Religious Artifacts." *International Journal of Historical Archaeology* 4 (2000): 281–313.

Ferguson, Leland G. "'The Cross Is a Magic Sign': Marks on Eighteenth-Century Bowls from South Carolina." In *"I, Too, Am America": Archaeological Studies of African-American Life,* edited by Theresa A. Singleton, 116–31. Charlottesville: University Press of Virginia, 1999.

———. "Looking for the 'Afro' in Colono-Indian Pottery." In *Archaeological Perspectives on Ethnicity in America,* edited by R. L. Schulyer, 14–28. Amityville, NY: Baywood, 1980.

Fields, Mamie Garvin, with Karen Fields. *Lemon Swamp and Other Places: A Carolina Memoir.* New York: Free Press, 1983.

Figueroa, Felix. Interview by author. 15 November 2001. New Orleans, LA. Notes and audio recording. Author's personal collection, Birmingham, AL.

Fischer, David Hackett. *Albion's Seed: Four British Folkways in America.* New York: Oxford University Press, 1989.

Flannery, Michael A. "Good for Man or Beast: American Patent Medicines from 1865 to 1938." *Alabama Heritage,* Winter 2001, 8–17.

Fontenot, Wonda L. *Secret Doctors: Ethnomedicine of African Americans.* Westport, CT: Bergin and Garvey, 1994.

Foster, Steven, and James A. Duke. *A Field Guide to Medicinal Plants and Herbs of Eastern and Central North America.* Boston: Houghton Mifflin, 2000.

Frazer, James G. *The Golden Bough: A Study in Magic and Religion*. 1922. Reprint, New York: Macmillan, 1951.

Frazier, Edward Franklin. *Black Bourgeoisie*. Glencoe, IL: Free Press, 1957.

Frey, Sylvia R., and Betty Wood. *Come Shouting to Zion: African-American Protestantism in the American South and British Caribbean to 1830*. Chapel Hill: University of North Carolina Press, 1998.

Fry, Gladys-Marie. *Night Riders in Black Folk History*. Knoxville: University of Tennessee Press, 1975.

Gainer, Patrick W. *Witches, Ghosts, and Signs: Folklore of the Southern Appalachians*. Morgantown, WV: Seneca Books, 1975.

Galke, Laura J. "Did the Gods of Africa Die? A Re-examination of a Carroll House Crystal Assemblage." *North American Archaeologist* 21 (2000): 19–33.

Gamache, Henri. *The Magic of Herbs throughout the Ages*. Plainview, NY: Original Publications, 1985.

———. *The Master Book of Candle Burning*. Rev. ed. Plainview, NY: Original Publications, 1998.

Gandolfo, Charles M. *Marie Laveau of New Orleans, the Great Voodoo Queen*. New Orleans: New Orleans Historical Voodoo Museum, 1992.

———. *Voodoo Vé-Vé's and Talismans and How to Use Them*. New Orleans: New Orleans Historical Voodoo Museum, n.d.

Genovese, Eugene. *Roll, Jordan, Roll: The World the Slaves Made*. New York: Random House, 1972.

Georgia Writers' Project, Savannah Unit. *Drums and Shadows: Survival Studies among the Coastal Negroes*. With an introduction by Charles Joyner and photographs by Muriel and Malcolm Bell Jr. Athens: University of Georgia Press, 1986.

Glassman, Sallie Ann. Interview by author. 14 November 2001. New Orleans, LA. Notes and audio recording. Author's personal collection, Birmingham, AL.

Gomez, Michael A. *Exchanging Our Country Marks: The Transformation of African Identities in the Colonial and Antebellum South*. Chapel Hill: University of North Carolina Press, 1998.

Gore, Barbara. Interview by author. 11 November 2001. New Orleans, LA. Notes and audio recording. Author's personal collection, Birmingham, AL.

Gorov, Lynda. "The War on Voodoo." *Mother Jones*, June 1990, 12.

Granberry, Edwin. "Black Jupiter: A Voodoo King in Florida's Jungle—Black Magic in the Turpentine Forests." With illustrations by Douglas Cleary. *Travel* 58 (1932): 32–35, 54.

Grieve, M. *A Modern Herbal: The Medical, Culinary, Cosmetic, and Economic Properties, Cultivation, and Folk-Lore of Herbs, Grasses, Fungi, Shrubs, and Trees with All Their Modern Scientific Uses*. With an introduction by C. F. Leyel and an index of scientific names by Manya Marshall. New York: Dover, 1971.

Griffen, Banks, and Dane Reugger. "What Is Voodoo?" 1997. The New Orleans Historic Voodoo Museum. www.voodoomuseum.com/whats.html (accessed 29 July 2002).

Grimm, Fred. "Ritual Sacrifices Turn Miami River Red." *Miami Herald,* 30 May 1981, 1B–2B.

Grimm, Jacob, and Wilhelm Grimm. *The Complete Fairy Tales of the Brothers Grimm.* Translated and with an introduction by Jack Zipes. With illustrations by John B. Gruelle. New York: Bantam Books, 1992.

Grossman, James R. *Land of Hope: Chicago, Black Southerners, and the Great Migration.* Chicago: University of Chicago Press, 1989.

"Hags and Their Ways." Folk-Lore and Ethnology. *Southern Workman* 23 (1892): 26–27.

Hamel, Paul B., and Mary U. Chiltoskey. *Cherokee Plants and Their Uses—A 400 Year History.* Sylva, NC: Herald, 1975.

Hand, Wayland. "Plugging, Nailing, Wedging, and Kindred Folk Medical Practices." In *Folklore and Society: Essays in Honor of Benjamin A. Botkin,* edited by Bruce Jackson, 63–75. Hatboro, PA: Folklore Associates, 1966.

———, ed. *Popular Beliefs and Superstitions from North Carolina.* Vol. 7 of *The Frank C. Brown Collection of North Carolina Folklore,* edited by Newman Ivey White. Durham: University of North Carolina Press, 1952–64.

Handy, M. P. "Witchcraft among the Negroes." *Appleton's Journal: A Magazine of General Literature* 8 (1872): 666–67.

Handy, Sara M. "Negro Superstitions." *Lippincott's Monthly Magazine* 48 (1891): 735–39.

Harris, Joel Chandler. *Uncle Remus: His Songs and His Sayings.* Rev. ed. With illustrations by Arthur Burdette Frost. New York: Grosset and Dunlap, 1921.

Harris, Joseph E. *Africans and Their History.* Rev. ed. New York: Penguin Books, 1987.

Harris, Marvin. "Death by Voodoo." *Psychology Today,* August 1984, 16–17.

Harvey, David. *The Condition of Postmodernity: An Enquiry into the Origins of Cultural Change.* Cambridge: Blackwell, 1990.

Haskell, Joseph A. "Sacrificial Offerings among North Carolina Negroes." *Journal of American Folk-lore* 4 (1891): 267–69.

Haskins, James. *Voodoo and Hoodoo: The Craft as Revealed by Traditional Practitioners.* New ed. Lanham, NY: Scarborough House, 1990.

Hauptmann, O. H. "Spanish Folklore from Tampa Florida: (No. VII) Witchcraft." *Southern Folklore Quarterly* 3 (1939): 197–200.

Hearn, Lafcadio. "The Last of the Voudoos." *Harper's Weekly Magazine* 29 (1885): 726–27.

———. "New Orleans Superstitions." *Harper's Weekly Magazine* 30 (1885): 843.

Heelas, Paul. *The New Age Movement: The Celebration of the Self and the Sacralization of Modernity.* Cambridge: Blackwell, 1996.

Herron, Leonora. "Conjuring and Conjure Doctors." Folk-Lore and Ethnology. *Southern Workman* 24 (1891): 117–18.

Herskovits, Melville J. *The Myth of the Negro Past*. With an introduction by Sidney W. Mintz. Boston: Beacon, 1990.

Hobsbawm, Eric, and Terence Ranger, eds. *The Invention of Tradition*. Cambridge: Cambridge University Press, 1983.

Hohman, John George. *Pow-Wows, or Long Lost Friend: A Collection of Mysterious and Invaluable Arts and Remedies for Man as Well as Animals—with Many Proofs*. 1855. Reprint, Brooklyn: Fulton Religious Supply, n.d.

Howard, James H., with Willie Lena. *Oklahoma Seminoles: Medicines, Magic, and Religion*. Civilization of the American Indian Series, vol. 5. Norman: University of Oklahoma Press, 1984.

Hudson, Charles. *The Southeastern Indians*. Knoxville: University of Tennessee Press, 1976.

Huggins, Nathan Irvin. *Harlem Renaissance*. London: Oxford University Press, 1971.

Hughes, Langston, and Arna Bontemps, eds. *The Book of Negro Folklore*. New York: Dodd, Mead, 1959.

Hughes, Louis. *Thirty Years a Slave: From Bondage to Freedom*. Milwaukee: South Side, 1897.

Hughes, Pennethorne. *Witchcraft*. London: Longmans, Green, 1952. Harmondsworth, UK: Penguin Books, 1973.

Hultkrantz, Åke. *Belief and Worship in Native North America*. Edited and with an introduction by Christopher Vecsey. Syracuse, NY: Syracuse University Press, 1981.

———. *The Religions of the American Indians*. Translated by Monica Setterwall. Berkeley and Los Angeles: University of California Press, 1979.

Hurston, Zora Neale. "Hoodoo in America." *Journal of American Folklore* 44 (1931): 317–417.

———. *Folklore, Memoirs, and Other Writings*. Selected and annotated by Cheryl A. Wall. New York: Literary Classics of the United States, 1995.

———. *Moses, Man of the Mountain*. Philadelphia: J. B. Lippincott, 1939.

———. *Mules and Men*. With a preface by Franz Boas, foreword by Arnold Rampersad, and afterword by Henry Louis Gates Jr. New York: Harper Perennial, 1990.

———. "The Negro in Florida, 1528–1940." Zora Neale Hurston Collection, Department of Special and Area Studies Collection, George A. Smathers Libraries, University of Florida, Gainesville.

———. *Tell My Horse: Voodoo and Life in Haiti and Jamaica*. With a foreword by Ishmael Reed and an afterword by Henry Louis Gates Jr. New York: Harper and Row, 1990.

———. "Uncle Monday." In *Folklore, Memoirs, and Other Writings*, selected and annotated by Cheryl A. Wall, 860–69. New York: Literary Classics of the United States, 1995.

"Husbands and Lovers Are Voodoo Sage's Specialty." *New Orleans Times-Democrat*, 29 October 1902, 10.

Hutchinson, George. *The Harlem Renaissance in Black and White*. Cambridge, MA: Harvard University Press, 1995.

Hyatt, Harry Middleton. *Folk-Lore from Adams County Illinois.* Memoirs of the Alma Egan Hyatt Foundation. New York: E. Cabella—French Printing and Publishing for the Alma Egan Hyatt Foundation, 1935.

———. *Hoodoo—Conjuration—Witchcraft—Rootwork.* Memoirs of the Alma Egan Hyatt Foundation. 5 vols. Hannibal, MO, and Cambridge, MD: Western Publishing for Harry Middleton Hyatt, 1970–78.

Institoris, Henricus. *Malleus Maleficarum.* Translated and with an introduction, bibliography, and notes by Montague Summers. New York: Benjamin Blom, 1928.

"Interesting Facts." *Chicago Defender,* 17 January 1920, 2.

Izard, George. "Diary of a Journey by George Izard, 1815–1816." *South Carolina Historical Magazine* 53 (1952): 67–76, 155–60, 223–29.

Jacobs, Claude F., and Andrew J. Kaslow. *The Spiritual Churches of New Orleans: Origins, Beliefs, and Rituals of an African-American Religion.* Knoxville: University of Tennessee Press, 1991.

Papa Jim and James e Sickafus. *Papa Jim Magical Herb Book.* 2nd ed. San Antonio: Papa Jim II, 1985.

Johnson, F. Roy. *The Fabled Doctor Jim Jordan: A Story of Conjure.* Murfreesboro, TN: Johnson, 1963.

Jones, Charles Colcock, Jr. *Gullah Folktales from the Georgia Coast.* With a foreword by Susan Miller Williams. Athens: University of Georgia Press, 2000.

Jones, Jacqueline. *Labor of Love, Labor of Sorrow: Black Women, Work, and the Family from Slavery to the Present.* New York: Vintage Books, 1995.

Jordan, Wilbert C. "Voodoo Medicine." In *Textbook of Black-Related Diseases,* edited by Richard Allen Williams, 715–38. New York: McGraw-Hill, 1975.

Joyner, Charles. *Down by the Riverside: A South Carolina Slave Community.* Urbana and Chicago: University of Illinois Press, 1984.

Keeney, Elizabeth Barnaby. "'Unless Powerful Sick': Domestic Medicine in the Old South." In *Science and Medicine in the Old South,* edited by Ronald L. Numbers and Todd L. Savitt, 276–94. Baton Rouge: Louisiana State University Press, 1989.

Kelley, Robin D. G. "'We Are Not What We Seem': Rethinking Black Working-Class Opposition in the Jim Crow South." *Journal of American History* 80 (1993): 75–111.

Kennedy, Stetson. "Ñañigo in Florida." *Southern Folklore Quarterly* 4 (1940): 153–56.

———. *Palmetto Country.* 1942. Reprinted with a new afterword by the author and an appreciation by Woody Guthrie. Tallahassee: Florida A&M University Press, 1989.

Kingsley, Mary. *Travels in West Africa: Congo Français, Corisco and Cameroons.* 5th ed. With an introduction by Elizabeth Claridge. London: Virago, 1982.

Klingelhofer, Eric. "Aspects of Early Afro-American Material Culture: Artifacts from the Slave Quarters at Garrison Plantation, Maryland." *Historical Archaeology* 21 (1987): 112–19.

Korstad, Robert, and Nelson Lichtenstein. "Opportunities Found and Lost: Labor,

Radicals, and the Early Civil Rights Movement." *Journal of American History* 75 (1988): 786–811.

Kramer, Victor A., and Robert A. Russ, eds. *Harlem Renaissance Re-examined: A Revised and Expanded Edition.* Troy, NY: Whitston, 1997.

Kulii, Elon Ali. "A Look at Hoodoo in Three Urban Areas of Indiana: Folklore and Change." Ph.D. diss., Indiana University, 1982.

———. "Root Doctors and Psychics in the Region." In *Indiana Folklore: A Reader,* ed. Linda Degh, 120–29. Bloomington: Indiana University Press, 1980.

Kyle, Richard. *The New Age Movement in American Culture.* Lanham, NY: University Press of America, 1995.

Lampe, H. U. *Famous Voodoo Rituals and Spells: A Voodoo Handbook.* New ed. Minneapolis: Marlar, 1982.

Lankford, George E., ed. *Native American Legends; Southeastern Legends: Tales from the Natchez, Caddo, Biloxi, Chickasaw, and Other Nations.* American Folklore Series, edited by W. K. McNeil. Little Rock, AR: August House, 1987.

Laveau, Marie. *Original Black and White Magic.* Los Angeles: International Imports, 1991.

Lawson, Steven F. *Black Ballots: Voting Rights in the South, 1945–1969.* New York: Columbia University Press, 1976.

———. *In Pursuit of Power: Southern Blacks and Electoral Politics, 1965–1982.* New York: Columbia University Press, 1985.

Lea, M. S. "Two-head Doctors." *American Mercury* 12 (1927): 236–40.

Lears, Thomas Jonathan Jackson. *No Place of Grace: Antimodernism and the Transformation of American Culture, 1880–1920.* New York: Pantheon Books, 1981.

"Lee Rails against Hollywood." *Gainesville Sun,* 7 February 2001.

Leone, Mark P., and Gladys-Marie Fry. "Conjuring in the Big House Kitchen: An Interpretation of African American Belief Systems Based on the Uses of Archaeology and Folklore Sources." *Journal of American Folklore* 112 (1999): 372–403.

"Letters from Hampton Graduates." *Southern Workman* 7 (1878): 28.

Levack, Brian P. *The Witch-Hunt in Early Modern Europe.* London: Longman, 1987.

Levine, Lawrence W. *Black Culture and Black Consciousness: Afro-American Thought from Slavery to Freedom.* New York: Oxford University Press, 1977.

Lewis, James R. "Approaches to the Study of the New Age Movement." In *Perspectives on the New Age,* edited by James R. Lewis and J. Gordon Melton, 1–12. Albany: State University of New York Press, 1992.

Lewis, James R., and J. Gordon Melton, eds. *Perspectives on the New Age.* Albany: State University of New York Press, 1992.

Lindroth, James. "Images of Subversion: Ishmael Reed and the Hoodoo Trickster." *African American Review* 30 (1996): 185–96.

Livermore, Mary A. *The Story of My Life, or the Sunshine and Shadow of Seventy Years.* Hartford, CT: A. D. Worthington, 1897.

Long, Carolyn Morrow. "John the Conqueror: From Root-Charm to Commercial Product." *Pharmacy in History* 39 (1997): 47–53.

———. *Spiritual Merchants: Religion, Magic, and Commerce.* Knoxville: University of Tennessee Press, 2001.

Lopez, A. L. "Nanigo Dance: Superstitions and Customs of Cuban Negroes in Tampa." In "Tampa." Tampa: Federal Writers' Project, [1938]. P. K. Yonge Library of Florida History, Department of Special and Area Studies Collection, George A. Smathers Libraries, University of Florida, Gainesville.

MacGaffey, Wyatt. *Religion and Society in Central Africa: The BaKongo of Central Zaire.* Chicago: University of Chicago Press, 1986.

MacRobert, Iain. "The Black Roots of Pentecostalism." In *African-American Religion: Interpretive Essays in History and Culture,* edited by Timothy E. Fulop and Albert J. Raboteau, 295–309. New York: Routledge, 1997.

"Madam Ida B. Jefferson." *Chicago Defender,* 7 July 1923, 18.

Maduro, Renaldo J. "Hoodoo Possession in San Francisco: Notes on Therapeutic Aspects of Regression." *Ethos* 3 (1975): 425–47.

"Magazine: Jackson Resorts to Voodoo." MSNBC, 2003. www.msnbc.com/news/880422.asp (accessed 11 March 2003).

Major, Clarence. *Dictionary of Afro-American Slang.* New York: International Publications, 1970.

———. *Juba to Jive: A Dictionary of African-American Slang.* New York: Penguin Books, 1994.

Malbrough, Ray T. *Charms, Spells, and Formulas: For the Making and Use of Gris-Gris, Herb Candles, Doll Magick, Incenses, Oils and Powders . . . to Gain Love, Protection, Prosperity, Luck, and Prophetic Dreams.* Llewellyn's Practical Magick Series. St. Paul, MN: Llewellyn, 1986.

Malcolm X, with the assistance of Alex Haley. *The Autobiography of Malcolm X.* With an Introduction by M. S. Handler and an epilogue by Alex Haley. New York: Grove, 1965.

Marie Laveau's Magic Herb Packets. New Orleans: Marie Laveau's House of Voodoo, n.d.

Mathers, S. Liddell MacGregor, ed. and trans. *The Key of Solomon the King (Clavicula Salomonis).* With a foreword by Richard Cavendish. York Beach, ME: Samuel Weiser, 1972.

McCracken, Grant. *Culture and Consumption: New Approaches to the Symbolic Character of Consumer Goods and Activities.* Bloomington: Indiana University Press, 1988.

McGowan, Pierre. *The Gullah Mailman.* Illustrated by Nancy Ricker Rhett. Raleigh, NC: Pentland, 2000.

McMillan, Timothy J. "Black Magic: Witchcraft, Race, and Resistance in Colonial New England." *Journal of Black Studies* 25 (1994): 99–117.

McNeil, W. K., ed. *Ghost Stories from the American South.* Little Rock, AR: August House, 1985.

McReynolds, Edwin C. *The Seminoles.* Norman: University of Oklahoma Press, 1957.

McTeer, James Edwin. *High Sheriff of the Low Country.* With an introduction by William L. Rhodes Jr. Columbia, SC: JEM, 1970.

———. *Fifty Years as a Low Country Witch Doctor.* Beaufort, SC: Beaufort Book, 1976.

"Md. Woman Facing Murder Charges Again." *Washington Post,* 5 January 2002, B1.

Mead, Margaret. *Coming of Age in Samoa: A Psychological Study of Primitive Youth for Western Civilization.* With a foreword by Franz Boas. New York: Blue Ribbon Books, 1932.

Melton, J. Gordon, Jerome Clark, Aidan A. Kelly, Dell deChant, Johnny Flynn, James R. Lewis, Suzanne Riordan, and Steve Shafarman. *New Age Encyclopedia: A Guide to the Beliefs, Concepts, Terms, People, and Organizations That Make Up the New Global Movement toward Spiritual Development, Health and Healing, Higher Consciousness, and Related Subjects.* Detroit: Gale Research, 1990.

Métraux, Alfred. *Voodoo in Haiti.* Translated by Hugo Charteris and with an introduction by Sidney W. Mintz. New York: Schocken Books, 1972.

Meyer Kallen, Horace. *Culture and Democracy in the United States.* American Immigration Collection, series 2. New York: Arno, 1970.

Miller, Donald, and Richard Miller. *Miller's* catalog. Atlanta, GA, ca. 2001.

Miller, Richard. Interview by author. 7 April 2001. Atlanta, GA. Notes. Author's personal collection, Birmingham, AL.

Millspaugh, Charles F. *American Medicinal Plants: An Illustrated and Descriptive Guide to Plants Indigenous to and Naturalized in the United States Which Are Used in Medicine.* Philadelphia: John C. Yorston, 1892. New York: Dover, 1974.

Mishkin, Tracy. *The Harlem and Irish Renaissances: Language, Identity, and Representation.* With a foreword by George Bornstein. Gainesville: University of Florida Press, 1998.

Mitchell, Faith. *Hoodoo Medicine: Gullah Herbal Remedies.* Columbia, SC: Summerhouse, 1999.

Mitchell, Margaret. *Gone with the Wind.* New York: Macmillan, 1936.

Moerman, Daniel E. "Anthropology of Symbolic Healing." *Current Anthropology* 20 (1979): 59–80.

Mooney, James. "Cherokee Theory and Practice of Medicine." *Journal of American Folk-Lore* 3 (1890): 44–50.

———. *Myths of the Cherokee and Sacred Formulas of the Cherokees.* Nashville: Charles and Randy Elder, 1982.

Moreau de Saint-Méry, Louis-Élise. *Description topographique, physique, civile, politique et historique de la partie française de l'île de Saint-Domingue.* 2 vols. Philadelphia, 1797.

Morrison, Toni. *Sula.* New York: Knopf, 1974.

Moss, Kay K. *Southern Folk Medicine, 1750–1820.* Columbia: University of South Carolina Press, 1999.

"Mother Mary." *Miami Times,* 4 July 1974, 37.

Mulira, Jessie Gaston. "The Case of Voodoo in New Orleans." In *Africanisms in American Culture*, edited by Joseph E. Holloway, 34–68. Blacks in the Diaspora Series, edited by Darlene Clark Hine, John McCluskey Jr., and David Barry Gaspar. Bloomington: Indiana University Press, 1990.

Mullins, Paul R. *Race and Affluence: An Archaeology of African American and Consumer Culture.* New York: Kluwer Academic / Plenum, 1999.

Murphy, Joseph M. *Santería: African Spirits in America.* Reprinted with a new preface. Boston: Beacon, 1993. Originally published in 1988 as *Santería: An African Religion in America.*

Naison, Mark. *Communists in Harlem during the Depression.* Urbana: University of Illinois Press, 1983.

Nash, Gary B. *Red, White, and Black: The Peoples of Early North America.* 4th ed. Upper Saddle River, NJ: Prentice Hall, 2000.

Neal, James C. "Legalized Crime in Florida." In *Proceedings of the Florida Medical Association: Session of 1891*, 42–50. Jacksonville: Times-Union, 1891.

"The Negro Cesar's Cure for Poison." *Massachusetts Magazine* 4 (1792): 103–4.

Nelson, Bruce. *Workers on the Waterfront.* Urbana: University of Illinois Press, 1988.

Newell, William W. "Myths of Voodoo Worship and Child Sacrifice in Hayti." *Journal of American Folk-Lore* 1 (1888): 16–30.

———. "Reports of Voodoo Worship in Hayti and Louisiana." *Journal of American Folk-Lore* 2 (1889): 41–47.

New Orleans Historic Voodoo Museum. New Orleans: New Orleans Historic Voodoo Museum, n.d.

Noll, Joyce Elaine. *Company of Prophets: African American Psychics, Healers, and Visionaries.* St. Paul, MN: Llewellyn, 1991.

Norrell, Robert J. *Reaping the Whirlwind: The Civil Rights Movement in Tuskegee.* New York: Knopf, 1985.

Norris, Thaddeus. "Negro Superstitions." *Lippincott's Monthly Magazine* 6 (1870): 90–95.

Novick, Peter. *That Noble Dream: The "Objectivity Question" and the American Historical Profession.* New York: Cambridge University Press, 1988.

Oliver, Roland, and J. D. Fage. *A Short History of Africa.* 6th ed. London: Penguin Group, 1988.

Opie, Iona, and Moira Tatem, eds. *A Dictionary of Superstitions.* Oxford: Oxford University Press, 1989.

Opoku, Kofi Asare. *West African Traditional Religion.* Accra, Ghana: FEP International, 1978.

"Opportunity Awaits You." *Miami Times,* 9 January 1960, 11.

Orser, Charles E., Jr. "The Archaeology of African-American Slave Religion in the Antebellum South." *Cambridge Archeological Review Journal* 4 (1994): 33–45.

Owen, Mary Alicia. "Among the Voodoos." In *The International Folk-lore Congress 1891: Papers and Transactions*, 230–48. London: David Nutt, 1892.

———. *Voodoo Tales as Told among the Negroes of the Southwest.* With an Introduction by Charles Godfrey Leland and illustrations by Juliette A. Owen and Louis Wain. New York: G. P. Putnam's Sons, 1893.

Owen, Nicholas. *Journal of a Slave Dealer: A View of Some Remarkable Axcedents in the Life of Nics. Owen on the Coast of Africa and America from the Year 1746 to the Year 1757.* Edited and with an introduction by Eveline Martin. London: George Routledge and Sons, 1930.

Page, Thomas Nelson. *Red Rock: A Chronicle of Reconstruction.* New York: Charles Scribner's Sons, 1898.

Park, S. M. "Voodooism in Tennessee." *Atlantic Monthly* 64 (September 1889): 376–80.

Parrinder, Geoffrey. *West African Religion: A Study of the Beliefs and Practices of Akan, Ewe, Yoruba, Ibo, and Kindred Peoples.* 2nd ed. With a foreword by Edwin Smith. London: Epworth, 1961.

Patten, M. Drake. "Mankala and Minkisi: Possible Evidence of African-American Folk Beliefs and Practices." *African-American Archaeology* 6 (1992): 5–7.

Pendleton, Louis. "Notes on Negro Folk-Lore and Witchcraft in the South." *Journal of American Folk-Lore* 3 (1890): 201–7.

Penkower, Monty Noam. *The Federal Writers' Project: A Study in Government Patronage of the Arts.* Urbana: University of Illinois Press, 1977.

Perdue, Charles, Thomas Barden, and Robert Phillips. *Weevils in the Wheat: Interviews with Virginia Ex-slaves.* Charlottesville: University Press of Virginia, 1976.

Peterson, Tracey. "The Witch of Franklin." *Southern Folklore Quarterly* 33 (1969): 297–312.

Pinckney, Roger. *Blue Roots: African-American Folk Magic of the Gullah People.* St. Paul, MN: Llewellyn, 2000.

Pitkin, Helen. *An Angel by Brevet: A Story of Modern New Orleans.* Philadelphia: J. B. Lippincott, 1904.

Pollack, Norman. *The Populist Response to Industrial America: Midwestern Populist Thought.* Cambridge, MA: Harvard University Press, 1962.

Porteous, Laura L. "The Gri-gri Case." *Louisiana Historical Quarterly* 17 (1934): 48–63.

Propp, Vladimir I. *Morphology of the Folktale.* Translated by Laurence Scott. 2nd ed. With a preface by Louis A. Wagner and an introduction by Alan Dundes. Austin: University of Texas Press, 1968.

Pryse, Marjorie, and Hortense J. Spillers, eds. *Conjuring: Black Women, Fiction, and Literary Tradition.* Bloomington: Indiana University Press, 1985.

"Psychic Readings by Niva." *Miami Times,* 26 March 1998, 5D.

Puckett, Newbell Niles. *Folk Beliefs of the Southern Negro.* Patterson Smith Reprint Series in Criminology, Law Enforcement, and Social Problems, 22. Chapel Hill: University of North Carolina Press, 1926. Reprint, Montclair, NJ: Patterson Smith, 1968.

R., L., G., and A. "Conjure Doctors in the South." *Southern Workman* 7 (1878): 30–31.

Raboteau, Albert J. *Slave Religion: The "Invisible Institution" in the Antebellum South.* Oxford: Oxford University Press, 1978.

Rawick, George P., ed. *The American Slave: A Composite Autobiography.* 41 vols. Westport, CT: Greenwood, 1972–79.

Reed, Ishmael. *Conjure: Selected Poems, 1963–1970.* Amherst: University of Massachusetts Press, 1972.

———. *Mumbo Jumbo.* Garden City, NY: Doubleday, 1972.

Reiss, Oscar. *Medicine in Colonial America.* Lanham, NY: University Press of America, 2000.

"The Religious Life of the Negro Slave." *Harper's New Monthly Magazine* 27 (September–November 1863): 479–85, 676–82, 816–25.

Renda, Mary A. *Taking Haiti: Military Occupation and the Culture of U.S. Imperialism, 1915–1940.* Chapel Hill: University of North Carolina Press, 2001.

Rhett, Nancy. Interview by author. 24 October 2001. Beaufort, SC. Notes. Author's personal collection, Birmingham, AL.

Rhodes, Jewell Parker. "Marie Laveau, Voodoo Queen." *Ms.* 28 (1983): 28–31.

Richardson, Martin. "Bolita," 17 August 1937. In "Negro Folk Lore and Custom," ed. John A. Simms. In "Florida Folklore & Customs." (Federal Writers' Project, [1938?]). P. K. Yonge Library of Florida History, Department of Special and Area Studies Collection, George A. Smathers Libraries, University of Florida, Gainesville.

Rigaud, Milo. *Secrets of Voodoo.* Translated by Robert B. Cross. New York: Arco, 1969. Reprint, San Francisco: City Lights Books, 1985.

Ritzer, George. *The McDonaldization of Society.* New Century Edition. Thousand Oaks, CA: Pine Forge, 2000.

Robinson, F. L.. Interview by author. 11 January 2002. Micanopy, FL. Notes and audio recording. Author's personal collection, Birmingham, AL.

Roller, David C., and Robert W. Twyman, eds. *The Encyclopedia of Southern History.* Baton Rouge: Louisiana State University Press, 1979.

Rondo, Mike, and Darren Rondo. *Rondo's Temple Sales Co.* catalog. Atlanta, GA, [2000?].

"'Root Doctor' Held in Murder of His Former Wife." *Jet,* 1 June 1987, 29.

"Roots and Herbs of All Kinds Bought and Sold." *Chicago Defender,* 10 September 1921, 3.

Rucker, Herman. *Black Herman's Secrets of Magic, Mystery, and Legerdemain.* 15th ed. Dallas: Dorene, 1938.

Russell, Jeffrey Burton. *Witchcraft in the Middle Ages.* Ithaca, NY: Cornell University Press, 1972.

Said, Edward W. *Orientalism.* New York: Vintage Books, 1979.

Saphir, J. Robin, Arnold Gold, James Giambrone, and James F. Holland. "Voodoo Poisoning in Buffalo, NY." *Journal of the American Medical Association* 202 (1967): 437–38.

Savage, Phoenix. Interview by author. Telephone. 28 July 2002. Notes. Author's personal collection, Birmingham, AL.

Savitt, Todd L. *Medicine and Slavery: The Diseases and Health Care of Blacks in Antebellum Virginia*. Blacks in the New World Series, edited by August Meier. Urbana: University of Illinois Press, 1978.

Saxon, Lyle. *Fabulous New Orleans*. New York: Century, 1928.

———. "Voodoo." *New Republic*, 23 March 1927, 135–39.

Saxon, Lyle, Robert Tallant, and Edward Dreyer. *Gumbo Ya-Ya: A Collection of Louisiana Folk Tales*. New York: Bonanza Books, 1945.

Schlesinger, Arthur M., Jr. *The Disuniting of America*. New York: W. W. Norton, 1992.

Scot, Reginald. *The Discoverie of Witchcraft*. With an introduction by Hugh Ross Williamson. Carbondale: Southern Illinois University Press, 1964.

Scott, Anne Firor. *The Southern Lady: From Pedestal to Politics, 1830–1930*. Chicago: University of Chicago Press, 1970.

Seabrook, William B. *The Magic Island*. New York: Harcourt, Brace, 1929.

Selig, Godfrey A. *The Secrets of the Psalms*. New ed. Arlington, TX: Dorene, 1982.

Shepard, Eli. "Superstitions of the Negro." *Cosmopolitan Magazine* 5 (1888): 47–50.

"Sister Lisa." *Miami Times*, 26 March 1998, 5D.

The Sixth and Seventh Books of Moses, or Moses' Magical Spirit Art. New ed. Arlington, TX: Dorene, n.d.

Smalley, Eugene V. "Sugar-Making in Louisiana." *Century* 35 (1887): 100–120.

Smiley, Portia. "Folk-lore from Virginia, South Carolina, Georgia, Alabama, and Florida." *Journal of American Folk-Lore* 32 (1919): 357–83.

Smith, Jonell, and Jazell Smith. Conversations with and overheard by author, 15 November 2001, New Orleans, LA. Notes and audio recording. Author's personal collection, Birmingham, AL.

Smith, Peter. *The Indian Doctor's Dispensatory*. Cincinnati, OH: Browne and Looker, 1813.

Smith, Theophus H. *Conjuring Culture: Biblical Formations of Black America*. New York: Oxford University Press, 1994.

Snake, Doktor. *Doktor Snake's Voodoo Spellbook: Spells, Curses, and Folk Magic for All Your Needs*. New York: St. Martin's, 2000.

Snow, Loudell F. "Mail Order Magic: The Commercial Exploitation of Folk Belief." *Journal of the American Folklore Institute* 16 (1979): 44–73.

———. "Sorcerers, Saints, and Charlatans: Black Folk Healers in Urban America." *Culture, Medicine, and Psychiatry* 2 (1978): 69–106.

"Some Conjure Doctors We Have Heard Of." Folk-Lore and Ethnology. *Southern Workman* 26 (1897): 37–38.

Sonny Boy Blue Book Guide to Success© Power©. 6th ed. Birmingham, AL, 2000.

Sparkman, James R. "The Negro." Sparkman Family Papers, Southern Historical Collection, University of North Carolina, Chapel Hill. Quoted in Charles Joyner, *Down by the Riverside: A South Carolina Slave Community* (Urbana: University of Chicago Press, 1984), 144.

"Special Judge Hears Case: Two Blacks Face Murder Charges in Voodoo Scheme." *Jet*, 17 July 1989, 52–53.

"A Spiritual Medium." *Chicago Defender*, 14 August 1915, 3.

Steiner, Roland. "Braziel Robinson Possessed of Two Spirits." *Journal of American Folk-Lore* 14 (1901): 226–28.

———. "Observations on the Practice of Conjuring in Georgia." *Journal of American Folk-Lore* 14 (1901): 173–80.

———. "Superstitions and Beliefs from Central Georgia." *Journal of American Folk-Lore* 12 (1899): 261–71.

Stine, Linda France, Melanie A. Cabak, and Mark D. Groover. "Blue Beads as African-American Cultural Symbols." *Historical Archaeology* 30 (1996): 49–75.

Stoyer, Jacob. *My Life in the South*. 4th ed. Salem, MA: Newcomb and Gauss, 1898.

Straight, William M. "Throw Downs, Fixin, Rooting, and Hexing." *Journal of the Florida Medical Association, Inc.* 70 (1983): 635–41.

Suttles, William C., Jr. "African Religious Survivals as Factors in American Slave Revolts." *Journal of Negro History* 56 (1971): 97–104.

Synan, Vinson. *The Holiness-Pentecostal Tradition: Charismatic Movements in the Twentieth Century*. 2nd ed. Grand Rapids, MI: William B. Eerdmans, 1997.

Tallant, Robert. "Chronology of Voodoo." Robert Tallant Papers, 245–58. City Archives, New Orleans Public Library, New Orleans.

———. *Voodoo in New Orleans*. New York: Macmillan, 1946. Reprint, Gretna, LA: Pelican, 1998.

———. *The Voodoo Queen*. New York: Putnam, 1956. Reprint, Gretna, LA: Pelican, 2000.

Taylor, Samuel C. "A Hoodoo Doctor, 30 April 1890." James S. Schoff Collection, William L. Clements Library, University of Michigan, Ann Arbor.

Thomas, Keith. *Religion and the Decline of Magic*. New York: Charles Scribner's Sons, 1971.

Thompson, Robert Farris. *Face of the Gods: Art and Altars of Africa and the African Americas*. New York: Museum of African Art, 1993.

———. *Flash of the Spirit: African and Afro-American Art and Philosophy*. New York: Random House, 1983.

Tinling, David C. "Voodoo, Root Work, and Medicine." *Psychosomatic Medicine* 5 (1967): 483–90.
Tivnan, E. "The Voodoo That New Yorkers Do." *New York Times Magazine*, 2 December 1979, 182–92.
Touchstone, Blake. "Voodoo in New Orleans." *Louisiana History* 13 (1972): 371–86.
Tsuzuki, Kyoichi. *Sam Doyle*. Los Angeles: Books Nippan, 1990.
Turlington, Shannon R. *The Complete Idiot's Guide® to Voodoo*. Indianapolis: Alpha, 2002.
Tyler, Varro E. "The Elusive History of High John the Conqueror Root." *Pharmacy in History* 33 (1991): 164–66.
Vogel, Virgil J. *American Indian Medicine*. Civilization of the American Indian Series, vol. 95. Norman: University of Oklahoma Press, 1970.
"Voodoo and Cemetery Tour." Haunted History Tours, 1996–2001. www.hauntedhistorytours.com (accessed 9 July 2002).
"Voodoo Kills by Despair." *Science News Letter* 67 (1955): 294.
Voodoo Spiritual Temple. New Orleans: Voodoo Spiritual Temple, n.d.
"The Voudou-'Fetish.'" *Daily Picayune*, 25 June 1873.
W. and C. "About the Conjuring Doctors." *Southern Workman* 7 (1878): 38–39.
Wacker, Grant. *Heaven Below: Early Pentecostals and American Culture*. Cambridge, MA: Harvard University Press, 2001.
Waite, Arthur Edward. *The Book of Ceremonial Magic: The Secret in Goëtia*. With a foreword by John C. Wilson. New York: Citadel, 1994.
Walker, Alice. *The Third Life of Grange Copeland*. New York: Harcourt, Brace, Jovanovich, 1970.
Ward, Martha. *Voodoo Queen: The Spirited Lives of Marie Laveau*. Jackson: University Press of Mississippi, 2004.
Waring, Philippa. *The Dictionary of Omens and Superstitions*. Rev. ed. Secaucus, NJ: Chartwell Books, 1986.
Warner, Charles Dudley. *Studies in the South and West, with Comments on Canada*. New York: Harper and Brothers, 1889.
"Warner's Safe Kidney and Liver Cure." *Key West Democrat*, 29 April 1882.
Watson, Wilburn H., ed. *Black Folk Medicine: The Therapeutic Significance of Faith and Trust*. New Brunswick, NJ: Transaction Books, 1984.
Weinstein, James. "Radicalism in the Midst of Normalcy." *Journal of American History* 52 (1966): 773–90.
"Welcome to the New Orleans Historic Voodoo Museum." The New Orleans Historic Voodoo Museum. www.voodoomuseum.com (accessed 9 July 2002).
"Welcome to Voodoo Authentica (TM)." Voodoo Authentica, 2000–2002. www.voodooshop.com (accessed 9 July 2002).

Weyer, Johann. *Witches, Devils, and Doctors in the Renaissance.* Translated by John Shea, introduction and notes by George Mora, and with a foreword by John Weber. Binghampton, NY: Medieval and Renaissance Texts and Studies, 1991.

"Where the Best Defense Is a Good Hex." *St. Petersburg Times,* 10 April 1995, 1B, 5B.

Whitney, Annie Weston, and Caroline Canfield Bullock. *Folk-Lore from Maryland.* New York: American Folk-Lore Society, 1925.

Whitten, Norman E. "Contemporary Patterns of Malign Occultism among Negroes in North Carolina." *Journal of American Folklore* 75 (1962): 310–25.

"Why Be Sick!" *Chicago Defender,* 17 January 1920, 2.

Wilkie, Laurie A. "Magic and Empowerment on the Plantation: An Archaeological Consideration of African-American World View." *Southeastern Archaeology* 14 (1995): 136–48.

Williams, Charles deV. "Gullah Tours." *Charleston Post and Courier,* 13 April 1999. Gullah Tours, 11 April 2002. www.gullahtours.com/courier.html (accessed 9 July 2002).

Williams, Claudia. Interview by author. 16 November 2001. New Orleans, LA. Author's personal collection, Birmingham, AL.

Williams, Marie B. "A Night with the Voudous." *Appleton's Journal: A Magazine of General Literature* 13 (1875): 404–5.

Williams, Thomas. Interview by author. 25 October 2001. Columbia, SC. Author's personal collection, Birmingham, AL.

Winkelman, Michael. "Magic: A Theoretical Reassessment." *Current Anthropology* 23 (1982): 37–66.

Winslow, David J. "Bishop E. E. Everett and Some Aspects of Occultism and Folk Religion in Negro Philadelphia." *Keystone Folklore Quarterly* 14 (1969): 59–80.

Wintrob, Ronald M. "The Influence of Others: Witchcraft and Rootwork as Explanations of Behavior Disturbances." *Journal of Nervous and Mental Disease* 156 (1973): 318–26.

Wolf, John Quincy. "Aunt Caroline Dye: The Gypsy in the 'Saint Louis Blues.'" *Southern Folklore Quarterly* 33 (1969): 339–46.

Wolman, Benjamin B., ed. *Handbook of Parapsychology.* New York: Van Nostrand Reinhold, 1977.

Woodward, C. Vann. *The Strange Career of Jim Crow.* New York: Oxford University Press, 1957.

Wyatt-Brown, Bertram. *Southern Honor: Ethics and Behavior in the Old South.* New York: Oxford University Press, 1982.

Yates, Irene. "Conjures and Cures in the Novels of Julia Peterkin." *Southern Folklore Quarterly* 10 (1946): 137–49.

Young, James Harvey. *American Self-Dosage Medicines: An Historical Perspective.* Lawrence, KS: Coronado, 1974.

———. *The Toadstool Millionaires: A Social History of Patent Medicines in America before Federal Regulation.* Princeton, NJ: Princeton University Press, 1961.

Young, Stark. *So Red the Rose.* New York: Charles Scribner's Sons, 1934.

Yronwode, Catherine. "Anointing Oils." Lucky Mojo Curio Company, 1995–2002. www.luckymojo.com/mojocatoils.html (accessed 29 July 2002).

———. "Blues Lyrics and Hoodoo." Lucky Mojo Curio Company, 1995–99. www.luckymojo.com/blues.html#performers and www.luckymojo.com/blueshoodoobrown.html (accessed 20 May 2002).

———. "Catherine Yronwode." Lucky Mojo Curio Company, 1995–2002. www.luckymojo.com/cat.html (accessed 29 July 2002).

———. "Hoodoo." Lucky Mojo Curio Company, 1995–99. www.luckymojo.com/hoodoohistory.html (accessed 20 May 2002).

———. *Hoodoo Herb and Root Magic: A Materia Magica of African-American Conjure and Traditional Formulary Giving the Spiritual Uses of Natural Herbs, Roots, Minerals, and Zoological Curios.* Forestville, CA: Lucky Mojo Curio Company, 2002.

———. "Hoodoo Magic Spells Correspondence Course 2003." Lucky Mojo Curio Company, 1995–2003. www.luckymojo.com/mojocourse.html (accessed 5 March 2003).

———. Interview by author. Telephone. 15 January 2001. Author's personal collection, Birmingham, AL.

———. "Lucky Mojo Curio Co." Lucky Mojo Curio Company, 1995–2002. www.luckymojo.com/luckymojocatalogue.html (accessed 29 July 2002).

———. "Secrets of the Psalms: The Kabbalist Influence on Hoodoo." Lucky Mojo Curio Company, 1995–2002. www.luckymojo.com/secretspsalms (accessed 18 June 2002).

———. "Sonny Boy Products at the Egypt Candle Store." Lucky Mojo Curio Company, 1995–2002. www.luckymojo.com/sonnyboy.html (accessed 18 June 2002).

Zamir, Shamoon. "An Interview with Ishmael Reed." *Callaloo* 17 (1994): 1131–57.

Index

Page numbers in italics refer to tables.

Aaron, Uncle, 79, 108
Abasi, *33, 35, 58*
Adam and Eve root, 70, 121, 125
Adams, William, 35, 60, 82, 94–97, 100, 111
Adefumni, Oba Oseijeman, 146–48
aerosol sprays, 119, 122, 129, 193
African Methodist Episcopal, 108
African religions, 28–49, 134, 143–44, 146–48
Afrocentrism, 165n64
Agoussou, 30, *32, 58,* 94
Akan, 27, 31
alchemy, 55
Alexander, 98
Alexander, King, 37–38, 64, 96, 101, 105–6, 108, 110, 116
Alfonso I, 35
altars, 46, 59, 91, 105–6
American nature of conjure, 72–74
Amish, 55, 58
ancestors. *See* dead, the
Anderson, Byrl, 56
Andrews, Samuel Simeon, 101, 105
Anglo settlement: and definition of cultural zone, 27–28, 31, 34–38, 45, 57, 71, 93–96, 99–100, 105–6, 108–9, 112–14, 121; origins of, 25–27
archaeology, 23, 40, 61, 73, 76, 85, 116, 194–95
arrowheads, Native American, 73
art, 12, 154–55, 191, 194, 198
Ashe, 144
Assonquer, 30–31, *32,* 59, 94
astrology, 54–55
Atlanta, Georgia, 117, 147
Aunt Sally's Policy Player's Dream Book, 120, 193
Ausly, Kenneth, 159

Bab, Old, 154
babalawos, 145
Bahamas, 92–93
Bambara, 28
Baptists, 117, 142, 146, 158
Barker, John, 84

221

Barnes, Doctor, 95, 98
Barrett, Harriet, 83
Bass, Ruth, 15, 44, 101
Batts, 53
beads, blue, 40
Beaufort, South Carolina, 14, 56, 98, 109, 118, 130–31, 151, 155
beef tongues, 106
Bell, John, 53
Bellile, Francisco, 51
Berendt, John, 21
Berry, Betty, 154
Berry, Tommy Lee, 154
Bibb, Henry, 38–39, 63–64, 84, 86, 102, 127
Bible, x, 56, 60, 69, 78, 96, 120, 123, 129, 132, 156
Bill, Railroad, 54, 89
Birmingham, Alabama, 120
births, unusual, 48, 96. *See also* cauls
Bishop, Ank, 94
Black, Jason S., 144, 148
black cats' bones, 41, 69, 105–6, 129
Black Hawk, 73–74, 157
Black Herman's Secrets of Magic, Mystery, and Legerdemain (Rucker), 193
Black Power, 20
black-to-white ratios, 31, 65, 167, 168n19
Blanc Dani, 30–31, 32, 34, 46, 57, 58, 59, 66, 92, 94
blood, xi, 9, 46, 93, 102
blues, ix, 135, 155, 190, 195
Bon Dieu, 35, 58, 95–96. *See also under* God
Bonaparte, Napoleon, 61
bones, x, 62, 69, 101, 168n27. *See also* black cats' bones
botanicas, 145–47, 159
bottles, 39, 61, 80, 102–3, 106. *See also* witch bottles
Boyle, Virginia Frazer, 8
Brazil, 144
Brisbane, Jimmy, 131
Brown, Bessie, 14

Brown, Eugenia, xiv, 131
Brown, William Wells, 7, 79, 86
Bruce, Philip A., 1, 7, 77, 79, 82, 86
brujas, 27
brujería, 144, 177n9, 185n36
Buddha, 129
Bug, Doctor, 109
Buzzard, Doctor, 14, 19, 42, 48, 56, 62, 78, 85, 98, 109–10, 118, 124–25, 129–31, 136, 151–52, 155, 164n47

Cable, George Washington, 9, 94, 115–16, 190, 194
Caesar, Julius P., 118, 129, 132, 152
Calvary Religious and Occult Store/Calvary Spiritual Temple, 122
candles, 46, 54, 59–60, 70, 91, 94, 99, 105, 118, 122, 126, 129, 139, 145, 158–59
Candomble, 18, 144, 161n2
cannibalism, 52, 54, 66
capitalism, 2, 11, 16
cards, 61, 69, 81, 102–3
Caribbean immigration, 27, 31, 34, 92
Carlos, 51
Carter, Ida. *See* Seven Sisters
Carter, Joseph William, 64
Castellanos, Henry C., 113
Catholicism, 18, 34, 50, 57–59, 65, 77, 95, 120, 146–47, 156–57
cauls, 44, 96
Cesar, 76
Chamani, Priestess Miriam, xiii, 142–43
Charleston, South Carolina, 62, 136
charms, feeding of, 38, 101
Charpentier, Mrs. Augustine Lombas, 78
Cherokee, 63–65, 72, 173n45
Chesnutt, Charles W., 8, 155, 194
Chewing John, 39, 70, 128
Chicago, Illinois, 12, 118–19, 156
Chicago Defender, 14, 124–25, 182n45, 193
Chickasaw, 63

chickens, xi, 41, 70, 93, 102, 107
Chireau, Yvonne, 166n76
Choctaw, 63
Christianity, 17, 35–36, 49, 51–52, 56–60, 79, 90, 92–96, 108, 129, 141, 143, 147, 156, 158. *See also* Catholicism *and* Protestantism
Church of God in Christ, 123, 158
Circle, the. *See* secret societies
civil rights movement, 16, 18, 20, 146–47, 152, 155–56
Civil War, 2, 4, 10, 51, 74, 76, 80, 83, 85, 87, 94, 103, 109, 113, 115–16, 120, 152–53
cold war, 16
commodification, 111–12, 126, 133, 135, 150
communism, 2, 11–12, 16, 23
Congo Hall, 93
Congo Square, 91, 135
conjure: African foundations of, 19, 22, 24–49, 134, 143, 150, 159; as an alternative religion, 133–34, 141–42; definition of, x–xi; effectiveness of, 75, 81–83, 89–90, 107, 144, 150, 191; European contributions to, 24–25, 50–63, 134, 150, 159; extent of belief in, 76–78, 84–86, 94, 136, 191, 193; function of, 7, 11, 81–86, 89, 106, 127, 150–52, 154, 159; and identity, 2, 5, 7, 11, 16–20; and language, 155–56; and marketing, 14, 90, 111, 193; Native American contributions to, 25, 62–74, 128–29, 134, 150, 159; and origin of term, 27–28, 57; removing, process of, 102–3, 110; scarcity of sources addressing, 51, 98, 150, 189, 197; survival of, 129; and women, 153–55. *See also* spiritual supplies
conjurers. *See* practitioners
Conquer-John. *See* John the Conqueror
consistency, principle of, 190
consumerism. *See* commodification
contagious magic, 103–5, 127–28
correspondences, 55. *See also* Doctrine of Signatures *and* sympathetic magic
Cortez, Enrique, 146

counterculture, 141–43
court cases and legal magic, 37, 60, 73, 85, 88, 103, 106, 128, 151–52, 159, 176n37
covens, 52–53
Covey, 84, 86. *See also* Frederick Douglass
Cracker Jack Drugstore, 117
creatures living in the body, 39–40, 68, 69, 80–81, 87, 102–3, 111, 115–16, 190–91
Creek, 63, 67–68, 72
creole and creolization, 25, 35, 73
cross marks, 40, 131
crossroads, 41, 98–99
Cuba, 18, 27, 34, 45, 92, 113, 120, 144–46
cultural pluralism. *See* relativism
cunning men/women, 54, 58, 79, 114
curanderismo, 144, 185n36

Da, 29–31, 65–66
Dahomey. *See* Fon
Dailey, Aunt Jenny, 131
dances, 45, 47, 49, 57, 66, 88, 91–92, 100, 114, 136
Dani (Danny). *See* Blanc Dani
Davis, Rod, 147
De Claremont, Lewis, 121
dead, the, x, 65, 101, 144. *See also* deities and spirits
Deborah, xiii, 146, 149
Dédé, Sanité, 109
deities and spirits, x, 28, 29–31, 32–33, 34–37, 38, 43, 48–49, 51–54, 57, 60–61, 66, 68, 79, 88, 94–97, 99–101, 103, 105, 109, 121, 123, 138–39, 142–44, 147, 156–57, 171n18, 190; animistic, 101; Marie Laveau as, 88; and payment, 37; and saints, 31, 34, 50, 57, 58, 59, 65, 73–74, 91, 106, 144, 157, 171n18. *See also names of specific deities, spirits, and saints*
DeLaurence, Lauren William, 118, 121
DeLaurence, Scott and Company, 118
devil, 48, 52–53, 57, 58, 79, 88, 93–99, 132, 136, 154, 171n18
devil's shoestring, 69

INDEX 223

Dipo. *See* secret societies
divining rods, 85, 124
Divinity, Old, 44, 68, 101
Doctrine of Signatures, 55
Domenech, Abbé Emmanuel Henri Dieudonné, 76–77
Donis, 97
Dorson, Richard M., 89
double-heads. *See* two heads
double-sighter. *See* two heads
Douglass, Frederick, 3, 84, 86, 102
Doyle, Sam, 155, 194
Dye, Aunt Caroline, 87, 130

Eagle, Doctor, 118, 121
East Asian immigration, 141
Eastern mysticism. *See* Orientalism
Efik, 45
eggs, 102, 113
egun, 144
Egypt, 122
Elegba, 29, 31, *33*, *58*, 93
Elihu, 60
Elixir Sulfanilamide, 125
English. *See* Anglo settlement
Episcopal Church, 134
Eshu, 29
Espiritismo, 18, 144
Everett, Bishop E. E., 122
evil eye, 62
Ewe, 26–30, *32–33*, 35, 38–39
Expedite, Saint, 73
Eye of the Cat, 117

F and F Botanica and Candle Shop, 117, 146
faith: and role in conjure, 81–83, 86, 89–90, 94, 106–7, 137, 144
Faith Doctor, 77–78
Farrakhan, Louis, 148
Father Jones, 157

feasts, 46–47, 91–92
Federal Food, Drug, and Cosmetic Act, 125–26
Federal Writers' Project, 11, 14, 16, 21, 76, 82, 84, 97, 116, 120, 129, 131, 154, 191, 197
Fields, Mamie Garvin, 131
Figueroa, Felix, xiii, 117, 146
five finger grass, 61, *70*, 125
fixing, 28, 85, 156
flannel, red, 41, *69*
folklore, professional, 5, 17
folktales, 5, 7–8, 89, 151
Fon, 26–30, *32–33*, 35, 38, 41–42, 49
footprints, 39, 41–42, 104
Foss, George, 99
Fowler, M. P., 124
Frank, Uncle, 86, 89
Franklin, Tom, 39
French. *See* Latin settlement
Fry, Gladys-Marie, 56
Full Gospel Church, 158
Funza, 39

Ga-Dangme, 27
Gamache, Henri, 120–21, 132
Ganda, 114
Gardner, Thomas, III, 151
gbo, 38, 68
Geffen, David, 159
Genovese, Eugene, 22
George, 103
Germans, 58, 61
gerregerys. *See* gregory bags
Ghana, 42, 44
ghosts, 30, 36, 41, 43, 54, 65, 101
Glassman, Sally Ann, xiii, 143–44, 148
Gnosticism, 142
God: Christian, 35–37, 48, 51, 57, *58*, 60, 94–97, 100, 105, 121, 123, 132, 139, 144
Gombre-work, 28
goopher, xii, 28, 36, 114
goopher dust. *See* graveyard dirt

Gore, Bishop Barbara, xiii, 157
Grand Zombie, *32,* 91, 93. *See also* Blanc Dani *and* Voodoo Magnian
Grandfather Rattlesnake, 31, 66, 92, 100
Grandfather Snake. *See* Grandfather Rattlesnake
grave goods, 36
graveyard dirt, x–xii, 36, 38–39, *69,* 101, 105–6, 113, 119, 122, 195
Gray, Josephine V., 159
Great Depression, 11, 76, 82, 116–17
Great Migration, 11, 112, 114–15
Great One, 45–46
Green Corn Ceremony, 71
gregory bags, 28, 38, 68, 113
gris-gris, 27–28, 37, 51
Guale, 63
Gullah, ix, 140

H., Rev. Mr., 108–9
hags, 42
Haiti, 6, 13, 18, 27, *32,* 34, 51, 90–92, 136, 143–44, 148, 159, 190
hands, 100–101
Harlem Renaissance, 12, 164n39
Harris, Doctor, 56, 62
Harris, Joel Chandler, 5, 7–8
Haskins, James, 20
Hearn, Lafcadio, 9
hell hounds, 84
Henderson, Harriet, 104
Henry, Herman, 124
herbal medicine, 49, 55–56, 65, 69–72, 81, 107, 128, 136, 140, 142, 152
Hercules, Doctor, 108
Herskovits, Melville J., 15
High John the Conqueror. *See* John the Conqueror
high men/women, 28, 58, 114
Hinduism and Hindus. *See* Orientalism
Holiness movement, 157–58

Holy Spirit, 96
homogenization, 2, 4
hoochie-coochie men/women, 156
hoodoo: definition of, x–xi; and origin of term, 27–28; and spread across South, 114
hoodoo doctors. *See* practitioners
horseshoes, 60, *69*
Hughes, Langston, 17
Hunter, Charles, 98
Hurston, Zora Neale, ix–x, 15, 28, 45–49, 53, 60, 72–73, 95, 98–100, 112, 114, 116, 120, 153–54, 196; reliability of, 169n56, 197
hush water, 80, 85
Hyatt, Christopher S., 144
Hyatt, Harry Middleton, 22, 53, 60, 77–78, 80–81, 99, 114, 117, 122, 126, 131, 191–92

Igbo, 27, 40
illness, 53, 66, 68, 81, 83, 102, 105–7, 115, 141, 151, 157–58, 191
incense, 119, 121, 124, 127, 129, 139
Indio Products, 119–20, 128
initiations, 44–49, 67, 98–100, 112, 142, 144, 147–48, 197
Islam, 142, 149
Ivy, John and Leroy, 151

Jack, Gullah, 87
jacks, 100
Jackson, Michael, 159
Jean Bayou. *See* John, Doctor
Jeff, 78
Jefferson, Ida B., 125
Jenkins, Sandy, 84
Jesus Christ, 36, 49, 60, 99–100, 133, 147, 156–57
Jews, 57, 117–19, 144, 195
Jim Crow system, 4, 10, 16, 84–85, 89, 135, 152–53, 189
Jockey Club Cologne, 118
Joe Moe. *See* mojo
John, Doctor, 8, 87, 97, 108, 129, 152

John, Old, 89, 107
John the Conqueror, 39, 61, 70, 105–6, 120–21, 125, 129, 179n56
Johnson, Lyndon, 141
Jones, Ava Kay, 146–48
Jones, Charles Colcock, Jr., 7, 8, 89
Jordan, James Spurgeon, 14, 129–33, 152
Jordan, Sam, 76
Journal of American Folklore, 6, 9, 17, 196
Joyner, Charles, 22
Jule, Old, 80–81
Julia, 93

Kabbala, 57, 118, 121, 127
Kenjji, 155
Key West, Florida, 93, 113–14, 124, 135
Keystone Laboratories, 119, 123, 135
King, Martin Luther, Jr., 17
King, Monroe, 107
King, Walter. *See* Adefumni, Oba Oseijeman
King Novelty, 121
Kingsley, Mary, 40
Kongo, 27–29, 31, 33, 35, 38–43, 49, 61, 65
Krobo, 44, 46–47
Kulii, Elon Ali, 115, 137, 151–53, 156

LaBas. *See* Lébat
Last Chance Medicine Company, 125
Latin settlement: and definition of cultural zone, 27–28, 30–31, 34–38, 43, 45, 47, 54, 57–61, 65, 71–72, 90, 93–95, 97–99, 105–6, 108–10, 112, 114, 120–21; during twentieth and twenty-first century, 18, 92, 134, 144–46; origins of, 25–27
Latour, Malvina, 109
Laveau, Marie, 20–21, 40, 64, 88, 91, 98, 108–9, 102, 115, 128, 132, 135–37, 154, 157
Lébat, x, 30, 32, 34, 58, 59, 94
Lee, Spike, 149
Legba, 29–30

Legends of Incense, Herb and Oil Magic (de Claremont), 121
Leland, Charles, 37–38
Levine, Lawrence, 22
Liba. *See* Lébat
Life and Works of Marie Laveau (Canizares), 120–21, 128
Lisa, Sister, 139
literature, 12, 19–20, 155, 190, 194–95
Livermore, Mary, 79
local color, 5, 10
locked bowels, 39, 80–81, 191
lodestones, 69
Long, Carolyn Morrow, xiii, 23–24, 112, 118–19, 169n56, 196–97
luck balls, xi, 37–38, 54, 89, 95, 100–101, 113
Lucky Mojo Curio Company, 119, 147
Lucky Star, 124
lynching, 88

Magic of Herbs, The (Gamache), 121
mail fraud. *See under* practitioners
mama-lois, 27–28, 93
mambo, 144
Mande, 26–28, 37–38, 44, 46–47, 68
Mandingo, 28, 37
Marie Laveau's House of Voodoo, 135–36
maroons, 73
Marron, Saint, 73
Mary, Virgin, 59, 91
Mason, Charles Harrison, 158
Mason, Ruth, 153
Master Book of Candle Burning, The (Gamache), 120, 132
Mawu-Lisa, 29, 35
McTeer, James, 19, 118, 130, 137, 139, 147
medicine: and practicing without a license (*see under* practitioners); traditional European, 55, 83
medicine bundles, 68

Memphis, Tennessee, 113, 119
Methodists, 158
Mexico, 77, 144
Meyer, Martin, 119
Miller, Donald and Richard, xiv, 117
Miller's Rexall, 117, 122
ministers. *See* preachers *and* Voodoo queens
minkisi, 30, 38–39, 61, 65, 68
Mitchell, Faith, 83, 140
Mitchell, Lorita, 146
mojo, 28, 89, 100, 155
mojo-man. *See* practitioners
Monday, Uncle, 63, 72
Montanet, John. *See* John, Doctor
Mooney, James, 64
Morrison, Toni, 155
music, 57, 66, 92–93, 135, 154–55, 195. *See also* blues

Nanga, 31, 33
Nañigo, 27, 31, 45, 57, 92–93, 113, 135, 177n9
Nanigro. *See* Nañigo
Nation of Islam, 149
nation sacks, 113, 195
nationalism, 12–13, 17, 19, 51, 146–48, 155, 159
Native American religions, 64–73, 134
neo-Voodoo, 147–48; and disagreements among practitioners, 148–49
New Age movement, 2, 18–19, 21, 51, 134, 140–44, 146–49, 159, 195
New Orleans, Louisiana, 20–21, 27, 30–31, 34–36, 40, 47, 50–51, 62, 64, 73, 77–78, 87–95, 97–100, 106–9, 112–19, 122, 129–30, 133–36, 143, 145–46, 148, 153, 156, 158, 190, 194, 197
New Orleans Historic Voodoo Museum, 135–36, 148
New York, New York, 12, 18, 87, 120–21, 134, 146
Newport, Arkansas, 130
Newton, Isaac, 55
Nigeria, 48

Niva, 139
noodoo, 27
Nzambi, 29

Obatala, 31, 33, 35, 58, 146
Obeah, 13, 18, 93, 161n2
offerings, 59, 91–92, 94, 106
Ogun, x
oils, 116–17, 119–20, 122, 126, 128–29, 145, 158–59
Olodumare, 144
Olorun, 29
Oriental Exclusion Act, 141
Orientalism, 118, 121–22, 129, 132, 141–42, 147–48, 182n33
Orisha Voudou, 147
orishas, 144
Oshun, 145
Owen, Mary Alicia, 2, 5, 7–8, 37, 61, 64, 72, 92, 95, 98–99, 101, 108, 110
Owen, Nicholas, 37
Oya, 143, 147
Oyotunji, 146, 148

Page, Thomas Nelson, 1–2, 5, 8–9
Palo Mayombe, 27, 144
papa-lois, 27–28, 93
parapsychology, 139–40, 147
patent medicines, 123–26, 132
Pentecostalism, 156–59
pepper, xi, 7, 41, 69, 72, 85, 95, 121, 127, 154
Peterkin, Julia, ix
pillow magic, 61, 104
Pinckney, Roger, ix
Pitkin, Helen, 8, 59, 94, 194–95, 197
poisons, 37, 79, 140, 151–52
Poro. *See* secret societies
Portuguese, 35
Posey, Martin, 78
possession by spirits, 48, 94
postmodernism, 2, 18–19

INDEX 227

powders, 38–39, 83–84, 100, 103, 107, 116, 119, 125, 151
powwow, 55, 58
practitioners: appearance of, 75, 91, 109; and apprenticeship, 45, 49, 99–100; as free blacks, 109; gifting of, 48, 67, 96–98; income of, x, 66, 68, 76, 79–80, 82, 86–87, 89, 118, 129–30, 152–53, 155, 191; and inheritance, 48–49, 64, 97–98; and isolation from community, 110, 151; and mail order, 118; and new names, 46–47, 100; prosecution of, 51–52, 113, 118, 126, 130, 133, 140, 149–50, 197; reputation of, 106–11, 122, 127, 151; social standing of, 48, 75–76, 79, 86, 89–90, 97, 108, 111, 129–30, 150, 152–53, 191; and specialization, ix, xii, 41–42, 49, 53, 66, 183n75; titles of, 37, 89, 100, 108–10, 123, 132–33. *See also names of specific practitioners*
prayer, 59, 68, 91, 93, 98–99, 117
preachers, 1, 79, 94, 108, 133, 158
proprietary medicine, 123
Protestantism, 26, 34, 50–51, 56, 96, 141, 157
psychics, 132, 134, 139, 162n12
puccoon root, 69, 72
Puckett, Newbell Niles, 10–11, 14–15, 20, 22, 41, 62, 107, 196–97
Puerto Rico, 144, 146
Pure Food and Drug Act, 125
Pyles, Henry F., 85, 101, 127, 154

Rabbit, 89
rabbits' feet, 60–61, 69, 83, 85
Raboteau, Albert J., 22
racial uplift, 5, 10
racism, 3–4, 13, 50, 62, 79, 84–85, 88, 115, 119, 133, 141, 149–50, 152–53, 155, 189
Rattlesnake. *See* Grandfather Rattlesnake
Reconstruction, 3–4, 11, 16, 135
Reed, Ishmael, 20, 155, 194
reincarnation, 43, 147, 156
relativism, 2, 18–19, 51, 142–44
Reverend Zombie's Voodoo Shop, 135

Rhett, Nancy, xiv, 130
ritual baths, 46–47, 57, 127, 129, 145, 157
Ritzer, George, 126
Robinson, Albert L., 83
Robinson, Braziel, 44, 54, 68
Robinson, Cornelia, 106
Robinson, Bishop Master F. L., xiii, 117, 128, 132–33, 153
Robinson, Stephaney. *See* Buzzard, Doctor
Robinson Hall, 117, 120
Rondo's Temple Sales, 117, 126
root doctor. *See* rootwork *and* practitioners
rooting, 28
roots, 39, 61, 67, 81, 84, 116, 119, 122, 127–28, 131–32, 139, 151
rootwork: definition of, xi–xii, 28, 73, 82–83, 86, 94, 114–15, 130, 132, 137–39, 147, 152. *See also* practitioners
Royal, Jim, 99
Rucker, "Black Herman," 124, 193

sacrifices, 31, 46, 52, 54, 88, 91–93, 105, 144–45
Saint Benedict Spiritual Church, 157
Saint John's Eve/Day, 57, 90–91, 93, 113, 135
Saint Joseph's Day, 46
saints, 60, 106, 145, 158. *See also* deities and spirits *and specific saints*
Salem, Massachusetts, 56, 76
Saloppé, Marie, 109
Samunga, 33, 94
Sande. *See* secret societies
Santería, x, 18, 58, 92, 143–47, 149, 159
sapiya, 72
Sarheed, Prophet Warkiee, 132
Satan. *See* devil
Sauk, 74
Savage, Phoenix, xiii, 140, 148
Schwab, Elliot, xiv
science, xii, 4, 55, 76, 78, 81, 123
scientific explanations for hoodoo, 134, 137–40, 147, 149, 193, 195; and medicinal properties,

81–83, 89, 115, 125, 137–38, 150–52, 193–94;
and psychological and psychiatric effects,
81–83, 115, 137–40, 147, 151–52, 193–94. *See also*
Voodoo death
Scot, Reginald, 60
secret societies, 44–45, 53, 66, 100. *See also*
covens
Secrets of the Psalms (Selig), 121, 132
segregation. *See* Jim Crow system
Selig, Godfrey, 121, 132
Seminole, 63, 67, 72
Senegal, 97
serpents. *See* snakes
Seven Sisters, 35, 99–100, 109, 129, 178n35
Seven Sisters of New Orleans, 128
Seymour, William J., 158
Shango, 18, 31, *33, 58,* 93, 143–44, 161n2
sharecropping. *See* tenant farming
Sheltun, J. T., 108, 116
shops, origin of. *See under* spiritual supplies
Simms, Father, 100
singing stone, 72. *See also* stones
Sixth and Seventh Books of Moses, The (Selig), 121–22, 132
slavery, 3–4, 10, 13, 21–22, 25–26, 30–31, 35–36, 47, 52, 56, 62, 65, 68, 73, 85, 87–89, 99–102, 111, 114, 128, 137, 150, 155, 190–92; and Native American masters, 63–64; resistance to, 34, 51, 71, 84, 86–87, 102, 105–6, 151
Smith, Jonell and Jazell, xiv, 158
Smith, Theophus, 22–23, 96–97, 156, 187n19
snakes, 29–30, 45–46, 65–66, 72, 88, 91, 102, 116, 136–37
Snow, Loudell, 126
soaps, 119, 129
Sonny Boy Products, 120, 122–23, 127–29
souls, multiple, xii, 43–44, 54, 67–68
Southern Workman, 3, 6, 9, 51, 79, 81, 87, 95, 102, 110, 196
Spanish. *See* Latin settlement
spearheads, Native American, 73

spells, turning back of, 83, 102–3, 111
Spielberg, Steven, 159
spirits. *See* dead, the *and* deities and spirits
Spiritual churches, 122, 142, 156–58, 161n2
spiritual hierarchies, 29–37, 42–43, 49, 54–55, 65, 144–45
spiritual supplies, 23, 112–35, 137, 153, 159; and antebellum free blacks, 115; and fidelity to traditional materials, 119–20, 128, 132, 147; and Internet, 115, 118–19, 136, 149; mail order, 111–12, 115, 118–19, 122, 126–27, 129, 131–34, 140; manufacturers of, 112, 117–19, 121–23, 126–28, 132–33, 135, 140; marketing of, 111–12, 122–25, 127, 134; and pharmacies, 117, 119, 122, 132; and publishing, 120–22, 126, 132; and shops, 23, 112, 115–16, 119, 121–22, 126, 132–35, 145–46, 148, 159, 195; and standardization of conjure, 126–27
Spiritualism, 156
Stanley Drug Company, 117
Steiner, Roland, 2, 6, 39, 68, 71, 80
stones, 70, 72, 173, 174n59
Stroyer, Jacob, 7
suppression. *See under* practitioners
sympathetic magic, 41, 55–56, 60, 65, 103–5, 128–29
syncretism, x–xi, 25, 57

Tallant, Robert, 11, 115, 135
Tampa, Florida, 93, 113
Taylor, Samuel, 75–76, 87, 89, 109–10, 192
tenant farming, 4, 87, 153
Thomas, Keith, 55
Thompson, Samuel, 45–47, 100
'Tit Albert, 56
Tituba, 56, 76, 171n14
Tiv, 48
Tlanuwa, 65
tobies, 27–28, 100
totemic animals and plants, 36, 109
transformation, 42, 53–54, 63, 67–68, 88
tricking (tricks), 28, 62, 79, 96, 100–102, 106, 110

Trinidad, 144
Truth, Sojourner, 96
Tull, Aunt Zippy, 52, 80, 83, 89, 103, 109–10
Turner, Nat, 87
two heads, xii, 15, 28, 114, 155. *See also* practitioners

Ubasi, *33*, 35
Uktena, 65, 72
Ulunsuti, 72
Undercover Man, 77

Valmor Company, 119, 121, 123, 132, 135
Vert Agoussou. *See* Agoussou
Vesey, Denmark, 87
Vietnam War, 141
Vodou, 6, 18, 89, 91, 143–44, 148, 159, 162, 163n17, 190
vodu, 28
Voodoo: definition of, x; and difference from hoodoo, x, 18, 90–91, 99–100, 113; and difference from Spiritual churches, 157; tourist variety of, 50, 113–14, 135–36, 148, 184n9
Voodoo Authentica, 135–36
Voodoo death, 81–82, 137–38
Voodoo dolls, 135–36
Voodoo Magnian, *32*, 34, 46, 91–92, 100
Voodoo queens, 30, 43, 54, 88, 90–91, 98, 108–9, 120. *See also specific queens*
Voodoo Rain, 136

wakes, 36
Walker, Alice, 155, 194
wanga, 27–28, 57, 100, 115
wangateur/wangateuse, 27–28
Ward, Martha, 21

Warner, Charles D., 56, 59, 91
washes, 100, 126
Washington, P. H. *See* Eagle, Doctor
White Hawk, 157
Whitehead, Aunt Mymee, 98, 109
whites, participation in conjure of, 2, 56, 62, 78, 88, 91, 113, 134, 136, 140–41, 143–44, 146, 148–50, 152
Wicca, 19, 142–44, 165n62
Williams, Mrs., 104
Williams, Claudia, xiii, 134, 143, 147
Williams, Robert, 97
Williams, Thomas "Pop," xiv, 117, 132–33, 137
Wilson, Woodrow, 130
witch balls, 53
witch bottles, 61
witches and witchcraft, xi, 29–30, 34, 40–43, 52–57, 60–62, 66–68, 78, 114, 132, 134, 136–37, 149, 154, 157, 159, 170n2
Woodpecker, 89
Works Progress Administration. *See* Federal Writers' Project
World War I, 11–12
World War II, 2, 16, 115, 119
Wyatt-Brown, Bertram, xiii, 78

Yamasee, 63
Yemaya, 31, *33, 58,* 93
Yoruba, 26–31, *32–33,* 35, 42–44, 67, 134, 144, 146, 148
Yronwode, Catherine, xii–xiii, 119, 121, 147–49

zinzin, 27–28
Zombie. *See* Grand Zombie
Zorro the Mentalist, 77

www.ingramcontent.com/pod-product-compliance
Lightning Source LLC
Chambersburg PA
CBHW031311150426
43191CB00005B/175